THE POLITICAL ECONOMY OF PUBLIC POLICY

A Concise Guide

The Political Economy of Public Policy

A Concise Guide

ALENA KIMAKOVA

UNIVERSITY OF TORONTO PRESS

Toronto Buffalo London

Toronto Buffalo London
utppublishing.com
Printed in Canada

ISBN 978-1-4426-1681-3 (EPUB)
ISBN 978-1-4426-2614-0 (paper)   ISBN 978-1-4426-1680-6 (PDF)

Library and Archives Canada Cataloguing in Publication

Title: The political economy of public policy : a concise guide / Alena Kimakova.
Names: Kimakova, Alena, author.
Description: Includes bibliographical references and index.
Identifiers: Canadiana (print) 20250277050 | Canadiana (ebook) 20250277085 |
    ISBN 9781442626140 (paper) | ISBN 9781442616813 (EPUB) |
    ISBN 9781442616806 (PDF)
Subjects: LCSH: Policy sciences – Textbooks. | LCGFT: Textbooks.
Classification: LCC H97 .K56 2025 | DDC 320.6 – dc23

Cover design: Heng Wee Tan

We welcome comments and suggestions regarding any aspect of our publications –
please feel free to contact us at news@utorontopress.com or visit us at utppublishing.com.

Every effort has been made to contact copyright holders; in the event of an error or
omission, please notify the publisher.

We wish to acknowledge the land on which the University of Toronto Press
operates. This land is the traditional territory of the Wendat, the Anishnaabeg, the
Haudenosaunee, the Métis, and the Mississaugas of the Credit First Nation.

University of Toronto Press acknowledges the financial support of the Government of
Canada and the Ontario Arts Council, an agency of the Government of Ontario, for its
publishing activities.

ONTARIO ARTS COUNCIL
CONSEIL DES ARTS DE L'ONTARIO
an Ontario government agency
un organisme du gouvernement de l'Ontario

Funded by the   Financé par le
Government   gouvernement
of Canada   du Canada

Canadä

MIX
Paper | Supporting
responsible forestry
FSC   FSC® C103567
www.fsc.org

Contents

Figures

Tables

Boxes

Preface to *The Political Economy of Public Policy: A Concise Guide*

While on leave from my doctoral studies, I worked as an analyst in investment banking, covering both macroeconomic and financial analysis and forecasting for Eastern European economies. I often received phone calls from traders, investment advisors, and reporters asking questions such as the following:

- Is the government going to intervene in the railway workers' strike? If yes, how long before that happens?
- Which political party is likely to win the next election? Is it going to be a majority government? What are the likely implications for financial sector regulations?
- Who is likely to be the nominee for the post of central bank governor? The rumour is that the finance minister will be nominated for the position: What policy changes, if any, can we expect from this person?
- Is the government going to address the projected shortfall in the national pension fund? When and how is this likely to occur?

Questions like these are commonplace across jurisdictions and made me realize that mainstream curricula at the undergraduate and graduate levels do not fully prepare students for the demands of careers such as policy analyst in the private, public, or not-for-profit sectors. There are several reasons for this shortfall. In the case of economics in particular, the mainstream representation of the field focuses on *normative* policy prescriptions, or what the optimal policy *should* be. This greatly confuses students by not reconciling the observed divergence between textbook policy recommendations and real-world government policies. As a result, economics as a field is often viewed by the general public as a largely theoretical exercise with lots of mathematics and assumptions, but basically irrelevant to policy-makers, business executives, and non-profit leaders as they go about their daily duties. Needless to say, this is very unfortunate since economic realities have a significant impact on private and public decision-making.

In a broader policy context, curricula in public administration, political science, and law programs at the undergraduate and graduate level are not immune to the normative doctrine either, but they typically aim to provide a more interdisciplinary approach. Nevertheless, what constitutes interdisciplinarity warrants further analysis. Often the adjectives "interdisciplinary" and "multidisciplinary" are used interchangeably. However, they are likely to yield differing learning outcomes for students.

When students simply take courses from a number of disciplines (multidisciplinary approach), they are left to reconcile the different frameworks and approaches on their own. In contrast, a truly interdisciplinary approach would provide structures in which economic, social, and political factors are integrated, and their interaction can be directly analyzed. This text aims to fill this persistent gap in university curricula as identified earlier in Kimakova (2008) by providing a methodological toolkit for students of public policy.

This book should appeal not just to undergraduate students in economics, but also to a wider audience including undergraduate and graduate students in public administration, political science, and law. The analysis in this text is not confined to economic policy; rather, it is a toolset that can be utilized to explore any public policy issue in any jurisdiction. The broad thematic scope of this text is a distinguishing feature, since most texts in the area of political economy typically focus on a narrowly defined policy area, industry, or geopolitical region. This book provides an intuitive understanding of public policy formation and its impacts that is also relevant for practitioners in the public sector, business, and non-profit organizations. We cover a wide range of policy areas using real-world examples that highlight key theoretical concepts and practical challenges in the design and implementation of public policy.

The textbook in its core aims to provide a general methodological framework for the qualitative and quantitative analysis of law and policy from a *positive* perspective – that is, aspiring to explain what actually happens in the realm of law and policy. The textbook itself is not a theoretical presentation, but connects various theoretical perspectives with empirical evidence. The book is filled with real-world policy questions (rather than hypothetical situations) and case studies on a wide range of law and policy topics. Therefore, the text is applied in nature, with case studies covering diverse jurisdictions such as the United States, Canada, European Union countries, and selected developing countries. In my experience, this approach instantly shows the applicability of the abstract concepts and engages students with diverse cultural backgrounds and disciplinary training in discussion.

It is equally important to outline what the text does not include. First of all, the book does *not* provide an overview of the history of political economy thought.[1] Similarly, no specific definition of "political economy" beyond a general juncture of economics, politics, and sociology will be stipulated since the term has different interpretations based on adherence to a particular school of thought or disciplinary affiliation. This approach should help maintain an unbiased frame of analysis. Keep in mind that different theoretical frameworks need to be applied in different contexts, depending on which framework's assumptions are met. If one were to adhere to one theoretical framework exclusively or predominantly, the analysis would likely be flawed and biased.

You will find that questions for discussion and further research by students are incorporated into the text at the end of sections rather than at the end of the chapters. This format serves to engage students in active learning and to provide immediate checks for students and the instructor to see if the students can understand the text covered

---

1   Readers interested in the history of political economy thought may refer to, for example, Blaug (1987), Buchholz (2021), Hancké et al. (2025), Heilbroner (1999), Innis et al. (2018), Nederman and Bogiaris (2024), Robbins and London School of Economics and Political Science (1998), Sandmo (2011), Stilwell (2011), and Whiteside (2020) for political economy in the Canadian context.

and if they can apply the relevant theoretical concepts to the given questions.

The text does not contain the answers to the questions at the end of the sections, but invites students to conduct further research and challenges them to identify and apply the relevant theoretical concepts from the text to answer the questions. Strong research skills and the ability to link theory and empirical evidence in an analytically sound manner are key requirements for policy analyst jobs, and the text is structured to help students develop those competencies. A technique I employ in a lesson plan is to allocate some class time for students to work in groups as they conduct basic research to help answer the questions posed. Working in groups helps students avoid shyness and anxiety and learn research skills from each other. The groups then report back to the rest of the class and get feedback from the instructor and classmates along with suggestions for further research. In general, policy analysts are routinely asked to make broad qualitative predictions about likely policy outcomes in their work without having the time and resources to conduct a full-scale research project. The exercise simulates that and prepares students for the workplace, where time and other resource constraints are prevalent.

Integrating student research into the learning process enhances the applied nature of the pedagogical approach employed in the text. Included at the end of each chapter is research advice for students to help them get started with research and avoid common mistakes at this stage of their learning and professional skill development.

CHAPTER ONE

Introduction to Political Economy of Public Policy

Public debates about the appropriate policy responses to emergent challenges are often complex, filled with tension, and fraught with competing or outright contradictory perspectives. You may often find that laws and policies implemented by governments are at odds with various expert recommendations or those found in your textbooks. How can we reconcile such contradictions?

Political economy aims to make sense of the complexities of government decision-making by taking into consideration the difficulties of aggregating varied opinions among citizens, and their ability to influence the policy-making process and its outcomes. This approach stands in contrast to the *normative* realm of policy analysis, which is devoted to the search for the "optimal" public policy that is meant to benefit the society at large. But how can we even define what is in a society's best interest if we – as individuals or groups – have diverse preferences about government policy, or if we are impacted by a particular policy stance in different ways?

The normative search for the optimal policy incorporates simplifying assumptions that political economy explicitly challenges and incorporates into the analysis. In this introductory chapter you will be acquainted with the main differences in the building blocks of normative versus positive political economy approaches to policy analysis. The defining characteristics and terminology of positive political economy inquiry are introduced in this chapter so that students will be able to do the following:

- differentiate between positive and normative questions of policy analysis
- understand key concepts in positive political economy theories, including agent heterogeneity, preferences, endowments, organizational ability, access to information, transaction costs, outcomes, incentives, and the principal-agent problem
- critically analyze commonly used terms such as "democracy" and "public interest," both at the conceptual level and in terms of empirical measurement
- explore the motivations to form a state (or other jurisdiction) with other individuals and groups, or to opt out of existing arrangements in favour of autonomous (self-governing, separate) formations

This chapter also includes a case study of abortion and contraceptive rights, which are a common and widely debated topic across several jurisdictions worldwide. Developments in the United States are utilized to highlight the driving forces behind the tensions while linking them to competing theories for explaining such developments on the public agenda.

To highlight the broad applicability of the theoretical concepts introduced in this book and to enhance your analytical skills, the text includes a wealth of suggestions for further research. This first chapter concludes with tips on how to get started with your own research on the political economy determinants of public policy or its likely course, including narrowing down the scope of your research and relevant sources of information.

1.1 THE DISTINCTION BETWEEN NORMATIVE AND POSITIVE PERSPECTIVES ON LAW AND POLICY DESIGN

While the area of law and economics has evolved greatly, most of the contributions have remained in the normative realm – that is, deriving optimal policy solutions to various economic and social problems (see, e.g., Posner, 2011; Cooter & Ulen, 2011). A positive perspective, on the other hand, aims to explain why certain laws and policies get implemented, while action on other issues of public interest is absent in practice. A positive analysis can also be utilized to draw predictions about probable future policy actions.[1]

The policy outcomes stemming from normative and positive analysis often diverge. This divergence cannot be explained easily, because the frameworks and theories utilized in the normative and positive realms of policy analysis are very different. Hence, it is important to be aware of what those fundamental differences are.

Mainstream normative economics involves several unrealistic assumptions that political economy directly addresses. For example, rather than assuming that a benevolent social planner maximizes some measure of welfare of a society made up of homogeneous representative agents, political economy explicitly acknowledges agent heterogeneity in terms of preferences, endowments, and/or organizational ability, which leads to conflicting interests. How these conflicting interests play out, and ultimately how they translate into law and policy, depends on the rules of the game, or the existing and evolving formal and informal institutional environment. Integrating economic concepts and tools with political and institutional elements explicitly will equip you with a general toolset to analyze or predict which laws and policies get implemented, and on which issues a government response will likely remain absent.

In a democratic society, more than one person decides on laws and policies, yet in normative economics a single "benevolent" dictator or social planner with an infinite time horizon makes all the policy decisions. The infinite time horizon implies that under a benevolent dictatorship, long-term intergenerational concerns are not ignored. In practice, political representatives often have short- to medium-term horizons as they consider the limited terms of their office and the likelihood of re-election.

---

1 For a concise overview of the historical development of law and economics, including normative, positive, and functional schools of thought, see Parisi (2004). For perspectives on positive political economy thought through the 1960s to 1980s, see Alt and Shepsle (1990).

The benevolent dictator or social planner also has a relatively easy job since all the members of the economy and society are assumed to be the same. Hence, it is enough to please one so-called representative agent – the average person – rather than take into consideration the myriad of opinions that a typical political representative or public servant faces. In other words, we have no aggregation problem in this case: If we are all the same, the average individual's best interest coincides with everyone else's best interest. In practice, societies can be politically and economically very polarized, with most of the people falling on one end of the spectrum or the other. In such cases, averages are not representative of the population at large. Even in cases when we actually have a statistically normal distribution of preferences, with the majority of the population in the mid-range, the issue of minority interests cannot be simply ignored.

Conflict is omnipresent. Even when actual laws have been formalized and implemented, we often cannot agree on their interpretation and let a supreme court make the final determination. Therefore, the key to political economy analysis is to think in terms of *incentives*. Incentives to endorse or oppose a particular policy stance can stem from personal beliefs or preferences, or from the distribution of costs and benefits of specific policy decisions. It is important to note that laws and policies do not have the same impact on everyone. The normative realm of welfare economics tests the desirability of a particular policy with the Pareto efficiency criterion: Is it feasible that everyone will be at least as well off as before, and nobody will be worse off, as a result of the policy?[2]

Pareto efficiency is often presumed to be achieved when the gains to the "winners" exceed the aggregate losses to others, thus allowing for the possibility that the "winners" can compensate the "losers," leaving everyone at least as well off as before. In practice, however, such compensation to the "losers" needs to be approved through the political process, not by a benevolent social planner, and that typically makes implementation unlikely. The political process or legal

---

2   The concept of Pareto efficiency is named after Italian economist and sociologist Vilfredo Pareto, who is generally considered to have laid the foundations of modern welfare economics, especially through his work in *Manuale d'economia politica* (1906).

challenges to decisions also entail so-called *transaction costs*. Hence, even if the "losers" would actually receive adequate compensation, there are inherently additional losses involved due to expending resources on the process of decision-making itself.

Policy-making – design and implementation – is a complex system with large information requirements. In addition to transaction costs, unintended consequences and unforeseen changes to the economic, social, and political environment often arise. Hence, uncertainty and informational problems also need to be carefully considered. Access to information and its quality may also be unequally distributed, which is commonly referred to as the *asymmetric information* problem. This is a problem because our decisions are only going to be as "good" as the information we base those decisions on, and because others can take advantage of their superior access to information.

Agent or *voter heterogeneity* simply means that we are different. Any given public policy decision can affect different individuals in varying ways – we may bear the costs or enjoy the benefits of certain government decisions in an uneven manner. The distribution of costs and benefits under different outcomes provides incentives to individuals to endorse or oppose a certain policy stance. We also have different likes and dislikes (or utilities), which we will call preferences. It is important to note that we have different preferences or opinions not only on what is "best" for us as individuals, but also in relation to what we prefer for society more broadly. Those preferences have been coined as *other-regarding* by Levine and Forrence (1990). Several words of caution are in order: Other-regarding preferences should *not* be interpreted simply as altruism for others. Even when one believes that they are acting in the interest of others, the affected individuals or groups may disagree with what is "best" for them. Hence, the term *other-regarding preferences* simply refers to opinions that affect others in society, not just us personally.

We also have different resources at our disposal, including income, wealth, access to information, technology, or other factors of production, including our own physical abilities. Since it is difficult for an individual to exert significant influence on collective decision-making, being able to identify like-minded individuals and inducing them to act on a certain matter of concern is very important, and we will refer to this phenomenon as *organizational ability*. Not all individuals or subgroups

Table 1.1. Key differences between normative and positive political economy analysis

Perspective	Normative	Positive
Research questions	What should the policy stance be? What is the optimal policy from a societal perspective?	How does the policy work? What impact does it have on different individuals and/or groups? How did the policy come about? Why is action in certain policy areas lacking?
Horizon	Infinite/long-term	Short- to medium-term
Decision-makers	Benevolent dictator	Elected officials and their designates
	Rational economic agents/ voters	No assumption of rationality or strict self-interest
Economic agents	Average/homogenous	Heterogenous preferences and endowments
Organizational ability	Homogenous	Varied/heterogenous
Information sets	Perfect	Imperfect/asymmetric information problem
Transaction costs	Negligible	Significant
Markets	Exist and are perfectly competitive	Market failures are common
Institutions	Assumed to function as intended and often ignored in analysis and policy recommendations	Play a significant role in decision-making and determining outcomes

in society have the same ability or potential to organize and thus to influence public decision-making (Olson, 1965; Grossman & Helpman, 1996). Collective action and the ability of minority groups to influence public policy will be explored in detail in chapter 5.

It is not easy to explain how individuals make decisions. Rational choice theory, often dominant in the literature, typically assumes that individuals are rational and make choices in their best self-interest. Hence, they will form educated expectations about the future and engage in strategic interaction with other agents. *Strategic interaction* means that we do not make decisions in isolation, but rather we take into consideration how our decisions are likely to influence others and their choices. In a way, we "think ahead." Formally, strategic interaction is typically analyzed in the context of *game theory*. While game theory is very useful to highlight the theoretical *incentives* for different types of action, the possibility of different outcomes, and whether they are likely to be stable or unstable, the framework is not easy to apply in practice. The reason is that the probabilities of different actions and outcomes crucially depend on the quality of information available to the participants. In practice, uncertainty about future costs and benefits is likely to prevail, and competing agents engaged in strategic interaction are also unlikely to share the information they have with their counterparts.

Contexts in which strategic interaction is relevant are often covert. They can encompass, for example, international and business espionage. Except for the globally publicized Wikileaks and other insider informants such as in the case of the National Security Agency (NSA) leak in the United States, there is very little publicly available and verifiable information to determine what information the parties had at any given point, what they expected their counterparts to know and do, and how that motivated their actions. Nevertheless, we are likely to be strategic in our daily lives as well. For example, we may vote in elections for our second-choice political candidate if we believe our first choice has a very low probability of winning and this would give our least-favoured political candidate an advantage.

QUESTIONS FOR DISCUSSION AND FURTHER RESEARCH

1 Can you provide other examples of strategic interaction?
2 What role does access to information play in these interactions?

Note: If you find it difficult to answer the above questions, form groups in class and/or conduct a basic Internet search to get you started. Then explain your answers by applying the theoretical concepts introduced in the section above. Practice formulating well-articulated arguments grounded in both theory and empirical evidence.

Rational choice theory and its applications have been challenged with the emergence of *behavioural economics*. Empirical methods such as surveys, interviews, observations, and simulations have been utilized to highlight inconsistencies in individual decision-making and divergence from "rational" choice. This has resulted in references to "bounded rationality" in the literature. In this text we will abstain from referring to choices as "rational" and "irrational" or exhibiting "bounded rationality." The reason is that, in my opinion, these labels can introduce bias into the analysis since one's "irrational" choice might simply be an indication of different sets of values, preferences, constraints, time horizons, expectations for the future, or access to information or other resources. Tversky and Kahneman (1986) have aptly summed up the inconsistencies between rational choice theory and empirical evidence: "the axioms of rational choice are generally satisfied in transparent situations and often violated in nontransparent ones" (p. S272). Nevertheless, the dominant view in the literature is that inconsistencies in individual decision-making are contradictory to rational choice. For example, intransitivity in preferences – which occurs when one prefers option *A* to *B*, *B* to *C*, but does not choose *A* over *C* when presented with this option – is typically considered inconsistent with rational choice. Cyclicality in preferences is likely to take place when the options are considered in relation to a given alternative rather than independent of each other, which arguably is often the case in practice. For a dissenting view from the mainstream assumption that preferences have to be transitive to be rational, see Anand (1993). Mandler (2005) also proposes that we should differentiate between choice behaviour, or *revealed preference*, and psychological preferences (individual likes and dislikes, attitudes). He argues that while it is easy to establish the rationality of transitivity in terms of psychological preferences, observed choices being intransitive can be consistent with rationality. This is because, for example, preferences can change over time as people change and their circumstances (endowments, choice sets, etc.) evolve, or if they exhibit a preference for maintenance or rejection of the status quo. Hence, intransitivity in observed choices should not necessarily, or automatically, be interpreted as irrational choice.

The above discussion highlights the importance of defining preferences in the broadest possible sense to account for potential complexities present in psychological preferences. Therefore, preferences should be understood in relation to actual, expected, perceived, self-, and other-regarding costs and benefits, clearly indicating an intention to go beyond the concepts of self-interest and pure rationality by including individually perceived costs and benefits, which may or may not be real. Analysis and findings stemming from both rational choice theory and behavioural sciences will be included in this text.

BOX 1.1. ABORTION AND CONTRACEPTIVE RIGHTS: A NEVER-ENDING PUBLIC DEBATE

Abortion and contraceptive rights are an example of other-regarding preferences. This is because, in general, people voice an opinion on the issue regardless of whether relevant laws directly affect them. It is not only women of child-bearing age, or fathers of unborn children, whose opinions are heard; post-menopausal women and men, without any possibility of ever getting pregnant, and with no relation to the affected women, also have the right to vote on the matter. These debates continue in most jurisdictions around the world, irrespective of income level and whether abortion has been legalized or not. How can we explain the persistent presence of abortion and contraceptive rights on the public agenda? And what is driving those individual other-regarding opinions and public policies?

There can be several possible explanations for the individual and public preferences on this issue. For example, the driving forces could be ideological – religion or altruism for the rights of those who do not have a voice – or the policies and public discourse could be a reflection on societal power relations. Specifically, in most societies the male population dominates decision-making at the household and government levels. Men also tend to dominate religious hierarchies and are thus likely to have more influence on the formation of ideologies as well. Yet women, rather than men, are more likely to bear the physical, economic, and opportunity costs of child-bearing and care. So, is it ideology, power relations, or the unequal distribution of costs and benefits of abortion legislation that drive public opinion and laws and policies?

A fascinating spectacle occurred on February 16, 2012, when the United States Oversight and Government Reform Committee debated the legitimacy of requiring health insurance coverage for contraception under President Obama's health policy mandate. Committee Democrats claimed they could only invite one witness, but when they chose a female witness, she was deemed unqualified to testify. As a result, all the committee members and witnesses, ten persons present at the hearing, were male (Daily Mail Reporter, 2012). Interestingly, in the United States, a high-income country that is proud to promote equal rights, the voice of the whole female population was not even considered for representation. It was also notable that all the witnesses testifying were religious leaders (Catholic, Jewish, Baptist, and Lutheran), which seems to stand in contrast to public beliefs about the influence of religion on politics. A 2006 survey found that 63 per cent of the respondents indicated that the "people's will" rather than "the Bible" should be a more important influence on US laws (Pew Research Center, 2006). Irrespective of the final policy outcome on this issue, the inequities in process and representation are most noteworthy in this case.

Similarly, on January 9, 2014, the Subcommittee on the Constitution and Civil Justice, an arm of the House Judiciary Committee, debated bill H.R. 7, the *No Taxpayer Funding for Abortion Act*, introduced in May 2013. The bill envisions a prohibition on the direct and indirect use of federal funds for abortion, including coverage under federal health care plans with the exception of instances of rape, incest, or threat of death to expectant mothers. Critics of the bill have argued that a direct prohibition on federal funding of abortion has been in place since 1976 under the Hyde Amendment (renewable every year) and that the bill had far-reaching implications not just for federal health insurance policy, but also for private health insurance coverage. This is due to the fact that the bill also eliminates tax credits for small business health insurance expenses that include coverage for abortion (Abbott, 2014). On January 28, 2014, the Republican-controlled US House of Representatives voted to approve the bill, which Democrats have argued has been "deceptively titled" to imply more limited reach in terms of public procurement (Peters, 2014). It was considered doubtful that the Democrat-dominated Senate would approve the bill, but it is noteworthy that state legislatures approved 70 restrictions on abortion in 2013 alone, and cumulatively the number for the 2011–13 period exceeded that for the previous decade (The New York Times, 2014).

Abortion rights continued to be challenged in subsequent years, and in 2022 the US Supreme Court overturned its *Roe v. Wade* (1973) ruling that granted abortion rights federally based on the right to privacy implied under the 14th Amendment to the US Constitution. The *Dobbs v. Jackson Women's Health Organization* (2022) ruling suggested that individual states should resolve the issue of abortion rights, which has led to the proliferation of new bans, invoking historical legislation as well as attempts to enforce extraterritorial bans by punishing the procurement or aiding of access to abortion services by travel to states that allow abortion.

It is important to note that the policy stance on abortion can differ not just by the decision-making body, but also in relation to affected populations. For example, while abortion had been legal in the United States and Canada (even covered by health insurance in some instances) and these countries provided foreign aid to low-income developing countries to improve health outcomes, safe abortions were often excluded from the funding scheme and the provision of services. This is despite the fact that abortions can be a life-saving necessity, and that complications from pregnancies and childbirth are a significant health risk to women in low-income developing countries. Was this a reflection on strategic interaction whereby the funding government did not want to antagonize local political support for maternal and child health initiatives, or was it an indication of power relations whereby women in poor countries have less political influence than their counterparts in high-income countries?

And why are people so vested in the abortion debate at all? Other life-and-death policy issues often receive much less public attention than abortion. Funding for cancer treatment or the so-called "right to die" by assisted suicide for terminally ill patients with low quality of life tend to receive comparatively less attention by the public. This is despite the fact that we are all, indiscriminately, far more likely to face these kinds of situations in our lives than consider an abortion. Can you explain why?

QUESTIONS FOR DISCUSSION AND FURTHER RESEARCH

1 Can you think of additional examples of other-regarding preferences?

1.2 DOES DEMOCRACY SOLVE ALL OUR PROBLEMS?

We have covered that we as individuals have a variety of opinions on public policy issues that affect all of us, even if in different ways. Hence, the question becomes this: How do we aggregate all these different opinions to come up with a single policy stance (action or inaction)? Democracy is supposed to be the answer to this question, but what does democracy mean and look like in practice?

It turns out democracy can take on different forms and meanings. For example, if democracy is simple majority rule, then what happens if you are a minority and get out-voted on every single policy issue? Would you be content with such a democracy? If you were a systematic or persistent minority, based on your preferences or some group affiliation, then you would likely feel very disenfranchised. For this reason, societies with systematic minorities (ethnic, religious, or other) can offer veto rights to those minorities on some key policy issues. These rights are typically embedded in a constitution because the standards for making constitutional amendments tend to significantly exceed the standards for ordinary laws. A simple majority can approve laws, while a qualified majority, which is typically set above 50 per cent, can only characteristically amend constitutions. Therefore, constitutional changes are harder to implement since they require near consensus on a given issue of fundamental importance.

We also have to differentiate between direct democracy, under which voters get to cast a vote on public policy issues through a referendum, and representative democracy, in which we elect political representatives who vote on our behalf. Under representative democracy, we again have an aggregation issue since your political representative may not vote in the same way as you would as an individual. Hence, we are likely to end up with different policy outcomes if the matter at hand is decided through a referendum or through a parliamentary or city council vote. Referendums are expensive and therefore relatively rare. Nevertheless, some jurisdictions put more emphasis on direct democracy than others. Switzerland and California, for example, stand out as jurisdictions where referendums are more routine.

While we have only covered veto rights and direct versus representative democracy so far, it is already obvious that policy outcomes are likely to differ depending on the rules of the collective decision-making process. This has been a very crude differentiation so far, but in practice there are a myriad of variations of the "rules of the game" in politics. Representative democracy can be broadly divided into proportional and majoritarian systems. Under majoritarian electoral systems (including Canada and the United States, for example), geographic areas are divided into electoral districts. The person with the highest share of votes in the electoral district then gets to represent everyone in that district, irrespective of their endorsement (or not) and ideological differences. How does this make sense? If geographic interests are important and unique, as tends to be the case with geographically dispersed countries, then a regional representative is more likely to have their interests allied with the local electorate. But this also means that fewer people in more remote areas are likely to have more weight in the collective decision-making than those living in more densely populated areas. Electoral district boundaries are artificial, determined by the political process, and can be manipulated to yield varying election results under majoritarian systems.

On the other hand, under proportional representation (adopted in some European countries, for example) regional differences do not matter, and all votes are simply added up with an equal weight. There are also countries that utilize some combination of majoritarian and proportional representation (for example, Germany). The important take-away of this very basic overview of electoral systems is that outcomes of elections can vary depending on the electoral system, or how you count the votes. Perhaps the most (in)famous and highly publicized case was the George W. Bush versus Al Gore US presidential election in 2000. Al Gore won the popular vote with 50,996,582 votes, compared to 50,456,062 votes for Bush, and under proportional representation he would have become the US president. But the result was less clear-cut under the US majoritarian system, as Bush had a higher count of electoral votes relative to Gore – 271 to 266, respectively (Office of the Federal Register, 2000). The US Electoral College awards Florida and its electoral districts a heavy weight. The result came down to a few votes, recounts, different interpretations of what constituted a valid vote, and a court battle. The final result was that

George Bush became the 43rd president of the United States, although many voters questioned his legitimacy because the US Supreme Court ruling played a significant role in the outcome (*Bush v Gore*, 2000).

And why does it matter who becomes president? The president in the United States (or prime minister in other jurisdictions) represents the head of the executive branch of government with significant powers to make decisions swiftly and even veto laws approved by the legislature. The courts – the judicial branch of government – are to provide checks on the legality and scope of executive powers by the president or prime minister, but challenging executive decision-making through the courts involves significant transaction costs for the challenging parties as well as delay, which means that in practice executive decision-making will have significant impact, which can be to a great extent irreversible.

If the judiciary is supposed to provide checks on executive and legislative actions, judges need to be able to form decisions independently and free from political, social, or economic pressures (e.g., the loss of their job or financial liability for their decisions). If the primary objective of judges is to uphold existing laws, they should also be free from political affiliation, ideological bias, or economic influence. The process for judicial nominations and appointments ought to be examined to determine the likelihood that these principles will be upheld in practice.

In summary, the above discussion highlights that the "rules of the game" in politics have a material impact on the policy outcomes. Yet they are largely ignored in mainstream economics, and only institutional economics devotes attention to the formal and informal structures that affect public decision-making. Chapter 4 will provide a more in-depth analysis of different voting rules and their impact on law and policy approval.

1.3 ON MEASURING DEMOCRACY, ITS DETERMINANTS, AND ITS IMPACT

There is a great deal of scholarly, political, and popular interest in determining the relationships between democracy and other political, economic, and social variables. Nevertheless, a great deal of caution should be exercised when conducting empirical research involving a measure of "democracy." Labels such as "democratic" or "undemocratic" are often the result of a political process and hence may be strategic or ideologically driven. Given the great degree of variation among political systems that would normally be characterized as "democratic," lumping them all together into a single category is likely to yield misleading results. A great deal of information is bound to be lost in such a crude aggregation, and one should aim to utilize more well-defined and directly comparable characteristics of political systems to be able to draw inferences about empirical relationships or the lack thereof.

Munck and Verkuilen (2002a, 2002b) provide an in-depth analysis of the conceptual, measurement, and aggregation problems embedded in democracy indices commonly used in empirical research. At the conceptual level, they argue that most indices utilize the attributes of "contestation or competition" and "participation or inclusion" to define "democracy," based on Dahl's (1971) framework. Contestation or competition is typically measured through indicators such as the right to form political parties and the freedom of the press or media more broadly. The main components of participation or inclusion have been identified as the right to vote, fairness of the voting process, and access to public funds by political parties, for example. Munck and Verkuilen (2002a, 2002b) call for special attention to be devoted to differentiating between official, or *de jure*, rights to vote and more informal, or *de facto*, obstacles to electoral participation that may exist in practice. Similarly, they highlight the importance of "agenda-setting powers by elected officials" and "constraints on the executive" that are often not included as attributes.

Even after the relevant defining attributes of democracy are conceptually identified, operationalizing these attributes into actual measurements remains a challenge. Often the attributes may not be observable or directly measurable in practice, and hence the measures rely on so-called proxies. There can be also multiple representations or interpretations of an attribute, and when these are not uniquely categorized, they can lead to problems of conflation (compounding different attributes into the same measure) and redundancy. Inevitably, a great deal of information is lost in the aggregation process, which is why Munck and Verkuilen (2002a, 2002b) advocate for the use of disaggregate data rather than broad, all-encompassing labels or single numerical representations of complex political systems and processes.

Despite the above outlined cautionary remarks about the broad analyses of "democracy," there is no shortage of empirical studies involving the concept and some measure of it. An additional common challenge in these studies is to determine the direction of causality between the measure of democracy and other variables. A correlation between "democracy" and other variables does not shed light on causality: Social and economic outcomes might be more or less conducive to creating an environment of participation or contestation, but democracy in turn may further affect these variables. Economists refer to such a two-way causality as an endogenous relationship, and endogenous variables are jointly determined through their interaction. Consequently, the challenge is to identify methodologies for predetermined or exogenous measurements of the relevant variables.

In terms of the determinants of democratic regimes, studies typically point to rises in per capita income, the middle class, and educational attainment as factors conducive to democratization. The reverse holds for dependence on natural resources: Countries rich in natural resources are less likely to be democratic (see Barro, 1999; Glaeser et al., 2007; Papaioannou & Siourounis, 2008; or Shafiq, 2010).

And is democracy conducive to positive developmental outcomes? Broadly speaking, yes. For example, positive health outcomes in terms of reduced infant mortality, increased life expectancy, and more equitable access to health care for marginalized groups (including the poor or HIV/AIDS-positive populations, for example) have been associated with more democratic regimes (see Altman & Castiglioni, 2009; Blaydes & Kayser, 2011; Justesen, 2012; Klomp & Haan, 2009; Lake & Baum, 2001; McGuire, 2010, 2013). Nevertheless, Ross (2006) argues that cross-national studies tend to suffer from selection bias, as they often exclude from their samples non-democratic regimes that have performed well in terms of developmental outcomes. After correcting for this sampling issue, Ross (2006) found a weak or no effect of democratization on infant and child mortality rates. Overall, the studies highlight the importance of closely examining the inclusiveness of samples, especially since data availability and reliability across different regimes can be an issue.

Nevertheless, Adam et al. (2011) found more broadly a positive relationship between public-sector efficiency and the level of democracy. Similarly, democratization tends to be the driving force for technological innovation and wealth accumulation (Coccia, 2010) and economic liberalization (Rode & Gwartney, 2012).

1.4 WHAT IS PUBLIC INTEREST? DO GOVERNMENTS ACT IN PUBLIC INTEREST?

The term "public interest" gets mentioned a lot by politicians, critics, and commentators in the media, but do we actually have a definition for this notion? It has been an elusive concept to define, not just in practice, but also in terms of political or philosophical thought. The diversity of opinions in society means that we can hardly reach consensus on any issue, so is there even such a thing as "public interest"?

Public interest theories have historically been part of the normative realm, focusing on the desired attributes of political representation or public service. Exploring normative theories of public interest is beyond the scope of this text,[3] but even within the positive realm it is difficult to come up with a definition of public interest. Having a definition of what constitutes public interest would be useful for identifying instances of deviations from public interest by politicians and/or public servants, and hence creating mechanisms for accountability.

In the political economy sphere, Levine and Forrence (1990) have defined public interest as "general-interest policies or actions adopted or undertaken by a regulatory agent that would be ratified by the general polity according to its accepted aggregation principles if the information, organization (including exclusion costs), and transaction and monitoring costs of the general polity were zero" (p. 176). Arguably, this definition still leaves us with some ambiguity. For example, what constitutes "accepted aggregation principles" can be subject to varying interpretations. Voters might disagree on the appropriate voting procedures for a particular issue, as some might argue that a referendum would be more appropriate than a vote in parliament on the matter, while others question whether proportional or majoritarian representation

---

3   For an overview of the literature on defining public interest, see King et al. (2010).

has legitimacy or if minorities should be given veto rights. We are also unlikely to ever reach the state of a perfectly informed electorate, making it impossible to test for the perfectly informed decision by the polity.

Nevertheless, the above definition by Levine and Forrence (1990) allows us to draw some basic inferences about what does not constitute public interest:

- Policies that only advantage a few with private benefits would not qualify as public interest and would be instead labelled as *private interests* or *regulatory capture by special interests*. Policies that only benefit the re-election of politicians, fraud, or corruption to subvert the powers of public office for private benefit would fall into this category.
- Public representatives who feel that they act in the best interest of society or their constituency – but are implementing unpopular policies that the polity would actually not support under direct democracy and a perfect information set at their disposal – are, under this definition, deemed not to be acting in public interest. This implies that ideologically or morally driven political representatives can be superimposing their values and opinions on society, and even if these are driven by "good intentions," they violate the principles of democracy and representation. Such representatives are labelled in the literature as Burkean, following the 1774 speech by Edmund Burke to the Electorate of Bristol on his views about the rights and duties of an elected representative (Burke, 1774).
- Autocratic regimes that involve absolute power through dictatorship or some forms of monarchy suppress and/or do not take into consideration the views of the population and therefore stand in clear contrast to public interest.
- The economic view of public interest as represented by the decision of the benevolent social planner (who maximizes aggregate social welfare and assumes that the losing segments of the economy will be compensated to achieve Pareto efficiency) is also not likely to coincide with the above definition of public interest because compensation is unlikely in practice. If the costs of compensation are dispersed among a large segment of the population, while the benefits are limited to a smaller group, the majority vote is likely to weigh against such a proposal.

In political economy analysis, it will be important to carefully differentiate between a technical definition of "public interest," like the one above by Levine and Forrence (1990), moral theories of public interest (what one believes to be in the interest of the general public), and colloquial or strategic references to "public interest," which may aim to influence public opinion on a particular issue.

In the next section, we turn to exploring the conditions conducive to deviations from public interest policies and the options available to limit the potential for such outcomes.

1.5 ASYMMETRIC INFORMATION, PRINCIPAL-AGENT PROBLEMS, AND ACCOUNTABILITY-ENHANCING INSTITUTIONS

Access to information – quality information obtainable at low cost – can yield a great deal of value and advantage. Above, we referred to the phenomenon of the *asymmetric information* problem, in which access to information is unequally distributed. Asymmetric information can arise in different contexts, but its common application is the so-called *principal-agent problem*. In the public realm, voters are the principals and their political representatives are supposed to be the agents with the mandate to act on their behalf. Similarly, public servants and program managers are supposed to be the agents acting on behalf of elected political representatives to implement the approved policies.

But can these principals trust the agents to act on their behalf? It is not possible for the principals, the voters for example, to monitor every decision politicians make. Voters can follow the news, but the news represents an aggregation of the relevant information and somebody's interpretation of that information. The voters do not have the time to research and follow every aspect of the decision-making process. After all, if they did have the time and resources to devote to public policy, they would not need the political representatives to do it on their behalf. This means that monitoring of the agents by the principals is imperfect. Politicians can be disciplined by not being re-elected, but that occurs infrequently, and they are thus likely to "get away" with some deviations from acting in the interest of their electorate.

Similarly, laws and policies may be deemed adequate, but if their implementation is ineffective, the public and the elected politicians are unlikely to be pleased with such outcomes. On this note, it is important to emphasize that principal-agent problems arise not just in the public or not-for-profit sectors, but also in the private sector. Business managers have a clear mandate to maximize profits for shareholders, but there have been plenty of examples of corporate mismanagement or outright fraud, such as skyrocketing bonuses and severance pay for CEOs of failed companies, or millions of dollars diverted from company pension funds. The early 2000s even yielded a few examples of corporate managers facing criminal charges.[4] Yet some political economy and development economics textbooks tend to use language suggesting that the principal-agent problem, mismanagement, and corruption are unique to the public sector, or that corruption is a problem that developing rather than high-income country governments face. Imperfect monitoring and enforcement are universally present in all sectors across the globe, and discussions of accountability are relevant for all.

Societies have developed formal and informal accountability-enhancing institutions to limit the potential for principal-agent problems and detect and punish instances in which deviations from assigned behaviour occur. Nevertheless, achieving perfect control and accountability is not feasible, and therefore discussions of asymmetric information and principal-agent problems are here to stay.

Accountability-enhancing institutions should be interpreted broadly and beyond the formal controls built into the political and administrative systems of governance. Free speech, investigative journalism, and limits on media ownership concentration are a few cornerstones of the public accountability-enhancing system. While anti-corruption initiatives tend to be popular among voters, the approaches taken to combat the phenomenon vary widely. For example, China even executes public officials found guilty of corruption, yet corruption remains

---

4   A wave of corporate scandals started with the case of the Enron Corporation in 2001. For a detailed overview of the subsequent criminal charges involving corporate leadership in the United States, see Jickling and Janov (2003). The scandals also led to the adoption of new legislation in the United States on corporate disclosure and CEO responsibility for verifying accuracy in financial reporting. See Congressional Research Service (CRS) Report RL31554, Corporate Accountability: Sarbanes-Oxley Act of 2002: (PL 107–204).

widespread.[5] How can we explain that? The payoffs to corruption in China, based merely on its economies of scale, are exorbitantly high, and are thus an attractive proposition. Combined with a low likelihood of punishment in an environment with widespread corruption, the expected punishment is rather low relative to the maximum punishment, and so is an ineffective deterrent. Such outcomes are well documented in the law and economics literature and consistent with the economic approach to crime and punishment as captured in Becker (1968), Becker and Stigler (1974), Friedman (1999), Garoupa and Klerman (2002) and Rajabiun (2009). Persson and Siven (2007) also show how in an environment of false convictions (type II errors) the democratization of the political environment yields to smaller punishments but higher probability of enforcement in a median voter framework.

Rather than focusing on extreme punishments for a few individuals, research shows that it is more effective to tackle the core of the accountability problem in a principal-agent setting, which is asymmetric information. In general, there is more scope for asymmetric information, and the potential to hide corruption, in complex systems that entail large costs for the public to obtain accurate information about the state of affairs and to interpret them. Therefore, simplifying political and administrative structures is conducive to limiting the scope for corruption. Initiatives explicitly aimed at reducing the costs of acquiring information by the public are equally important. Requiring public-sector organizations to publish procurement tenders is one example of such initiatives intended to reduce information asymmetries. Granting private individuals the right to access to government information on demand is another.[6] Publishing sources and amounts of private and corporate contributions to political campaigns can similarly help enhance accountability in policy-making.

Advances in technology and the rise of the Internet have made a significant contribution to enhancing access to information and reducing the costs of obtaining such information. Nevertheless, the sheer volume of available information, combined with the open-access

---

5 According to Transparency International, China received a score of 43 on the public sector Corruption Perception Index in 2024, on a scale of 0–100, with 0 representing high corruption. See the Corruption Perceptions Index at https://cpi.transparency.org/.

6 See, for example, the 1985 Canadian *Access to Information Act* (RSC, 1985, c A-1), updated with amendments at https://laws-lois.justice.gc.ca/eng/acts/A-1/.

nature of the Internet, create challenges for distinguishing quality information from noise, which can be unintentional errors or intentional misinformation by special interests aiming to influence public opinion. Special interests can masquerade as think tanks, independent research institutions, or quasi journalists, and this is underscored by the rise of the Internet and its pluralistic character. Therefore, as students of political economy, you will need to pay close attention to assessing the credibility of your sources. The research guide at the end of the chapter offers some advice in this regard. For further analysis of the impact of the Internet on "the destabilization of political communication systems," see Dahlgren (2005).

In addition to more accessible information, the Internet also provides a new platform for collective action and advocacy. It allows people concerned about particular issues to more easily make complaints and submit petitions to policy-makers and government agencies. While social media provides a novel platform for activism, it can create echo chambers and enhance political polarization (Terren & Borge-Bravo, 2021). Online and off-line activism tend to complement each other. The online sphere provides public- and private-sector interests with new opportunities to monitor and control dissenting voices (Greijdanus et al., 2020).

QUESTIONS FOR DISCUSSION AND FURTHER RESEARCH

1 Can you list additional examples of both formal and informal accountability-enhancing institutions?
2 Discuss how these mechanisms are common or varied across jurisdictions, cultures, or communities with different income levels. Do you think they are effective in practice? Why?

1.6 HOW DO PEOPLE COME TOGETHER TO FORM A STATE (OR OTHER JURISDICTION)? WHAT DRIVES THE SECESSION DECISION?`

We often take the boundaries of jurisdictions, especially at the country level, as given. But it is interesting to explore with whom we are willing to share the decision-making on issues of public interest. Arguably, we inherit a historical legacy from our ancestors, but there have been examples of secession and breakups of countries in the late twentieth and early twenty-first centuries, while other cases remain widely debated or result in violence. Examples include the civil war and division of Yugoslavia, the separation of Sudan and South Sudan, recurring civil wars in a number of African countries, lingering calls for referendums in Quebec and Basque Country, and the more unusual case of the peaceful breakup of Czechoslovakia.

Post–Cold War examples of secession have motivated theoretical and empirical research by Alesina and Spolaore (1997, 2003) on the size and number of independent countries. They emphasize that borders are human-made decisions that result from a cost-benefit analysis. Larger jurisdictions benefit from economies of scale, both in the private and public sector, thus offering cost savings, more power, and security. On the other hand, more people create the potential for greater heterogeneity in preferences, and hence more conflict. Therefore, Alesina and Spolaore (1997, 2003) find that democratization leads to secession and an increase in the number of states or countries. Greater economic integration or globalization also leads to calls for political independence in their framework, since the benefits of economies of scale can be reaped by smaller jurisdictions if access to external markets is not linked to their political integration. In practice, though, access to markets is often linked to political integration, largely due to the existence of preferential trading arrangements rather than indiscriminate free trade. This can explain the main counter-example to country breakups in the late twentieth century, which is integration under the European Union (EU) and its iterative expansions. Nevertheless, we should also highlight that the 2016 United Kingdom (UK) referendum led to the decision to leave the EU and is commonly referred to as Brexit. This development raises several interesting questions: Can you hypothesize what led the UK in particular to leave the EU? What were the internal tensions behind the outcome of this referendum? What has been the impact of Brexit on different groups within the UK and the EU?

Most African states had their borders drawn by their colonial occupiers, and so they are a reflection of force rather than choice of unity. This historical legacy yielded countries with a high degree of ethnic, linguistic, and religious heterogeneity. Applying the framework of

Alesina and Spolaore (1997, 2003), such a great deal of heterogeneity is likely to lead to conflict. If we further take into consideration heterogeneity in resources – since many African countries are rich in natural resources, but these are inherently unequally distributed across regions – we have all the ingredients for conflict and civil war within national boundaries, which often spill over to neighbouring jurisdictions with closer ethnic ties. According to measures by Alesina et al. (2003), the 13 ethnically most diverse countries in the world are in sub-Saharan Africa, followed by the former Yugoslavia, and then seven more sub-Saharan African countries. Interestingly, religious diversity is highest in South Africa, the United States, and Australia, according to their measures.

Fearon and Laitin (2003) posited that it is poverty rather than ethnic or religious fractionalization that leads to conflict. However, their empirical methodology raises some concerns since prolonged conflict will arguably impede growth and yield low income per capita, and therefore income per capita cannot be regarded as an independent variable. This is especially the case if per capita income is only lagged by one year prior to the start of new civil conflict, as it does in their empirical study. The indicator of prior war (war in the previous year) is also statistically significant among their control variables, along with large populations, mountainous terrains, and being a newly independent state. They show that instability leads to conflict, but they do not explain what causes political instability in the first place. In the language of economic analysis, the study seems to be afflicted by the problem of endogeneity, which means there is a two-way causality between the dependent and independent or explanatory variables, thus yielding inconsistent estimators of the parameters.

1.7 ANARCHY VERSUS ORDER: PRIVATE AND PUBLIC SOLUTIONS TO ANARCHY IN TRADITIONAL AND MODERN SOCIETIES

It is equally interesting to explore why we come together to form states and governments at all, rather than just minding our own business and carrying on with our lives as individuals and families. Why do people tend to congregate and form towns and other associations? History suggests that strength and security are in numbers, and costs are also likely to decline with increases in economic scale. But we do not necessarily need to resort to analyzing primitive societies to explain why a modern person would still want to belong to a state. Even in contemporary societies, we can explore the counterfactual to the organization of a state. In other words, we can identify recent instances of state failure that illustrate what happens if we are on our own, without government and the rule of law. Instances of state failure occur at times of war, political unrest, or natural disaster, or they persist in very remote areas where more traditional social organizations still prevail beyond the control of modern states. War-torn Iraq, Sudan, and Somalia, the jungles of Colombia and Nigeria, post-earthquake Haiti, and remote tribal areas of Afghanistan and Pakistan are just a few examples from the early twenty-first century that are out of the reach of the state.[7] Similarly, illegal underground activities pose a significant challenge to state control in many Latin American countries such as Mexico and Guatemala, or low-income urban areas of Brazil or Colombia.[8] Piracy in international waters is another phenomenon that we used to read about in the annals of history, yet it also remains a twenty-first-century occurrence.

So, what happens in instances and regions beyond formal state control? They would be commonly characterized by chaos, violence, and lawlessness. People's lives and property would be at risk. Since strength is in numbers, people would typically aim to form groups. A closer examination would also likely reveal some type of organization, rules, and order, at least within these groups, even if the groups themselves may be in conflict with each other. In traditional societies, for example in remote tribal areas, the bonds within groups are likely to be strong due to family relations and the repeated interactions among a relatively small number of people, which foster conditions for long-term reputation-building and trust. In more modern settings that are urban, more mobile, and less isolated, the interactions become more short-term, anonymous, and continuously changing. This means the conditions for building trust and stability are less than ideal, and the situation becomes more volatile. This evolution from

---

7   See, for example, Ahmed (2007), Bakonyi (2013), Brands (2011), Castetter (2003), Kraxberger (2005), and Mumtaz (2010).
8   See, for example, Brands (2011) and Moncada (2013).

traditional to modern societies also illuminates the need and demand for centralized provision of security, as well as predictable laws and their enforcement, to establish stability for productive activity.

Wars, unrest, and power struggles are inherently inefficient since they only diminish the productive capacity of assets. The rule of law that creates a more stable and predictable environment for work and investment should therefore be productivity-enhancing and conducive to growth. Even criminal organizations apparently have an appreciation for this phenomenon, since research reveals that they exhibit strict, often ruthless, enforcement of their internal rules and agreements among each other.[9] Affiliation with a group offers protection in return. Individuals signal their group affiliation in a variety of ways, including tattoos, uniforms, or street graffiti – not unlike armies with their flags and uniforms representing specific countries.

The efficiency-enhancing aspect of government is a juncture where normative and positive political economy analyses come together. Political economy is concerned with costs, and inefficiency is costly to individuals and societies.

QUESTIONS FOR DISCUSSION AND FURTHER RESEARCH

1 Based on the above discussion of the incentives for individuals to organize into groups, can you explain why political parties exist?
2 Why are independent political candidates so rare in practice?

RESEARCH ADVICE: GETTING STARTED WITH YOUR OWN RESEARCH

You will find the subject of political economy all the more fascinating if you conduct your own research on a related issue. Here are some helpful tips on how to get started:

- If you do not already have a topic in mind, just turn on the news and you will find plenty of inspiration.
- Don't be afraid to pick a topic that you are not familiar with. In fact, for a junior researcher it can be most helpful to start in unfamiliar

9 See, for example, Reno (2009), Rodgers (2006), Sanchez-Jankowski (2003), Skarbek (2011), and Venkatesh (2008).

territory in order to have an open mind and avoid preconceived notions, potentially biasing the analysis.

- Political economy is not limited to the analysis of economic policy; hence, you can select *any* public policy issue for your research.
- The time frame of the public policy under investigation may affect the quality of the information available. Both historical and very recent public policy issues may pose challenges in terms of data availability, reliability, and validity.
- Similarly, while you can explore issues at all levels of government, problems under local government mandate are likely to have a relatively thin literature compared to issues of country-level interest. This text is not limited to any particular jurisdiction, and the concepts can be applied to any country, as well as to international interaction.
- Remember to maintain a *positive perspective* on the design and implementation of a specific public policy (or lack thereof) – that is, you should explain actual policy conduct.
- It will be helpful to formulate your proposed research in terms of a question. It will help you stay focused and analytical.
- Formalize your research plan in a written research proposal. This will help illuminate whether your plan is well defined or needs rethinking.

RESEARCH PROPOSAL GUIDELINES

- You cannot write a research proposal without conducting some preliminary research.
- A simple Internet search will not be enough. You need to be able to search the scholarly journal literature.
- In political economy, you will most likely need to conduct interdisciplinary research and utilize specialized search engines for scholarly publications in several disciplines, including political science, economics, sociology, and other social sciences, but you may need to venture into other disciplines as well.
- Given the significant variation in the scope of coverage of individual search engines (e.g., the number of journals indexed, whether working papers are included or not, etc.), please remember to use several of them, even within the same discipline.

- You should provide a minimum of ten references based on your literature search on the subject matter in your proposals.
- Comparative literature (i.e., research on the same area of public policy, but in the context of a different country) is also a good source of information and can be added to your reference list.
- The proposal should provide a brief context and motivation for the question to be analyzed. It is most convincing if you can motivate your research with some basic facts and statistics.
- You should also elaborate briefly on the unique contribution of the research to the literature, along with the methodology and potential data sources to be utilized.
- Consider carefully the quality of your data and their sources. Private interests have an incentive to influence public opinion and policy. Governments may have superior access to information, but keep in mind that politicians and public servants may have vested interests in what becomes published information and influence the methodology used to compile datasets. Independent non-government organizations with a reputable track record may provide more reliable information.[10]
- Referencing formats vary across disciplines and publication outlets. It is important to maintain consistency in the formatting of citations.
- Ask your instructor and peers for feedback on your proposal.

QUESTIONS FOR DISCUSSION AND FURTHER RESEARCH

1 Can you explain why, in general, analysis in scholarly journal publications is considered more credible than Internet postings or government reports?
2 How does the institution of tenure for faculty members at universities affect the credibility of scholarly publications?
3 Does this imply that faculty members and scholarly journal editors are free from ideological bias?

---

10 For example, Amnesty International is generally recognized as a more reliable source of information on human rights abuses than government sources. Investigative journalism more broadly is another example of non-scholarly information and analysis that is built on reputational capital.

CHAPTER TWO

Role and Size of Government

Why do governments exist? At the most basic level, the incentives for forming groups and formal and informal structures to govern them (rather than tackling challenges on our own) include cost savings and other benefits stemming from coordination and the pooling of resources. Conceptually, the motivations for governments can be summarized under the headings of correcting for market failure and inefficiencies and creating scope for redistribution.

The size of government and the degree of government involvement in the economy and society also change over time and vary across jurisdictions based on a number of factors. These factors include both demand and supply elements. For example, demographic changes and preferences for redistribution affect the demand for government, while revenue-generating capabilities affect the supply of government services.

In general, governments entail a hierarchy of decision-making and administrative powers and responsibilities. What are the trade-offs involved in allocating authority to local, regional, or national/country-level/central[1] governments? And to what extent are government decisions driven by ideology and partisanship rather than data or mainstream public opinion?

---

1   Note that terminology may vary by jurisdiction or database.

Upon reviewing this chapter, you should be able to do the following:

- differentiate conceptually between the different motivations for forming governance structures involving market failure, inefficiency, and redistribution
- identify different types of market failure, the scope for efficiencies, and redistribution
- understand the intersections and divergence of normative and positive analyses of public policy
- appreciate that social justice is only one form of redistribution and that it is a fundamentally subjective concept that can take on varied interpretations, thus leading to diverse preferences
- analyze the impact of ideology, demographic changes, economic development, and globalization on the demand for government as well as on public revenue-generating capabilities
- identify the trade-offs involved in centralizing or decentralizing decision-making and administrative authority across different levels of government

The box example in this chapter explores if ideology or economic conditions drive the revealed preference for sons over daughters in some South Asian communities. The research tips at the end of the chapter provide guidance on methods for gathering information on preferences and ideology. The concepts of validity and reliability in data collection are introduced, along with the building blocks of research ethics protocols and cultural competence for research involving human participants.

2.1 MARKET FAILURE, INEFFICIENCY, AND REDISTRIBUTION AS MOTIVATION FOR GOVERNMENT

In the previous chapter, we discussed briefly the counterfactual to the presence of government using the examples of state failure at times of war or in the context of criminal organizations. The main drawback of chaos and lawlessness is the unpredictability of outcomes and lack of security for persons and property. Under such conditions, a substantial portion of resources have to be devoted to security, which is from an economic point of view unproductive activity and use of resources, since it entails opportunity costs in terms of foregone alternative forms of investment and output. To save on security costs, individuals are motivated to form groups, which provide strength in numbers and lower costs of security per person, since security services can be shared among group members. In economic terms, the declining cost of protection per person as the size of the group increases represents *economies of scale*. Conceptually, this motivation for forming states (or other jurisdictions) and structures to govern them can be put under the heading of efficiency, since it would be very costly, and thus inefficient, for each of us to look after our own security interests alone. There would be fewer resources left over for other productive activities and investment, thus stifling growth.

Similarly, markets sometimes fail, and we would not be able to obtain certain goods and services in markets unless society's resources are pooled specifically for such a purpose. The case in point is *public goods*, which provide shared benefits to all in society. As individuals, we might have incentives to free ride on the contributions of others to the provision of public goods, and hence governments are created to compel us to make contributions to the common resource pool. Chapter 3 will analyze the provision of public goods in detail.

Examples of market failure can be less extreme than the non-existence of markets for a particular good or service and may include, for instance, dominant sellers or buyers in markets that lead to deviations from competitive pricing and distort incentives for investment and innovation. Such outcomes entail inefficiency and costs to the rest of the economy and society, and therefore we have incentives to organize and address those issues through public regulation.

In addition to inefficiency and market failure, a third general motivation for government is redistribution. Given the enforcement powers to pool resources, there exists scope for significant redistribution in society. Nevertheless, it is essential to note that redistribution is not limited to transfers from the "rich" to the "poor," or some form of social justice. Redistribution can simply mean the appropriation of funds or resources from one group to the benefit of others. As chapter 6 will explain in detail, it is not necessarily obvious, or easy to determine, who bears the actual burden of redistribution even when tax law explicitly specifies who will be paying the tax. Implicit transfers of the burden of redistribution are common. In general, though, the theoretical political economy literature highlights that as voter heterogeneity increases, so do redistributive conflict and the size of government as a means of building political alliances (Persson et al., 1998; Persson & Tabellini, 1999; Annett, 2001, Tridimas & Winer, 2005).

It is important to note that motivations for government along the dimensions of redistribution, efficiency, and correcting for market failure are likely to compete for resources or be outright contradictory in terms of desired outcomes. Therefore, decision-making on public policy issues will always be a balancing act, weighing conflicting interests at the level of the individual and the collective.

We can identify areas of concern common to positive and normative analysis of public policy. Efficiency is of primary concern to normative economics, for example. Social justice is on the agenda of social sciences in general. However, it is especially difficult to define what social justice is since it is the ultimate normative concept based on subjective value systems.[2] Different individuals or groups may emphasize different aspects of justice, including procedural equality, equality of opportunities, equality of outcomes, or rewarding effort or competence, for example. Varying interpretations of justice in society yield different outcomes and are likely to be contradictory at some level to each other. For instance, an equal degree of criminal liability for a healthy individual and one with schizophrenia would contrast with the principle of equality of opportunity. Equality of economic outcomes emphasized under communist ideology clashed with the principle of rewarding effort and motivation. Only rewarding effort and productivity, on the other hand, would infringe on the principle of equal opportunity and outcomes in the case of severely disabled individuals.

Overall, preferences along the dimensions of social justice are complex. While students are often tempted to use the terms "fairness" and "justice" interchangeably, I like to caution against the use of the terms "fair" or "fairness" because of their great degree of vagueness and subjectivity. It is possible to dissect the concepts of justice or equity in more

---

2 Students should be careful not to confuse normative concepts with normative analysis, introduced in chapter 1. Normative concepts, such as an individuals' value systems, are very much part of positive analysis because they capture agent heterogeneity.

detail and pinpoint their key functional elements in a more analytical manner, rather than just referring to some perception of "fairness."

It is interesting to explore the determinants of one's preferences related to social justice and how life experiences, group affiliation, and the surrounding formal and informal institutional environment might shape them. For more, turn to research in areas of sociology, anthropology, psychology, and behavioural economics. More on methods employed in sociological research can be found at the end of this chapter.

In the next section, we turn to exploring how shifts in economic development have shaped preferences for government involvement in the economy and society more broadly.

2.2 THE SIZE OF GOVERNMENT AND ECONOMIC DEVELOPMENT

Economists typically measure the size of government by the ratio of government revenue or expenditure relative to gross domestic product (GDP) in a given year.[3] There is a clear positive relationship between the size of government and income per capita both historically, over the developmental path of a given jurisdiction, and in cross-country comparisons, as wealthier countries tend to have larger governments, holding other things equal, as shown in figure 2.1.

There are several possible explanations for this trend. First of all, government can only be as significant as its size or revenue-generating powers. Taxes are the most significant form of public revenue generation,[4] and taxable capacity is closely linked to income. If most of the population is very poor and spends all its income on food, shelter, and other necessities of life, there is little scope for government taxation.

On the demand side, several demographic trends have contributed to increased demand for government over time. As per capita income and the level of economic development increase, women gain more education and work outside the household, and the birth rate

---

3 In general, government expenditure as a percentage of GDP tends to be a more stable and readily available measure of the size of government than the revenue-to-GDP ratio.

4 State-owned enterprises tend not to be a significant source of government revenue. Similarly, printing money or inflationary taxation is not a sustainable form of revenue generation.

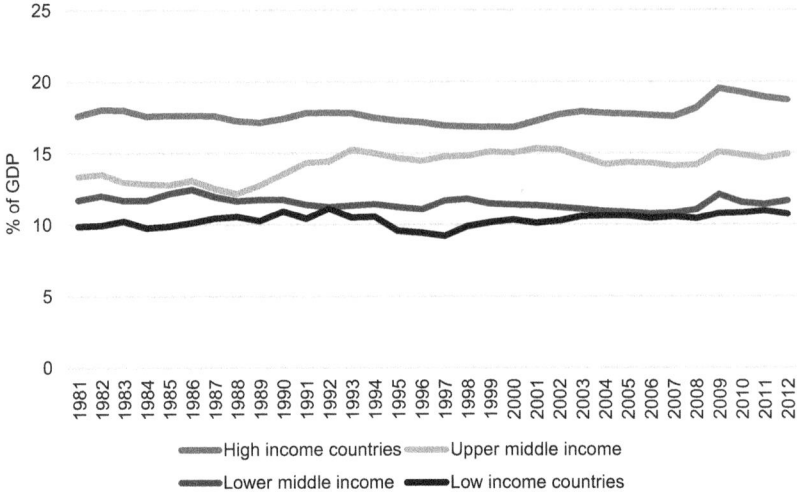

Figure 2.1. Size of government: general government final consumption expenditure, % GDP

Source: World Bank (2025b).

declines. This is a well-documented global phenomenon, as illustrated in figure 2.2. Possible explanations for this trend include factors such as more education leading to later age of first marriage (which reduces total fertility), work for pay increasing the opportunity cost of having children, and improving the bargaining position of women with regards to fertility control. Positive developmental outcomes, such as a decline in infant mortality rates, have also been linked to declining birth rates. If families target a certain number of surviving children, then the reduction in infant mortality would imply more fertility control.

Once fewer children are born, their survival prospects improve, child labour recedes, and children spend more time in school instead. Becker (1981) theorized that under such conditions parents have more incentives to invest in the "quality" of their children – for example, in terms of education – rather than quantity, since children transition from being a source of income to cost-generators. Becker's theory is consistent with observed empirical trends, as shown in figure 2.2. The traditional social contract, under which children would

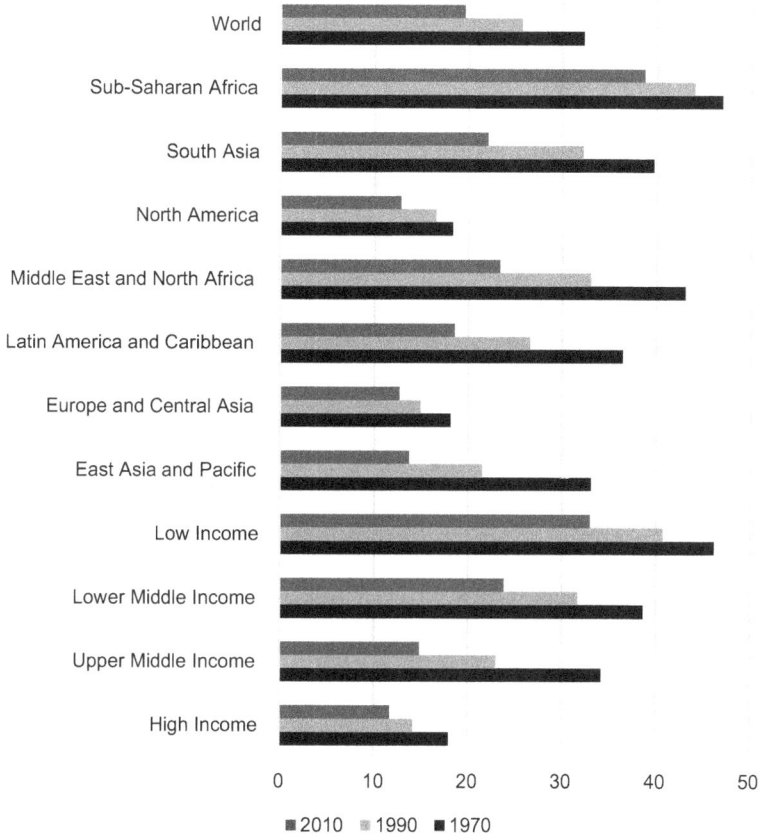

Figure 2.2. Crude birth rate (per 1,000 people)
Source: World Bank (2025a).

take care of their parents in old age, has also changed as a result of economic development. The rise of industry led to migration and urbanization, disintegrating traditional family-centred settings. The opportunity cost of taking care of the elderly has increased (especially for women), while expected lifespans have expanded substantially. Between 1970 and 2010, average life expectancy in high-income countries increased from 70 to nearly 79 years, while in low-income countries the increase was even larger, from 51 to nearly 66 years (World Bank, 2025b) The issue of old age security on the public agenda has grown in tandem with these demographic trends. The elderly are also among the most active voters in many jurisdictions, especially in high-income countries. For example, in federal elections in Canada since 2004 voter participation rates have been the highest for the 65–74 age group (Elections Canada, 2011).

Other aspects of social security also gained importance in the course of the twentieth century. With the onset of the Great Depression in the 1930s, calls for government involvement in the provision of a systematic social safety net intensified in the face of economic hardship. Basic welfare support, unemployment and health insurance, and macroeconomic stabilization emerged on the public agenda. Today, social protection and health-related expenditure account for the largest difference in the structure of government expenditure across poor and high-income countries (see, e.g., Fan et al., 2008; OECD, 2013).

Globalization has also had a profound impact on government. The late twentieth-century wave of globalization is only one among many in the history of humanity, but a historical analysis is beyond the scope of this text. We will limit our attention to the wave of economic liberalization since the late 1980s. Most empirical studies on the impact of globalization have focused on trade integration, but the liberalization of capital flows and their dramatic surge in the 1990s has had the most dramatic impact around the world. Economic theory has predicted benefits primarily from the potential for international risk-sharing in a liberalized environment, but capital market imperfections and the volatility of capital flows have in fact propagated the spillover of financial crises across jurisdictions in the 1990s and 2000s. Given public "demand" for macroeconomic stabilization to limit the fallout of economic downturns on living standards, financial crises have renewed interest in the question of whether more open economies tend to have larger or smaller governments.

Smaller government size under globalization would be consistent with the theoretical propositions for risk-pooling, while larger governments are likely to be symptomatic of compensating government spending in response to economic downturns and financial sector bailouts. Empirical evidence is somewhat mixed in this area of research, but this can also be explained by methodological differences and sample size, since many studies have focused only on high-income OECD countries, which typically benefited from financial integration until the financial crisis that erupted in the United States in 2008. In addition to such sample selection bias, openness has traditionally been measured only as trade openness (i.e., exports plus imports as a percentage of GDP), thus ignoring international capital flows, which have arguably been an even stronger determinant of economic outcomes. Once financial openness is taken into consideration in a large sample of developed and developing countries, as in Kimakova (2009), evidence reinforces Rodrik's (1998) finding that more open economies tend to have larger governments.

The liberalization of international capital flows has also negatively affected the tax capacity of governments and the distribution of the burden of taxation between labour and capital. Chapter 6 on fiscal policy will provide a detailed analysis of the matter, but it is interesting to note that political critics, researchers, and media commentators have typically attributed such policy changes to neo-liberal ideology rather than changing economic realities. The collapse of the Soviet Bloc and socialism was an ideological victory for more liberal policies, but the preceding restrictions on international capital flows were just as much driven by ideology, nationalism, and politics as economics and public interest. This highlights that, in practice, it is very difficult to differentiate between ideology, private special interests, or changing economic realities driving public policy, especially when the accompanying rhetoric by various stakeholders is strategic and politically motivated.

QUESTIONS FOR DISCUSSION AND FURTHER RESEARCH

1 What has been the effect of technological advancement on the size of government and its involvement in the economy and society more broadly?
2 Update figure 2.1 above to see how the COVID-19 pandemic affected government size, specifically government expenditure relative to GDP. Were the changes temporary or do you detect some persistent trends?
3 Has technology affected the democratic process in developed and developing countries? If yes, how?
4 In countries like China and Cuba, which oddly combine a mixture of communist party rule and elements of market economy, is there still a battle between communist ideology and economic interests, or is it simply incumbents holding on to power and its payoffs? Which variables would you look at to answer this question?

2.3 TO CENTRALIZE OR DECENTRALIZE?

An interesting aspect of government is the degree of its centralization versus the delegation of authority to lower levels of government. The Decentralization Theorem states that lower levels of government are "closer" to their electorate, and therefore have a greater potential to represent the heterogeneity of their interests (Oates, 1972). Closer monitoring also has the potential for limiting principal-agent problems. On the other hand, central governments have greater taxable capacity and face more competing interests, hence making it potentially more difficult for special interests to capture government.

Whether more centralized or decentralized governments are more prone to corruption is theoretically ambiguous, and thus ultimately an empirical question. But empirical analyses of the determinants and effects of decentralization have suffered from a lack of quality data. Economists typically approximate the degree of decentralization by the share of sub-national government expenditure (or revenue) in total public spending (or revenue). Such crude approximations do not account for the degree of actual decision-making authority by lower levels of government or political decentralization. A large share of revenue or spending for sub-national governments is made up by transfers from central government (due to its greater taxable capacity), but these funds often come with strings attached that limit decision-making autonomy by lower levels of public representation and administration. It is possible to have a high proportion of sub-national government expenditure combined with very little decision-making powers, and therefore a great deal of caution should be exercised when interpreting empirical studies on government decentralization.

There exists a great deal of variation across jurisdictions along the dimension of political decentralization. Federalism has typically emerged in reaction to geographically diverse interests stemming from unequally distributed natural resources, ethnic and religious diversity, or divergent economic interests. The functional distribution of government responsibility across levels of government also varies greatly, which has implications for economic and social outcomes. Defense tends to be a central government responsibility, but education, health, and industry regulation can fall under different levels of government. In the absence of equalizing payments and national/country-level standards, inequality can prevail across sub-national areas of control, but these can be a reflection of the diversity of preferences or power relations.

Since direct democracy is more likely to be exercised at the level of local or municipal governments, local referendums have been utilized to draw comparisons between policy outcomes under direct versus representative democracy. Referendums are also more likely to reveal individual preferences rather than strategic political bargaining on a multitude of issues undertaken by political representatives. Since some jurisdictions favour referendums more than others (e.g., Switzerland, California), they are also more heavily represented in the literature. Hainmueller and Hangartner (2013) found that when immigration and naturalization decisions were switched from local referendums to decisions made by elected politicians on local councils in Switzerland, the approved naturalization rates showed a dramatic increase of 50 per cent. The authors argue that referendums allow citizens to vote with their anti-immigrant prejudices, while elected representatives are held accountable to justify their decisions, thus limiting the potential for discriminatory rejections. In line with individual self-interest and expectations of tax liability, evidence suggests that referendums also tend to limit government revenue growth and income redistribution (see, e.g., Park et al., 2010; Feld et al., 2010).

QUESTIONS FOR DISCUSSION AND FURTHER RESEARCH

If sub-national governments possess strong veto rights, policy changes at the national level can be difficult to achieve.

1 Can you provide examples of such countries and affected policies?
2 Would the policy outcomes likely be different under one centralized government?

2.4 PARTISANSHIP AND POLITICAL POLARIZATION VERSUS MIDDLE-OF-THE-RANGE POLITICS

An interesting question to explore is to what extent extreme political views have the potential to drive political agendas and actual policies. The traditional *median voter model* suggests that middle-of-the range politics are more likely to prevail since political candidates have incentives to appeal to the middle of the political spectrum to capture the most votes.[5] But such an equilibrium can be unstable, depending on the number of major political candidates in the running. Several practical implications can be drawn from the median voter model. The model can explain the often-observed opportunism by political leaders to sacrifice principles and move towards compromise. In such situations, it can be difficult to differentiate among political party platforms. On the other hand, principled politicians with inflexible positions will always lose in a median voter framework because more flexible opponents can position themselves to appeal to a larger proportion of the electorate.

If certain parts of the electorate are more active voters than others, then it can create uncertainty about the identity of the median voter and their preferences. If more extreme parts of the electorate are more active or influential politically, then polarization can prevail in political representation. Partisanship is often analyzed in the context of the United States, not just because it is a large and internationally influential country, but also because its two-party system makes it easier methodologically to identify partisan leanings and consistency in views with party platforms. A 2014 survey by the Pew Research Center (PRC) clearly showed that the degree of political polarization is greater in the politically active population than in the general population.[6] The PRC (2014a) report also provides a look at the changes in political polarization in the United States over a 20-year span between 1994 and 2014. The results confirm the stylized fact that political polarization has in fact increased over the studied period: Partisans have moved further apart from each other, and the share of the US public with mixed views has diminished. The ideological shifts towards more partisan views, or even divergence and polarization within parties, have occurred both among Republicans and Democrats, and not just on social issues, but also with respect to economic policy and size of government. It is not surprising, then, to see deadlock rather than compromise

---

5   For an account of the historical development of the median voter model, see Congleton (2004).
6   You can view a graphical illustration of the difference at PRC (2014b).

in the US Congress and Senate, which even led to the shutdown of a range of federal government services in 2013 amidst a stalemate about budget approval and raising the debt ceiling. A decade later, the stalemate about raising the debt ceiling and disagreements about fiscal spending/cuts and revenue are more frequent and severe, with hostile polarization and deep ideological divisions even within the same political parties.

Ideological differences exist across countries as well. Even among high-income countries in the western hemisphere, encompassing the United States and Western European countries, we can identify stark differences. For example, when presented with the question of whether individual freedoms without state interference or state guarantees for social justice are more important, 58 per cent of the US public chose individual freedom compared to only 30 per cent in Spain, and 36–8 per cent in Germany, France, and Britain (Pew Research Center, 2011). Strikingly, 70 per cent of German respondents agreed with the statement that "success in life is determined by forces outside our control," compared to only 36 per cent of US respondents (Q15a and Q61, Pew Research Center, 2011). Similarly, nearly half the US and German public believe in their cultural superiority,[7] compared with only 27 per cent in France (Q15b, Pew Research Center, 2011). Religion plays a much more significant role in the US belief system when compared to Western European countries: Morality and belief in "God" are estimated to be aligned for roughly half the population in the United States, compared to only 15 per cent in France (Q17, Pew Research Center, 2011). Religion is "very important" to about half the population in the United States, and there is no major difference in this regard for those with or without college education. Only with respect to the assertion that "it is necessary to believe in God to be moral" do we see differentiation by educational attainment: 59 per cent of respondents without a college education agree with the above statement, compared to 37 per cent of those with a college education (Q17 and Q118, Pew Research Center, 2011).

---

7   The belief in American cultural superiority has actually declined, having been held in 60 per cent of the population roughly a decade earlier in 2002 (Pew Research Center, 2011).

QUESTIONS FOR DISCUSSION AND FURTHER RESEARCH

1 Can you formulate other questions aimed at measuring ideological beliefs?
2 On which public policy issues are ideology and partisan politics likely to be more influential than other factors, such as the state of the economy, scientific evidence, or embedded costs and benefits to individuals and groups?

BOX 2.1. THE PREFERENCE FOR SONS OVER DAUGHTERS: IS IT DRIVEN BY POVERTY OR IDEOLOGY?

The sex ratio at birth is naturally slightly skewed towards male children, with 1.05 male births per female birth in most parts of the world. However, the sex ratio at birth has been higher and on the rise in South Asia, increasing from 1.075 in 1990 to 1.097 in 2010 (World Bank, 2025b). The preference for male offspring in South Asia and China has manifested itself in gender-based abortions, neglect of female babies, and infanticide. The dominant hypothesis aimed at explaining such harsh realities has focused on poverty and deeply entrenched economic and social discrimination against women. In other words, if sons have a significantly greater earnings potential than daughters, and parents rely on their children to provide welfare in old age, then parents will have a strong preference for male children.

Almond et al. (2013) aimed to control for the effect of poverty on the decision for selective abortion of female fetuses by analyzing 2001 and 2006 Canadian census data for South and East Asian immigrants. They found that the data still revealed a preference for sons over daughters, even after facing vastly different economic circumstances and the earnings potential of female children being much improved and closer to that of male children.[1] The authors concluded that it was cultural or ideological partialities, rather than harsh economic conditions, driving the preference for sons. This is also consistent with another finding in their study that the selective preference for male children was not detected among Christian and Muslim immigrants from South and East Asia, who shared the same economic environment, but differed in terms of their religious beliefs regarding abortion.

---

1   Pay equity for women has not been achieved in Canada, either. For example, in Ontario, the estimated gender wage gap in 2011 was 26 per cent (Pay Equity Commission, 2012).

2.5 REDISTRIBUTION AND ITS FORMS

As mentioned earlier, social justice is only one rather limited form of redistribution that entails transfers from the "rich" to the "poor" or from the "young" to the "old" under so-called pay-as-you-go pension systems. Redistribution should be more broadly understood as the appropriation of assets by one group at the expense of others, or the redistribution of costs and benefits associated with a particular public policy stance. The costs and benefits can be explicit or implicit, actual or opportunity costs, for example.

Common forms of redistribution have been taxation, the appropriation of natural resources from Indigenous populations by colonizers or other dominant population groups, and racial, gender, and other types of discrimination in labour markets. Other less obvious forms of redistribution include government borrowing, inflation, or trade regulations, for example.

Government borrowing and the accumulation of debt imply that current taxes are lower, but unless there is significant growth in tax revenue to alleviate the relative burden of the nominal debt (i.e., the debt to GDP ratio), future tax rates will have to increase as a result. Higher taxes in the future will have to be paid by future generations; hence, the accumulation of government debt is a form of redistribution from the "young" or future generations to the "old" or current generation.

Inflation is a general rise in price level over time, which means that if we just hold on to our money in the form of cash, the purchasing power of this given nominal sum of money diminishes over time as prices increase. While inflation affects everyone in the economy, it does not affect everyone the same way. Those who are on fixed incomes – for example, pensioners or workers – lose purchasing power as a result of inflation. This is because even if pensions and wages get adjusted to inflation, there is typically a time lag involved in the adjustment, and uncompensated losses occur in the meantime. Business owners, on the other hand, can respond to increases in the cost of inputs in a timelier manner and pass on the costs of inflation to consumers. Inflation also leads to redistribution between lenders and borrowers. Borrowing costs in the form of interest rates incorporate expected inflation, but if actual inflation overshoots its expected level, then lenders are not fully compensated for the resulting loss in purchasing power upon repayment of debt and borrowers benefit instead – at least in the short run. In the medium to long term, inflationary expectations adjust upwards, and in light of uncertainty may even overshoot, overall increasing the costs of borrowing or even reducing the availability of loanable funds. In general, inflation tends to hurt the poor rather than the wealthy, because the incomes of the wealthy are more likely to adjust in line with inflation.

Overall, government debt accumulation and inflation are examples of inter-temporal redistribution since the impact is over time. The role of time in the distribution of costs and benefits, and resulting incentives, will be explored in detail in chapter 3.

Government regulations in general have a redistributive effect. One area of government regulation that we are all inevitably exposed to as consumers is international trade policy. The effects of this particular category of regulation are publicized and debated widely, but their true redistributive effects are not necessarily obvious or well understood among the public. Tariffs and quotas on imports are typically justified on the basis of protecting domestic jobs. However, since trade regulations are very much sector-specific, they tend to protect a small minority, while imposing costs on domestic consumers and those employed in the exporting sectors by exposing them to potential retaliatory measures and reducing their competitiveness by inducing currency appreciation.

2.6 PROPERTY RIGHTS, DISCRIMINATION, AND REDISTRIBUTIVE CONFLICT

The ability to assert, secure, and transfer property rights has historically varied greatly across and within jurisdictions in relation to attributes such as gender, race and ethnicity, economic class, and political affiliation. While progress has been made with development, at least in terms of official declarations of equality in most jurisdictions, de facto variations in the enforcement of property rights remain widespread.

For instance, Sargeson (2008) analyzed instances of land expropriation in the Chinese province of Zhejiang between 2001 and 2006 and found significant discrimination in terms of the compensation paid to female landowners. Often the property appropriated by the government was communal farms, for which the women worked and held shares. The compensation was frequently at below-market values or in less liquid non-monetary forms. Since household property is typically registered in the name of the male head of household alone, intra-family redistribution of the compensation was also an important determinant of the value of the compensation women received and led to great variation. Arguably, this situation illustrates gender-based discrimination in property rights in the twenty-first century, but it is just another example of an all too common story that has played out countless times throughout history across the globe and still persists. In the context of sub-Saharan African countries, Whitehead and Tsikata (2003) outline the main policy discourses in relation to the protection of women's land rights. They highlight the resurgence of preference among national and international policy-making institutions for so-called customary systems of land tenure, which ignore the persistent power inequities between men and women in political representation as well as in households. Therefore, the dissenting voices argue for better statutory law protection for women's property rights, rather than a return to customary law.

Khadiagala (2001) provides evidence in support of this dissenting view from Uganda by analyzing adjudicating decisions for property disputes by traditional local councils. The paper also highlights that the discrepancy between the theory and practice of popular or traditional justice arises from the tendency to assume some inherent morality on the part of local communities. Such a normative view of policy-making stands in contrast to the political economy approach adopted by Khadiagala, who shows that if marriage is patrilocal – meaning that women relocate to live with their husband's family – then family land disputes will end up being adjudicated by local male elites who have personal ties to their husband's family, and thus a clear conflict of interest. Overall, the women involved in the study perceived the local courts to be biased against them.

The broader implication of the analysis of developing country contexts and traditional forms of conflict resolution is the rise in demand for statutory law protection for property rights and their enforcement through an independent judiciary. Although modern states are better equipped to provide such protections to their citizens, conflicts of interest and discrimination do not simply vanish. Expropriations of property still occur in developing and developed countries, with the only potential difference being the degree of difficulty and costs associated with such expropriation.

When the exercise of property rights is aimed primarily at the exclusion of others, it is referred to as *anticommons*. There are symmetric inefficiencies associated with both anticommons and commons (or communal property) in the form of underutilization and overuse of assets, respectively, as shown in Buchanan and Yoon (2000), but the implications for political power relations are just as important. Heller (1998), for example, illustrates several applications of the anticommons in the context of the transition from socialism to market economy in Russia and the fractionation of Indigenous land.

The expropriation of land, other natural resources, and even personal freedom from Indigenous populations by colonial powers or other dominant ethnic or religious groups has undoubtedly led to economic devastation and the absence of resources to maintain autonomous governments in Indigenous societies. In the absence of such political and resource autonomy, implications for regulating education and language use emerged, which further exacerbated power imbalances. Many children from these minority groups then underperform in the formal educational system (if they have access to it) and ultimately as economic participants, thus propagating the cycles of poverty, discrimination, and disenfranchisement. The contexts in which to analyze the linkages between expropriation, power imbalances, language and cultural identity, and discrimination are widely available around the world, and the research spans over different disciplinary areas including sociology, linguistics, anthropology, political science, law, and economics. For example, Skutnabb-Kangas (2012) argues that while we have increasingly seen proclamations of respect for Indigenous rights, especially in the international arena, they are likely to lack substance in the face of persistent power inequities and a lack of resources to support cultural autonomy.

The issue of Indigenous rights has received a great deal of attention in the context of mineral mining, property rights, and the environmental and economic externalities of mining activities. Warden-Fernandez (2001) provides an overview of mining development on Indigenous lands and legal challenges to such activities in Australia, Canada, New Zealand, and several Latin American countries including Colombia, Argentina, Peru, Ecuador, and Bolivia. The common elements in these conflict-prone situations include the fact that Indigenous populations typically only have the rights of consultation but not veto; the mineral rights tend to be separate from land rights and rest with the state, and hence only a small fraction of the profits generated reaches the Indigenous populations. All the while, the direct environmental impact of mineral extraction is borne by the Indigenous communities, and is a representation of a *negative externality*. Such an asymmetric distribution of the costs, benefits, and decision-making powers related to mining activities provide all the ingredients for conflict, whether through court challenges or violence, but invariably with significant long-term economic and political implications.

Conflicts in the context of biodiversity, commercialization of genetic resources and the sharing of those proceeds, patent law, and sustainability, both globally and in the circumstances of Indigenous communities where most of the world's untapped genetic resources remain, have also intensified around the world. In this context, US patent law sets the stage. This is because US patent protection is generally considered to be the strongest around the globe, due to the public and private enforcement capabilities provided by US law, amplified internationally by the economic powers of the United States as a large economy and major actor in international politics. Nevertheless, the US Patent and Trademark Office has been widely criticized for its low standards for the granting of rights when very small rather than significant innovation is demonstrated by the submitting parties seeking protection. In such circumstances, patent and trademark protection would represent exclusion rights or anticommons motivated by abnormal profits rather than reward for innovation and the investment involved in it.

For example, in 1997 the United States granted a Texas company a patent over a type of basmati rice, to the outrage of the governments and people of India and Pakistan, who view the basmati rice variety as part of their Indigenous biodiversity. The patent legally limited the ability of Indian and Pakistani producers to market their produce under the well-recognized basmati name, and hence infringed on their rights and profits by distorting the current competitive conditions in the world market for basmati rice. The outrage turned global and ignited opposition against the World Trade Organization and globalization more broadly. After protracted legal and political opposition, the US patent was revised in 2001 to provide protection only for a few variants of the rice. The Indian government viewed it as a victory and a cautionary tale at the same time, since the case highlighted the potential for further redistributive conflict between developing countries and corporations (Rai, 2001).

The theoretical concept often applied in property disputes involving externalities is the so-called Coase Theorem, which implies that as long as transaction costs are low, the initial assignment of property rights is irrelevant because through bargaining the parties will arrive at an efficient outcome (Coase, 1960). It is important to note that the "efficient outcome" in this context is purely in terms of the efficient use of resources and irrespective of the redistributive implications, since it is aggregate social welfare that matters in this framework, rather than the welfare of the individual parties involved. In other words, social justice would not be a consideration in this setting. Moreover, the conditions for arriving at an economically efficient outcome are unlikely to be met in practice to begin with. For example, transactions costs involved in bargaining are non-trivial, especially for marginalized communities. The information requirements for efficient bargaining are also high, while in practice imperfect information is likely to prevail. The number of negotiating parties also matters: It is easier to arrive at a solution between two parties than many, and the parties in the dispute may differ in organizational ability to present a united front. It matters if the bargaining is an iterative process or a one-time offer, also referred to as an ultimatum game. Slonim and Roth (1998) showed, through an experimental design with actual cash payouts to participants, that learning takes place in high-stakes ultimatum games. Offers for the division of proceeds between two parties (in an unspecified context to avoid psychological reactions to situations with different perceived ethical connotations) declined over time with learning. At the same time, the frequency of rejections of offers in high-stakes games was low, despite the low offers. The implications for potentially arriving at mutually satisfactory outcomes between expert negotiators with significant resources at their disposal, such as large corporations, and low-income families or marginalized communities are grim in practice. The potential for redistributive appropriation is significant in such contexts, and hence the initial assignment of property rights will matter in practice, as well as the protections provided through statutory laws rather than just private bargaining.[8]

QUESTIONS FOR DISCUSSION AND FURTHER RESEARCH

1 In the context of colonialism, can you provide historical examples of artificially created monopolies by colonial powers, and the implications for inequities in wealth accumulation and power relations?
2 Which theoretical concepts would you utilize to explain the emergence of those inequities?

RESEARCH ADVICE: GATHERING INFORMATION ON PREFERENCES

AND IDEOLOGY

As discussed above, measuring voter preferences is a difficult task. Election results do not necessarily reveal voter preferences since they may reflect strategic behaviour, the bundling of different issues into one political representation, the disengagement of certain voter groups, or disenfranchisement of others.

The methodologies employed in gathering information on individual preferences include surveys, ethnographies, critical discourse analysis, or controlled experiments and simulations. These methods typically involve subjective elements in terms of self-evaluation on the part of the research subjects, and design and interpretative discretion on the part of the researchers. For example, if we aim to measure the

---

8 In the context of experimental designs, Henrich (2000) further demonstrated cultural differences in bargaining and offers in ultimatum games. He hypothesized that cultural differences in concepts of "fairness" and what is expected behaviour among their counterparts yield variation in offers from more equal to more skewed, self-interested distributions of proceeds.

prevalence of racism in society, it is hardly going to be sufficient to ask individuals in a survey if they are racist. Awareness of racism is not a prerequisite for holding such beliefs and declarations to that effect are also likely to be strategic, even in the context of an anonymous survey. Therefore, caution should be exercised when designing and interpreting surveys and research based on them. A few broad elements to look out for include the following:

- Examine closely the survey questions for any signs of ambiguity or biased wording.
- Look for control questions – that is, questions asking about the same key issues in different questions from different perspectives. If the answers are inconsistent, consider it a red flag and explore potential explanations for such inconsistencies.
- Check for validity: Are the questions actually measuring what we intended to measure or are they a reflection of something else?
- Check for reliability: Can we measure the same concepts consistently over time and across different populations with varied educational, linguistic, and cultural backgrounds?

Sampling is another important aspect of data collection to consider. The size of the sample and the representativeness of the target population are the key elements to explore. Therefore, online polls by media outlets that rely on self-selection cannot be relied on for accuracy. Random selection or stratified random selection are desired for scientific evidence. However, there are circumstances when it is not possible to achieve random sampling due to access or ethical considerations. For example, some target populations can be small, largely inaccessible, or over-researched. These are typically ethnic minorities or subcultures, often marginalized groups. Random selection and sample size typically become secondary considerations in those cases. Ethnographies generally rely on smaller sample sizes but look for common elements in the information gathered.

Accuracy in the interpretation of results ought to be critically evaluated. In the context of subcultures and marginalized communities, the issue of cultural competence or understanding has been receiving growing attention. Some researchers and program evaluators require cultural competence to entail lived experience rather than just academic or professional credentials. This also raises the issue of to what extent stakeholders, rather than just notional independent researchers, should be involved in the design phase of information gathering. Philosophical and ethical concerns range from limiting the potential for conflict of interest to aiming to correct for traditional power inequities by empowering marginalized communities with a voice in the design process.

To enhance validity and reliability in data collection and interpretation, feedback mechanisms can be employed, including, for example, peer evaluation and stakeholder feedback, which is also called "member checks."

Research involving human participants inevitably raises ethical considerations. You need to make sure to receive approval from the relevant research oversight authority at your academic institution, and potentially other organizations involved, prior to commencing research. Research ethics policies may vary across institutions, but key common elements include the following:

- informed consent by research participants outlining process expectations and potential harms involved
- voluntary participation and leave to withdraw consent at any time without negative repercussions
- anonymity and confidentiality guarantees
- considerations of potential benefits and harms to participants, and minimizing risks

QUESTIONS FOR DISCUSSION AND FURTHER RESEARCH

1 Pick a public opinion poll and closely examine its design elements. Do you think the given poll meets the standards for validity and reliability? Explain your answer.
2 In a number of jurisdictions, including Canada, providing personal information in a government-sanctioned public census is mandatory and refusal to participate is a criminal offense. This stands in stark contrast to the principle of voluntary participation commonly engraved in academic research protocols or libertarian values more broadly. Research the factors that led to the adoption of such laws in a given jurisdiction.

CHAPTER THREE

Public and Private Goods under Government Mandate

What are public goods? Do governments fund only public goods? How does the way in which goods are supplied affect their costs, quantity, and quality? How do factors such as external effects, uncertainty, and time affect the decision to provide or not provide certain goods under a government mandate? What is the likely degree of government involvement in the provision of various goods?

Questions like this can be very confusing. The first step to tackling these questions is to master the technical definitions of key economic concepts and to keep in mind that the colloquial understanding of some terms – such as "public good," for example – can be very different from their technical definition in the field of economics. The objective of this chapter is to provide key definitions and methodological tools for students to be able to do the following:

- define clearly and understand key economic concepts such as public and private goods, positive and negative externalities, moral hazard, and market competition
- differentiate the government decision to fund a good from the decision to supply the good, and recognize the variety of goods that may fall under a public mandate
- analyze the implications of the different combinations of funding and supply decisions for public and private goods in terms of their availability, their quality, and the distribution of costs and benefits associated with the goods

- understand the impact of time on the valuation of costs and benefits associated with goods and apply basic methods of discounting
- analyze the implications of uncertainty for government policy in terms of expectations, unintended consequences, contingencies, and the time-inconsistency problem facing policy-makers

The box example in this chapter covers the key characteristics of socialism as the example of the highest degree of government involvement implemented in some economies. The tensions involved in the choice of privatization methods and transitions from central planning to market economy implemented in a number of jurisdictions since 1989 are also explored.

The chapter concludes with advice on how to approach and utilize scholarly journal articles in the field of economics in light of their typically very technical nature and the challenges they pose to those without advanced training in economics.

3.1 THE NATURE OF GOODS

This section aims to dispel common misconceptions about what public goods are, what types of goods governments fund, and the connections (or the lack thereof) between funding and supply decisions. We will begin with the following concepts:

- public versus private benefits of goods, and positive and negative externalities
- the funding decision: public versus private funding
- public versus private supply, market structure, and regulatory implications

First of all, it is important to provide a few crucial definitions:

The term *goods* should be interpreted as broadly as possible to include tangible and intangible goods and services that provide utility or disutility to individuals and groups in the economy and society more broadly, irrespective of whether they are tradable in a market or not.

The term *public goods*, on the other hand, should be applied only to goods that satisfy the following criteria:

- *non-rivalry in consumption*, which means that if one individual enjoys the benefits of a good, it does not diminish the amount available to others, so we can all enjoy the same level of consumption of the given good
- *non-excludability*, which refers to the fact that it is impossible or too costly in practice to exclude anyone from the consumption of the given good

Several caveats are in order with respect to the above definition. For example, there can be limits to the non-rivalry criterion, as reaching a certain threshold number of users may diminish the level of benefit from a public good available to everyone. When that happens, the public goods are characterized as *congestible*, a common example being traffic jams on public roads during rush hour. On the other hand, when public goods are not subject to congestion, they are referred to as *pure* public goods.

The non-excludability characteristic of public goods implies that property rights would be very difficult or impossible to enforce for this type of good. It follows that private individuals will not be able to trade such a good, the good will not have a market value, and hence private entities will typically not have an incentive to invest in a public good. This is the reason that the provision of public goods would normally fall under a government mandate. Nevertheless, it is possible for private individuals to provide public goods. For example, if you volunteer to help clean up a public park, that serves as an example of private provision of a public good.[1]

Perhaps the purest form of a public good is information. Once the breaking news hits the media headlines or the informal village gossip channels, it is impossible to exclude anyone from the consumption of the news, and everybody can enjoy the same level of news intake. But does this imply that governments will pay for the collection of relevant

---

1   In general, one should consider altruism as only one possible motive for the private provision of a public good. Other motivations may include tax incentives, enhancing one's self-image (and the subjective utility derived from that), or signalling for political and/or career purposes, for example. For more insight and empirical evidence, search the literature on volunteering and charitable donations.

information or actually be involved in the supply or dissemination of the information? Not necessarily. For instance, government agencies may collect information about earthquakes and issue tsunami warnings through municipal sirens, but in other instances, governments may choose not to be involved in the supply of the public good or even its funding.

Consider the example of regulations governing the dissemination of information about publicly traded companies. With the aim of protecting investors and promoting market efficiency, publicly traded companies (in financially developed jurisdictions) are required to periodically disclose financial information and guarantee the accuracy of balance sheets, which are compiled according to set accounting standards. The cost of collecting this information remains private,[2] while public costs to taxpayers are limited to enforcement costs when violations of the regulations are detected and prosecuted.

Another example of a public good is transportation infrastructure. Roads and bridges are standard examples of publicly funded public goods, but is this infrastructure built and maintained by state-owned enterprises and public sector employees, or by private companies hired by municipal or regional governments? Increasingly, we see more and more examples of the *private supply of publicly funded public goods*. The motivations for this shift are diverse and the outcomes also vary widely.

The classic motivation for the public supply of public goods is the natural monopoly argument. When the population needs only one set of sirens for a tsunami warning, it makes sense to avoid inefficient duplication and waste of resources and have only one public warning system installed. But when we have to rely on one supplier only, the risk involved is that this monopoly supplier has no incentive to limit costs or deliver high-quality goods since its client base and funding are guaranteed due to the lack of other alternatives for the public to turn to. If the public monopoly supplier systematically runs a budget deficit, the only possible response (at least in the short to medium term)

---

2   The owners of the company and the consumers of its products and services bear the private costs of accounting standards and information disclosure. The distribution of the costs between owners and consumers depends on the relative elasticities of investor supply and consumer demand. This issue will be analyzed in detail in chapter 6, which deals with fiscal policy. For now, it is important to simply note that the legal obligation by an entity to pay a tax or to comply with regulation does not necessarily coincide with the incidence or burden of taxation and regulatory compliance.

is to continue to fund the deficit and maintain so-called soft budget constraints. Economists refer to this incentive problem as *moral hazard*.

In order to eliminate the problems of moral hazard and soft budget constraints, low quality due to lack of competition, and potentially also supply shortages associated with public supply, governments have increasingly turned to procuring goods in markets through competitive bidding, or privatizing public monopolies and regulating their supply and prices. The definition and understanding of natural monopoly has also shifted over time, especially since the late 1980s to early 1990s, due to an ideological shift towards more market-oriented solutions following the collapse of the socialist bloc, as well as innovations in technology and regulation.

While it might seem like ancient history, it was not that long ago that national state-owned telecom companies and airline carriers dominated markets in many countries. These state monopolies have been privatized and markets were opened so that new entrants could compete. Consumers benefited greatly from these shifts, especially in the telecom sector. Besides the fast pace of technological innovation and the need for new capacity and investment, the regulatory innovation that made this possible was the requirement to grant third-party access rights to new market participants on existing infrastructure networks owned by incumbents at regulated prices (Rajabiun & Middleton, 2015). Nevertheless, the success of this regulatory shift hinged on the creation of competition in the telecom markets. In more remote areas with lower population density, and hence greater potential for market failure, the demand for public-private partnerships has persisted (Hambly & Rajabiun, 2021). In other sectors, the move towards privatization, and hence private rather than public supply of public goods, was not so successful. Utility companies – including, for example, electricity and water supply and distribution companies – turned out not to be good candidates for privatization. The infamous California electricity blackouts of 2000–1 were linked to collusion and market manipulation by power generators and traders,[3] and public sentiment quickly turned against utilities privatization. From an economic point of view, the inability to create effective markets and competition drove the results.

---

3   For an account of the market manipulation practices by Enron and other companies, see Leopold (2002). Criminal charges and convictions followed for a few corporate executives.

It is also important to note that while clean drinking water and electricity do exhibit attributes of public goods, at least to some extent, we do pay the bills for our water and electricity consumption privately. This is dictated by the need to provide private incentives to conserve these scarce resources. In the absence of private usage-based payments, inefficient overconsumption and potentially shortages would arise, as in the case of common resources, also referred to as the *tragedy of commons*.[4] At the same time, in many jurisdictions the supply of water and electricity is subsidized to some extent by public funds. The motivation for the subsidy in this case can be partly social justice, to ensure affordability by poor households and communities, and partly the fear of potential negative spillover effects stemming from the lack of access to clean water and electricity by segments of the population. For example, clean drinking water is a necessity of life and the lack of access to clean water by the general public would lead to the spread of infectious diseases, hence reducing societal welfare. Similarly, the lack of access to electricity by the public at large would negatively affect public safety and inhibit the smooth functioning of the economy. Hence, goods with negative and positive spillover effects for society at large, also known as *negative and positive externalities*, provide an impetus for government involvement in their funding and/or supply.

In general, externalities – positive or negative – represent benefits and costs that accrue to the general public in addition to the private benefits and costs that they provide to individuals. Since selfish individuals consider in their decisions to consume, produce, or invest only the private benefits and costs of goods, they will ignore the external spillover effects to society at large. In the case of positive externalities, the private decision-making leads to a provision of goods that is lower than socially optimal, and vice versa in the case of negative externalities. Since governments have the mandate to represent the interest of the public at large,[5] they have the mandate to internalize the externalities

---

4   Classic examples of the tragedy of commons include over-grazing on communal lands, over-fishing in lakes and oceans without fishing quotas, and their effective enforcement.

5   Note that there is no clear definition of what constitutes the "public at large." Is it our neighbourhood, region, or country? And do we care about the rest of the world? Do we even care equally about all populations and regions within our own country? When externalities have an impact beyond the boundaries of a given jurisdiction, they are referred to as extraterritorial, transnational, or global.

and try to correct for the under- or oversupply of goods in private markets. For instance, education entails both private and public benefits. The private benefits of education are represented by the positive correlation between earnings and educational attainment, and these provide the incentive for individuals (and/or parents on their behalf) to invest in schooling and informal education. But the benefits of an educated population well exceed those represented by higher earnings and consumption levels. Arguably, positive health outcomes,[6] greater degree of innovation and technological progress,[7] and positive social outcomes such as respect for human rights and democracy[8] have been linked to educational attainment, which implies that education exhibits positive externalities for society at large. If the decision to invest in education by individuals and families is based only on the private benefits in terms of higher expected earnings, then the investment in education will be lower than the level desirable from a social perspective. This provides a rationale for public subsidies to fund educational services and reduce the explicit and implicit costs of education that are borne privately, as well as to mandate minimum years of schooling.

Another argument for public funding for education is social justice. Educational attainment can provide, at least in theory, a channel for upward economic and social mobility. In practice, racial and class discrimination, immigration, and structural changes in the demand for labour market skills have been shown to limit the positive effect of education on social mobility. Nevertheless, the social justice argument is that if children from poor households and poor communities are able to complete a university degree, they might be able to transition

---

6   For example, Ferreira and Walton (2006) highlight that infant mortality rates vary greatly even within developing countries in relation to mothers' educational attainment. According to Demographic Health Survey data, children born to uneducated mothers in low- and lower-middle-income countries are typically two to three times more likely to die before the age of one than those born to mothers with secondary or higher education in the same country.

7   See, for example, Blundell et al. (1999) and Knight et al. (2003).

8   For example, Barro (1999) found that "democracy" is positively correlated with primary education and more even primary school attainment between males and females.

to middle-income status.[9] In this case, it is the private benefit of education in terms of higher earnings that we are considering, rather than the public good/positive spillover aspects of education, yet it can still provide a rationale for public funding based on society's endorsement of social justice and social mobility.

Similarly, public social security systems, in terms of old-age pensions or welfare benefits to disabled or unemployed individuals, are further examples of publicly funded private benefits or private goods. The associated eligibility requirements imply excludability, and rivalry in consumption is present in this case since the more is spent on private benefits for one group, the less is available for other groups and causes. Essentially, these goods with private benefits entail income redistribution, but social justice is only one possible motivation for redistribution. Redistribution can also represent the appropriation of public funds by special interests.

In summary, the above examples illustrate that taxpayers fund goods with both public and private benefits, and the decision to provide the goods is separate from the decision to fund them and to supply them. In other words, when analyzing the provision of a certain good, we need to address three separate questions:

- the nature of the good (public vs. private goods)[10]
- the funding decision (public vs. private funds)
- the supply decision (public vs. private suppliers)

These three criteria create different combinations of goods involving a government mandate in some form. Some examples of these are summarized in table 3.1.

---

9 Unfortunately, most research shows that inequities in opportunity related to parental wealth and education from early childhood through the years of formal schooling limit the chances of poor students for upward economic mobility and other social outcomes, including health, later on in life (see, e.g., Barnett & Belfield, 2006; Burger, 2010; Hayward & Gorman, 2004). Hence, intergenerational persistence in outcomes can be strong. Among OECD countries, d'Addio (2007) shows that persistence in economic outcomes is greater in the United States, the United Kingdom, and Italy relative to the Nordic countries, Canada, and Australia. In general, intergenerational persistence is strongest at the extremes of the income distribution.

10 Some goods can exhibit the characteristics of both public goods and private benefits to varying extents, as discussed in the example of education.

Table 3.1. Combinations of public versus private goods, funding, and supply

Type of good or service	Funding	Supply	Example
Public good	Public	Public	Security services provided by national armies and police*
Public good	Public	Private	Public road construction funded by government, but completed by private construction companies
Public good	Government mandated, but privately funded	Private	Disclosure of financial statements by publicly traded companies
Public good	Private	Public	National flood insurance in instances of unavailability of private insurance or market failure
Private goods/ benefits	Public	Public	Social welfare, corporate subsidies
Private goods/ benefits	Public	Private	National/state health coverage combined with private health service providers at regulated prices
Private goods/ benefits	Government mandated, but privately funded	Private	Mandatory car liability insurance procured from private insurance companies, car seat belts
Private goods/ benefits	Government mandated, but privately funded	Public	Protection from international imports through trade tariffs and quotas, paid for by consumers through higher domestic prices
Private goods/ benefits	Privately and publicly funded	Public	Enforcement of a private contract through the court system, public real estate registry†

* The traditional boundaries of providing national defense have been pushed by the hire of defense contractors by the US Department of Defense, for example, during the Iraq and Afghanistan wars in the 2000s. Domestically in the United States, privately operated prisons and immigrant detention centres are another example of the shift towards outsourcing public security services to private suppliers.

† The last combination of private goods – privately funded, and privately supplied – is acquired through private decisions and transactions in markets. Nevertheless, government involvement may affect these markets and transactions through a whole host of laws and regulations including, for example, quality standards, international trade restrictions, competition regulations, or licensing requirements.

QUESTIONS FOR DISCUSSION AND FURTHER RESEARCH

1 Can you think of other examples for each of the above combinations of public versus private goods, funding, and supply? If not, research the answers as part of your homework!

Why is it important to explore the three dimensions of the nature of the benefits from goods, their funding, and supply in public policy analysis? The reason is that each combination of the three criteria has unique implications for the amount and quality of the goods supplied, the associated market structure in terms of the degree of competition or lack thereof in the provision of the goods, and the distribution of the costs and benefits stemming from the provision of the goods. Tracing the distribution of these costs and benefits will help shed light on the incentives to support the provision of these goods and thus help explain why certain goods are provided through a government mandate and others are not. Of course, we have yet to discuss decision-making rules and procedures, which also have a material impact on public policy outcomes. This analysis will follow in chapter 4.

QUESTIONS FOR DISCUSSION AND FURTHER RESEARCH

1 Can you think of examples of controversial government funding for certain goods or examples when government involvement is lacking?
2 Analyze the distribution of costs and benefits from those decisions, as well as the resulting incentives to support the public provision of those goods or not.

BOX 3.1. SOCIALISM, PRIVATIZATION METHODS, AND THEIR REDISTRIBUTIVE IMPLICATIONS

From an economic point of view, the defining characteristic of socialism is state ownership of the means of production. In practice, this had been manifested by the state ownership of land and capital, and not just the right, but also typically the legal obligation to work for the working-age population.

How does socialism differ from communism? While most socialist countries of the twentieth century had the word "communist" in their governing or political regime, communism essentially remained the unreached ideal that would have entailed the complete elimination of private property (including personal property), and income distribution based on "needs" rather than any measure of work effort or productivity. There was a general emphasis on social justice and equality of economic outcomes under social-ism, with varying degrees of oppression in different jurisdictions. Demonstrated achievements typically included mass improve-ments in education and health outcomes, as well as rapid indus-trialization, at least in the early periods (Kornai, 1992).

Putting aside issues of freedom (personal, political, and eco-nomic) and ideology, why did socialism fail from an economic per-spective? Under socialism, all the production decisions were made under a central plan, typically with a five-year horizon. There were no markets, and hence no market-determined prices, to guide the decisions as to what to produce more of because it is in demand, or which input should be used less because it is in limited supply. Such decisions had to be made for every possible consumer and investment good, and intermediate input – overall, a large scale, complex problem-solving exercise with little independently deter-mined information to go on. In a market economy, producers are required to make decentralized decisions only for their individual companies, while utilizing market-determined prices as signals. If the price of a good is high, as consumers we aim to cut down our use of it. If prices are high, it is a signal to producers to supply more of the good, or to find a substitute for it because demand is strong. Hence, central planners were at a fundamental disadvantage given the enormous informational requirements of a large-scale input-output-consumption problem to solve. It is not surprising, then, that mistakes were made: Shortages of basic consumption goods often prevailed, while other resources such as fossil fuels were used inefficiently with a negative environmental impact.[1]

Besides the misallocation of resources, quality problems were also present. If you are the only supplier of a good, and consum-ers have no other choice but to purchase your goods, then why bother to ensure that the goods meet high quality standards? Or, if the company you work for is pretty much certain not to be shut down even if it is making a loss, then why worry about the efficiency of production? Competitive markets, in which no single seller or buyer has the ability to affect the market price, provide incentives for enhancing efficiency and innovation. In the absence of such incentives under central planning, it is not surprising that productivity, and hence growth, stagnated in the latter periods of socialism in the 1970s and 1980s (Kornai, 1992).

Following the political disintegration of socialist regimes from 1989 onward, the transition from central planning to market economy proceeded and inevitably involved the privatization of state-owned productive assets. The methods of privatization varied widely depending on the scale of the production units and across jurisdictions. Small-scale privatization typically involved restitution to the original owners or sell-off at auctions. A closer examination of large-scale privatization methods is warranted given their implications for wealth redistribution and the development of market economies.

A common characteristic of socialist economies was the low degree of income inequality. This changed following the transition to market economy, especially in a subsection of the former socialist economies (Milanovic, 1998). While arguably a configuration of factors led to the rise in income and wealth inequality (including unemployment, inflation, and structural changes in the economy and public finances), the methods of large-scale privatization helped shape the economic and political environment to a significant extent. Allegations of corruption – bribery of public officials or selling off state-owned assets at below-market valuations – were common across jurisdictions,[2] but the privatization methods still varied to a great extent in their emphasis on equity (or the lack thereof). For example, the so-called voucher privatization scheme was adopted in the former Czechoslovakia (and its successor states the Czech Republic and Slovakia) for a subsection of large companies that needed relatively little restructuring and new investment to be viable in a market economy. Under the voucher scheme, every citizen over the age of 18 was entitled to obtain, for a nominal fee, a number of vouchers for the purchase of company stocks. The price of the company stocks in terms of vouchers was determined by demand from voucher-holders. The vouchers were then converted into shares, which were subsequently tradable for money at the emerging stock exchanges. Hence, the average citizen became a shareholder and could share in the wealth of the country. The shares did not translate into large sums of money for individual citizens, but the emphasis was on equity and social justice rather than get-rich schemes. Measures of income inequality did not change drastically during the transition in Slovakia and the Czech Republic, especially when compared to other formerly centrally planned economies going through the same types of processes (Milanovic, 1998).

In contrast, the privatization methods adopted in Russia and other former members of the Soviet Union were markedly different. While there were nominally forms of voucher privatization to employees, the sell-off of companies to incumbent managers at below-market valuations was common and "a defining feature of Russia's privatization process," as critically noted by Sachs (1993, p. 185). This resulted in a small number of individuals becoming incredibly rich in a very short period of time. Industrial composition and market structure (i.e., the degree of market competition, or lack thereof) also played a role in this outcome. While Czechoslovakia was not rich in natural resources and manufacturing companies dominated the economy, many of the former Soviet Union countries were well endowed with natural wealth including oil and gas reserves. Since natural resources are not evenly distributed around the world, their producers often possess market power, which means that individual producers are large enough to be able to influence the market prices with their strategic actions. Monopolies and oligopolies tend to dominate the natural resource sector and thus create the potential for the rate of profitability to be higher than in competitive industries. Abnormal profits (also referred to as *economic rents*) in turn attract opportunistic behaviour by economic and political agents resulting in relentless power struggles, corruption, or even violence. In the context of Russia and other former members of the Soviet Union, the combination of natural resource wealth and favouring incumbent state-appointed managers in the privatization process led to the emergence of the *oligarchy*, an elite group of individuals with a great deal of personal wealth, also resulting in political influence. In Russia, for example, it is estimated that the richest 10 per cent of the households received about 45 per cent of national income in 2010, down from about 50 per cent in the early 2000s (Neef, 2020).[3]

China also stands out as an interesting case study with the Communist Party still in power, while the number of Chinese nationals, especially political representatives, on the list of the world's richest people is skyrocketing. In 2013, the Chinese-based Hurun Global Rich List identified 83 billionaires, in US dollar terms, in the Chinese parliament (Anderlini, 2013). In 2011, the estimated net worth of the 70 richest members of China's National People's Congress was USD $89.8 billion according to the Hurun Report, which was roughly 12 times higher than the combined net worth of all 660 top officials in the three branches of the US government around the same time (Bloomberg News, 2012).

In this case of China, the state maintained partial ownership (typically majority share) of large state enterprises, but partnered with foreign multinational companies to benefit from capital injections, managerial know-how, technology transfer, and marketing under well-recognized global brands. The strategy has brought about benefits in terms of productivity increases and mass employment opportunities in labour-intensive industries. The export orientation of production also required maintaining competitiveness, and the growth performance of the economy has been strong. The components for growth with equity seem to have been in place, so what has been driving the rise in income inequality? The answer lies in market segmentation, specifically the separation of production for exports and domestic markets, and the corresponding discrimination in trade policies. Export processing zones were created for the production of goods destined for foreign markets. To ensure their competitiveness, inputs can be imported into the export processing zones free of tariffs and other trade restrictions. At the same time, imports to the domestic market remain subject to trade restrictions, which drive a wedge between the prices of goods in the export processing zones and the domestic economy more broadly. Those with political and economic connections, and thus access to both segments of the economy, have the opportunity to profit from the price difference based on the simple strategy to buy at low world prices and resell in protected markets. Such prospects represent so-called *arbitrage opportunities*, which in this case are created by government regulation and benefit well-connected elites. The case also highlights that it is of utmost importance to include market structure, and the natural or artificially created impediments to free competition, in political economy analysis. Governments have historically contributed to the creation of monopolies and their exclusionary effects have had long-standing implications for economic and political power inequalities.

QUESTIONS FOR DISCUSSION AND FURTHER RESEARCH

1 Vladimir Putin consolidated political power as president in Russia, ultimately leading to autocracy and severe oppression of dissent. What role did the economic structure and political ideologies play in the process of political power consolidation?
2 In general, what linkages can be drawn between natural resource wealth and political and economic outcomes? Have natural resources been a blessing or curse for developing and developed countries?
3 What are the implications of China's growing income inequality for its economic and political future?

---

1 See, for example, Kuskova et al. (2008) for the long-term analysis of energy use and political regime changes in the Czech Republic and Slovakia throughout the twentieth century, and Petri et al. (2002) exploring the countries of the former Soviet Union.
2 For example, Arikan (2008) found a statistically significant positive relationship between privatization and perceived corruption in former socialist economies.
3 The corresponding inequality measure provided by the World Bank in its World Development Indicators is 32–4 per cent share for the richest 10 per cent of the households in 2008–9, but this measure is consumption-based. In general, consumption-based measures tend to underestimate inequality relative to income-based measures. Survey methodologies also vary by country, and therefore direct cross-country comparisons should be exercised with caution.

3.2 THE IMPACT OF UNCERTAINTY ON THE PROVISION OF GOODS BY GOVERNMENTS: PERSONAL BELIEFS VERSUS SCIENTIFIC EVIDENCE

It is not uncommon for anyone – individuals, political representatives, or scientists – to fail to adequately assess the true nature and extent of the benefits and costs stemming from public and private goods currently, or potentially, under a government mandate. When such uncertainty prevails, it will have implications for government decision-making, as well as the effectiveness of the delivery of those goods.

Consider, for example, the state of children's vaccination programs from across North America to Pakistan. Even before the emergence of the COVID-19 pandemic, the World Health Organization (WHO) had noted an increase in a number of infectious diseases, and in fact declared the renewed rise in polio cases in 2014 a global emergency (WHO, 2014). These developments came on the heels of a global push to eradicate polio through vaccination programs. Empirical evidence shows that it is in fact possible to eradicate at least certain diseases through the vaccination of the general population, with the case of smallpox eradication being perhaps the most widely known health policy achievement of modern medicine in the twentieth century. Yet children's vaccination rates have plateaued in both low- and high-income countries despite educational campaigns, government funding, and accessibility programs to reach underserviced populations. In Pakistan, it has been reportedly alleged that the vaccines have been deliberately tainted by Western governments to cause infertility in Muslim populations, even leading to the slaying of several health workers and the refusal of parents to allow the vaccination of their children. In North America, an often-cited reason for the rise in parental refusal to have children vaccinated has been the hypothesis that the rise in autism cases can be linked to a chemical ingredient in vaccines. Numerous scientific studies have since provided evidence against the hypothesized link between vaccines and autism (Stehr-Green et al., 2003; DeStefano, 2007; Price et al., 2010); yet public skepticism persists to a large extent, and children's vaccination rates remain negatively affected, along with their health outcomes. Negative externalities in terms of increased health risks for wider populations are also present. It is noteworthy that this situation prevails in countries with high average income and educational attainment. Therefore, it suggests that personal beliefs (warranted or not) play a significant role in ensuring public support for government policy and the effectiveness with which it is implemented.

3.3 DISCOUNTING THE FUTURE

The impact of uncertainty is further exacerbated when the costs and benefits of government action or inaction accrue with some considerable delay. A commonly noted case in point is carbon dioxide emissions, global warming, and the resulting climate change predicted by scientists with various degree of intensity since the late 19th entury.[11] Yet action on environmental protection has typically been lacking by governments across the globe. How can we explain the current status quo? The scientific predictions about the future impact of climate change have typically involved an extended time horizon over generations, and the estimates of the costs have varied widely across studies. Furthermore, the methodology involved in arriving at estimates has been highly complex and technical, and hence largely not verifiable first-hand by the average person in society. This complexity and the resulting *asymmetric information* problem between scientists and the general public have created room for divergent interpretations of the scientific evidence by various special interest groups that may be differentially affected by government action on this issue, or based on partisanship and ideology. In 2013, a global survey covering 39 countries showed that on average 54 per cent of the population considered global warming a major threat to their respective countries. Notably, the corresponding figure in the United States was only 40 per cent (Pew Research Center, 2013). The ideological divide on the issue in the United States is well documented. According to a 2014 Pew Research Center survey, 68 per cent of Democrats considered climate change a

---

11 For an overview of the historical development of global warming research, see Maslin (2008).

major threat to the United States, compared to only 25 per cent among Republicans and 44 per cent among independents (Motel, 2014). More recent data suggest that this divergence and polarization has in fact become more pronounced over time. Survey data from 2024 by the Pew Research Center indicate that only 12 per cent of Republican or Republican-leaning voters consider dealing with climate change a top policy priority. This stands in sharp contrast to the growth in concern among Democrats or Democratic-leaning voters, 59 per cent of whom say climate change should be a top priority (Kennedy & Tyson, 2024).

The distribution of costs and benefits of environmental regulation over time also plays an important role in determining policy outcomes. Government regulation on the emission of pollutants into the atmosphere by producers and individual consumers has immediate costs and is likely to yield opposition. Benefits of environmental protection, on the other hand, tend to be more long-term and dispersed across populations domestically and internationally, as well as across various species in the ecosystem. So who is likely to care about these benefits?

In order to care about environmental protection, one needs to care about the future rather than dismissing it as unimportant. Economists capture the emphasis we put on the present time versus the future through the concept of personal discount rates, which can vary greatly and are difficult to measure. For example, if your life expectancy is short due to a lack of adequate sanitary conditions and the potential for infectious diseases, you might be more likely to discount heavily the possibility that you might develop cancer 20 years from now as a result of the toxic pollution in your environment. Nevertheless, *intergenerational altruism* should be also considered: If you have children or grandchildren, and you care about their future well-being, then the future of the planet might be important to you even if you will not be alive by then. If you care about the well-being of the rest of the ecosystem, you will be concerned about the immediate and future impact of humankind on the environment and will not discount the future heavily. In general, the less you discount the future, the more likely you are to act today in a responsible manner with long-term sustainability in mind.

In practice, economists typically approximate personal discount rates with market-based interest rates. Is this reasonable? We know that discount rates vary from one individual to the next, but on average, within an economy or society, can we make any generalizations? Interest rates tend to be lower in high-income economies than in developing countries as a result of diminishing returns at higher levels of capital accumulation.[12] The lower interest rates and economic growth rates in high-income countries broadly correspond to less discounting of the future and more calls for environmental protection by the public, even if the rhetoric is not necessarily backed by action.[13] On the other hand, developing countries with rapid growth (as well as global investors) face a large opportunity cost of devoting limited resources to environmental protection rather than investing in economic growth. The exception to this broad generalization of developing countries is isolated traditional societies, which have their survival closely linked to the ecosystem, and thus the discount rates are likely to be lower. Nevertheless, these traditional societies or communities tend to be too small in economic terms to have any significant impact on collective decision-making.

Consider the following hypothetical example to illuminate the concepts of *discounting* and the *time value of money*: Suppose your friend has borrowed $1,000 from you. Will you be indifferent as to whether you get paid back next week, a year from now, or ten years later? Will your friend be indifferent in this regard? Most likely not: You will prefer to get your money back as soon as possible and your friend will favour paying you back later rather than sooner. Why is that? Well, most likely you have limited resources, and therefore not having the $1,000 at your disposal today will entail an *opportunity cost* for you. If you had the $1,000 at your disposal today, you could invest the money

12 The law of diminishing returns states that as we keep adding one factor of production (e.g., capital), while holding all other factors of production constant (e.g., labour and land), the marginal product of this factor of production declines. It follows that high-income countries with a large degree of capital accumulation face diminishing marginal productivity, making developing countries with a relative scarcity of capital an attractive alternative for investment. This phenomenon is often referred to as outsourcing. Real interest rates represent the marginal product of capital, and hence real interest rates tend to be relatively lower in high-income countries and vice versa.

13 The reasons for collective inaction, even if most individuals approve of a particular public policy solution, can be manifold, including free-riding and coordination problems. These will be explored in detail in chapter 5, on collective action problems.

in an interest-bearing account or make another investment, which you expect to appreciate over time. Either way, assuming you could earn 5 per cent return in one year, you would expect to have $1,000 × (1 + 0.05), or $1,050 dollars, a year from now.

It is important to note that the difference between the present and future value of $1,000 (i.e., $50 in this case) exists even in the absence of inflation or a rise in prices over the given time period. This is because the *opportunity cost drives the wedge between the present and future value.*

If inflation is likely to prevail over a given time period, then your purchasing power decreases over time, making the loss in value even greater. As a result, the market interest rate (also known as the nominal interest rate) would need to be adjusted upward to compensate investors for the expected loss in purchasing power due to inflation over time. This is captured by the relationship between nominal and real interest rates as outlined below in equations (3.1a) and (3.2a).

A few important things to note about present value analysis:

- In order to be able to weigh the various costs and benefits of goods against each other, it helps if we are able to put a dollar value on them. Monetization then becomes the common denominator. However, monetization can be a very difficult task for many reasons. Market prices can be used as the first approximation, but they may not necessarily represent the true scarcity value of the underlying good. For example, what is the price of a balanced ecosystem or species near extinction?[14] Markets can fail, and hence markets may not exist, may not be competitive, or prices may not reflect true scarcities and externalities. In economic or social analysis from a policy-making perspective, the emphasis should be on including all these broader, external, hard-to-measure elements. Economic analysis thus poses a more

---

14 On January 12, 2014, the Associated Press reported that the hunting permit to kill an endangered African black rhino was auctioned off in Dallas for $350,000. Five hunting permits are sold annually in Namibia alone, while poaching and loss of habitat continue to threaten the viability of the species. It is estimated that less than 5,000 rhinos remain on the planet. Is this market price likely to represent the true scarcity and social value of an endangered animal? Conservationists also highlighted the negative externality stemming from such an auction taking place at all, as it sends the message to the public that hunting endangered species is acceptable if one is wealthy enough.

complex challenge than business analysis, which can simply rely on market prices to determine viability.

- In order to represent true values and scarcities in economic analysis rather than just relying on market prices, economists often utilize so-called *shadow prices* instead to monetize benefits and costs. It is important to realize that shadow prices are simply estimates, which may vary widely according to their sources, assumptions, and value judgment. Therefore, they introduce another element of uncertainty into analysis. It needs to be emphasized that some degree of subjective value judgement can be unavoidable: If we were to simply exclude shadow prices from analysis and use market-based valuations only, the analysis and the inferences drawn will be erroneous in instances of market failure.

- Hard-to-monetize costs and benefits are often excluded from formal analysis, which warrants caution when examining methodological approaches used in studies and the conclusions drawn from them. Nevertheless, I would like to emphasize that as individual voters we would certainly take into consideration all the hard-to-monetize tangible or intangible costs and benefits that we personally care about. Such implicit calculations should not be disregarded when attempting to gauge public opinion on policy issues.

- If we use market interest rates to proxy for discount rates, how do we choose among the many? In general, interest rates vary depending on the time horizon in question. If we use annual projections of costs and benefits, we should use annual interest rates, which may also change over time. For the sake of simplicity, a constant annual interest rate is often assumed.

- It is also crucial to differentiate between real and nominal interest rates. Keep in mind that market-posted interest rates are nominal interest rates, as they incorporate compensation for expected inflation. *When the projections of costs and benefits capture expected inflation, nominal interest rates (i) should be utilized for discounting. However, when the projections of costs and benefits are net of inflation (i.e., assume zero inflation), real interest rates (r) should be used instead.* This is captured by the relationship between nominal and real interest rates. As an approximation, for small levels of inflation, the nominal interest rate (i) simply equals the real interest rate (r) plus the rate of expected inflation (π^e), as shown in equation

(3.1a). As the inflation rate gains in magnitude, the approximation becomes inaccurate; the so-called Fisher equation should be used to capture the relationship between real or nominal interest rates, as shown in equations (3.2a) and (3.2b).

$$i \cong r + \pi^e \tag{3.1a}$$

or

$$r \cong i - \pi^e \tag{3.1b}$$

$$1 + i = (1 + r) \times (1 + \pi^e) \tag{3.2a}$$

or

$$r = \frac{(1+i)}{\left(1+\pi^e\right)} - 1 \tag{3.2b}$$

- The main point to note about the time value of money (or the costs and benefits these dollar amounts represent) is that since a dollar today is not worth the same as a dollar tomorrow, a year from now, or two years from now, we cannot directly add up costs and benefits that accrue at different times. To make dollar amounts from different time periods directly comparable, we need to first convert them into one particular time period. We typically utilize the present time as the default for time conversion and calculate the present value of costs and benefits. When weighing the costs and benefits against each other, we search for the bottom line by calculating the net present value (NPV) according to equation (3.3).

$$NPV = \sum_{t=0}^{n} \frac{(B_t - C_t)}{(1+r)^t} \tag{3.3}$$

- Present value calculations are sensitive to the choice of the interest rate as the discount rate. How does one choose the appropriate interest rate among the many posted even for the same time period? The discount rate should aim to represent the relevant context – for example, the opportunity cost for the decision-maker.

QUESTIONS FOR DISCUSSION AND PROBLEM SOLVING

1 If your friend does not pay you back in a week, but gives you your $1,000 a year from now, how much is that worth to you today?

Table 3.2. Template for net present value (NPV) calculations

Time period (t)	Benefits in period t (B_t)	Costs in period t (C_t)	Present value (PV) of net benefit (NB) from period t ($NB_t = B_t - C_t$)	Comments
$t = 0$ present time	B_0	C_0	$PVNB_0 = B_0 - C_0$	By default no discounting is involved in present.
$t = 1$ one period from now, typically one year	B_1	C_1	$PVNB_1 = \dfrac{(B_1 - C_1)}{(1+i)^1}$	Remember to add up only costs and benefits in the same row (i.e., the same time period).
$t = 2$ two periods from now	B_2	C_2	$PVNB_2 = \dfrac{(B_2 - C_2)}{(1+i)^2}$	This assumes a constant nominal interest (i) over time.
t t periods from now	B_t	C_t	$PVNB_t = \dfrac{(B_t - C_t)}{(1+i)^t}$	
Net Present Value (NPV) =			$PVNB_0 + PVNB_1$ $+ PVNB_2 + \cdots + PVNB_t$	Add up the present value of net benefits from different periods, t, in the preceding column. If the final NPV > 0, benefits outweigh costs.

Important: If the projected costs and benefits do not include inflation, replace the nominal interest rate i in the above formulas, with the real interest, r, as per equations (3.1b), (3.2b), and (3.3).
Sensitivity analysis: How much does the present value change if the discount rate changes?

2 Will you still feel that you got back all your money when you could have been $50 richer a year later?

3 How much will the difference amount to if you get paid the $1,000 dollars back only ten years later? For simplicity, assume that the nominal interest rate on saving will remain 3 per cent per year over the next ten years. How would the results change if the interest was 7 per cent per year instead?

For a more complicated structure of benefits and costs over time, I recommend utilizing the template provided in table 3.2 to keep track of the calculations and avoid mistakes.

In the case of environmental policies, the costs of protection tend to be immediate (both in terms of expenditure and opportunity cost), while in general the benefits are expected to be removed far into the future and geographically dispersed. Thus, when we incorporate the discounting of future for such a structure of costs and benefits, favouring environmental protection is not necessarily apparent, and this is consistent with the currently dominant public policy stance across the globe.

Even if we were to assume for a moment that governments are willing to take immediate action and invest in environmental protection, what should those policies look like? Arguably, there is no definitive answer to this question that would guarantee an effective and efficient outcome. Should governments subsidize electric cars? What energy sources will be utilized for the electricity generation and how much pollution will be produced? What is the expected lifetime of an electric car battery, and how sensitive is it to regular use and charging? What about the environmental impact of toxic materials contained inside batteries? Can they be safely recycled or disposed of?

Or should governments subsidize sustainable biofuel instead? Several governments have experimented with this option, including the United States and Brazil. However, some unintended consequences of the policy emerged. Since growing crops for biofuel became relatively more profitable as a result of government subsidies, many producers switched from producing crops for food to fuel instead. Given the limited availability of arable land, the switch to biofuel production contributed (among other factors) to a decline in the output of basic food staples and an increase in their prices in 2007–8 (Rosegrant, 2008; Zilberman et al., 2012). The rise in food staple prices had a negative impact on poor populations around the globe, and as a result, the World Bank, the World Trade Organization, and other international agencies have since then recommended that governments end subsidies to biofuel production (Dunmore, 2011).

When such uncertainty persists about what the "right" public policy solution is, it can also be exploited by opportunistic private interests arguing that their research and development (R&D) is the one with the most promise, and so should be subsidized. But given the great degree of uncertainty, such claims are difficult to verify or disprove in practice, and evidence may become available only after a substantial period of time. In the meantime, if resources are devoted to specific government-favoured R&D projects, this will entail an *opportunity cost* since public funds are limited and expenditure on other programs may need to be curtailed or postponed instead. Will it also misdirect scientists to focus on a limited range of potential solutions that make them eligible for government funding, rather than consider a wide range of innovative solutions? This would be another representation of misallocation of resources and opportunity costs, and an argument for an R&D subsidy program that would be wide in scope rather than based on narrow targets driven by limited information at best, or worse, by special interests.

Asymmetric information about the nature and magnitude of environmental pollution provides special interests with opportunities to shape public opinion about the risk of pollution, thereby shaping public policy. A notable example of the informational problem in building political support for policies that counteract climate change can be found in recent research on the level of pollution from the Alberta tar sands in Canada. Using aerial surveys, He et al. (2024) show that the levels of actual pollutants from this source of oil are vastly higher than those reported by industry and government agencies (up to 63 times higher). The magnitude of this gap might appear substantive and shocking. However, from a political economy perspective, the strategic incentives of industry and governments in countries that export fossil fuels to underestimate their negative impact on local populations and at the global level is not surprising. This example highlights the importance of independent empirical research as a constraint on powerful special interests with asymmetric capacity to shape data, policy narratives, public opinion, and public policy.

3.4 CONTINGENCY AND THE TIME INCONSISTENCY OF GOVERNMENT POLICY

Another very interesting element of uncertainty in government decision-making takes place when the government's preferred policy choice changes over time as circumstances change or after certain commitments have been made by others. This leads to strategic interaction between government and private agents, or internationally with respect to other governments. For example, in order to encourage the influx of investment into a certain region, the government may promise a corporate tax break for new companies for a number of years. Once the investment has been made, and especially if it would be difficult to relocate the business in the short to medium term, then the government may be tempted to renege on such a previous commitment and reap the benefits of raising corporate tax revenue after all. Arguably, if the government acts on such a temptation it loses credibility and will discourage future investment, potentially reducing its taxable capacity over the long term. Hence, while the optimal policy from a long-term perspective is to have a stable and predictable tax policy, the short-term benefit of higher tax revenue today may outweigh the costs from the loss of credibility over time if the government discounts the future heavily.

Governments that face a low probability of re-election are more likely to behave in an opportunistic or short-sighted manner. Strotz (1956) introduced the problem of *dynamic inconsistency* into the economic literature, and later Kydland and Prescott (1977) applied the concept to argue for rules rather than discretion in government decision-making since limiting the government's options or discretion can actually raise welfare over the long term. The *time inconsistency of optimal policy* in mainstream economics is typically illustrated in the context of monetary policy or investment, but I believe the concept has been greatly underutilized, since it can be applied to the analysis of a wide range of policies, not just economic ones.

Finally, an obvious element of uncertainty affecting public policy is when something unexpected happens and the government is compelled (by public opinion or self-interest) to take action in response. There are clearly numerous examples of such unexpected shocks, ranging from natural disasters or terrorist attacks to stock market crashes. Such large-scale events can turn the state of public finances around in an instant, as we have seen numerous times in the late twentieth century or in the early years of the twenty-first century, for example. Government revenue typically declines dramatically as a result of such shocks, while spending is required to curb the economic fallout from such events. This type of government spending can be characterized as a *contingent liability*, since the government has not committed to it a priori and it is not planned expenditure, but as the circumstances change, the explicit or implicit liability emerges.

Consider the example of the COVID-19 pandemic or the 2008–9 global financial meltdown, which started with liberal lending practices, the overvaluation of the United States housing market, and the sale of high-risk mortgage-backed securities to banks and pension funds and ended with massive layoffs, the failure (or near-failure) of a number of large financial institutions, and a surge in government spending, deficits, and debt.

Government bailouts represent a contingent liability as a result of a crisis. Nevertheless, typically not everybody gets bailed out, the bailout packages vary in size, and some are also more popular among the public than others. For example, during the 2007–9 financial crisis, pension funds and individual mortgage holders bore heavy losses in the United States. Most banks and other financial institutions did get bailout packages, but these were typically not very popular among the public. Meanwhile, car manufacturers, who have far fewer linkages to the rest of the economy than financial institutions – and so their demise would imply a more limited impact on the national economy – enjoyed only slightly lower public support than the financial sector bailouts in the United States. The public support for car manufacturer bailout has actually increased from 37 per cent to 56 per cent between 2009 and 2012. At the same time, public support for bailing out banks and other financial institutions has remained virtually unchanged over the same period (Pew Research Center, 2012). Potential predictors of public support for specific government bailouts according to Smith (2014) include factors such as economic self-interest, ideology and partisanship, the degree of perceived culpability of distressed firms for the situation at hand, and other-regarding or sociotropic preferences.

QUESTIONS FOR DISCUSSION AND FURTHER RESEARCH

Utilizing the concepts introduced in this chapter, try to explain the following:

1 The varying degrees of public support for the different bailout packages implemented by various governments in the aftermath of the United States housing market collapse in 2008 and during the COVID-19 pandemic.

2 The refusal by the US government to cover the medical expenses
   of emergency workers (firefighters, paramedics, police, and others)
   responding to the terrorist attacks on the World Trade Center in New
   York on September 11, 2001. Many of the first responders have
   subsequently suffered serious chronic illnesses, but the government
   claimed that it is not possible to establish a causal link between
   their exposure to toxic substances during this particular event and
   their subsequent illness. Do you think this scientific uncertainty
   drives the decision, or are there other factors to consider?

3 The European Union bailout of Greece with most of the financial
   burden falling on German taxpayers. Why would the German
   government and taxpayers be willing to cover the costs of bailing
   out the systematic public overspending in another country?

RESEARCH ADVICE: HOW TO READ SCHOLARLY JOURNAL ARTICLES

IN ECONOMICS WITHOUT A GRADUATE DEGREE IN THE FIELD

Unfortunately, there are very few publication outlets for economists
that are non-technical in nature and hence more accessible to general
readership. At the same time, non-scholarly (not peer reviewed) publications on economic issues tend to be driven by political agendas or
simple misinterpretations of economic concepts by non-experts. Since
the general public participates in the economy, most people feel qualified to comment on economic issues. Yet most answers in economic
analysis are not clear-cut or obvious at first glance. Therefore, a warning is in order: Beware about your sources of economic analysis and
get at least a basic education in economics.

Since it is unlikely for anyone to be able to conduct sound economic
analysis without reading scholarly journal articles in the field, here are
a few pieces of advice on how to approach these often very technical
readings:

• Begin with identifying the assumptions of the theoretical
  framework. The implications and conclusions drawn based on a
  theoretical model are only as good as its assumptions.
• The assumptions define the limits of the validity of the findings. If
  your context does not match the assumptions of the theoretical

model, you cannot use the model in question for your analysis. Otherwise, you are just "comparing apples and oranges," as economists like to point out.

- Are the assumptions ad hoc or justified? Even if the theoretical assumptions seem reasonable, are they likely to be satisfied in practice? If not, the model is not useful for your analysis and you cannot draw conclusions based on this model.
- Every model of economic activity is a simplification of a very complex reality, and thus inherently wrong. However, the objective is to isolate the key elements that drive the phenomena. Identify the key driving forces behind the results in the theoretical model. Then the question becomes empirical: Can we draw causal inference between the theoretical driving forces and the observed outcomes in reality? Keep in mind that correlation does not necessarily imply causation. Two-way causation is also often present between variables in the economy, which economists refer to as endogeneity.
- You should critically ask: Is there a factor that was not included in the theoretical analysis, but you suspect might be actually driving the results in practice? Can you link areas of research that have not been linked before? In general, keep in mind that economics is a very introverted discipline,[15] and hence there is scope for interdisciplinary inquiry and widening the perspectives. Most mainstream economic analysis disregards political factors, for example.
- Empirical testing of the theoretical propositions then typically follows. However, many theoretical economic concepts are not observable or easily measured in practice. The key question to establish validity in the data is to ask the following: Are we measuring what we intended to measure?

---

15 This stylized fact is supported by Pieters and Baumgartner (2002), who found that 90 per cent of all scholarly citations in leading economics journals during the period of 1995–7 were confined to the discipline. While the remaining 10 per cent of citations were characterized as interdisciplinary, the vast majority (79 per cent) of them came from finance. Notably, only 14 per cent of interdisciplinary citations in economics could be attributed to political science. This is despite the fact that 67 per cent of interdisciplinary citations in political science were assigned to economics.

- Empirical results often vary or are outright contradictory even when testing the same theory. How can we reconcile them? You need to take a closer look at the empirical sample – size, period, diversity – and the methodologies employed.
- Remember that statistical significance does not necessarily imply practical significance. Politicians, not economists, make policy decisions, and hence you should also take into consideration the practical significance of the findings and the feasibility of policy actions.

CHAPTER FOUR

Voting Rules and Their Impact on Law and Policy

The rules that specify how collective decisions are to be taken can and do have a material impact on the decision-making outcomes. In other words, different outcomes – laws, policies, candidates elected, etc. – may come about under different decision-making rules even if the voters or decision-makers are the same and their preferences and other circumstances remain unchanged.

This chapter aims to do the following:

- provide an overview of the basic collective decision-making structures spanning consensus voting and veto rights, majority voting, and strategic interaction
- highlight the relationships between decision processes and outcomes and their stability
- demonstrate the importance of agenda-setting powers
- critically analyze the relationship between voting, democracy, and economic efficiency
- provide a basic understanding of strategic interaction and game theory concepts
- highlight the challenges of applying game theory in empirical contexts

4.1 CONSENSUS VOTING AND VETO RIGHTS

At first glance, it seems an ideal situation would be to make decisions by consensus – that is, everyone would agree on a particular policy stance. It would seem to satisfy the Pareto efficiency criterion in that everyone would be at least as well off under the new policy than before, and no one would be worse off (assuming all the affected parties were actually involved in the decision-making, and no affected groups were excluded from the decision-making). Of course, in practice, such direct inclusion of all the affected groups and individuals in decision-making is unlikely, and people are affected by any decision in a variety of ways depending on their particular characteristics and circumstances. Hence, in practice, even if there is a collective decision taken by consensus, it is important *not* to assume it complies with Pareto efficiency since some parties affected by the decision could have been excluded from voting on it. For example, voters in a given country make decisions that affect citizens in other parts of the world, but the rest of the world is not eligible to take part in a national vote. Similarly, a jury's decision in a criminal trial is typically required to be unanimous, but it is unlikely that the guilty party would have been in favour of it.

Consensus voting is typically required when the decision has significant repercussions; allowing any individual party to reject the decision against all the other parties' wishes is therefore important. Such veto rights protect minorities, but there can be a downside to them: Given that it is unlikely that we can all agree on things, decision-making can be stalled when veto rights are granted. As a result, the status quo or inaction is likely to persist. The number of voters also matters – the higher the number of voters or parties to the decision-making, the less likely that a consensus can be reached and the more likely the status quo will prevail. Those with veto rights can also hold out not just for their own protection, but strategically, in an effort to extract rents or favourable votes from other parties on other, even unrelated, issues. Therefore, veto rights can also create scope for the abuse of the system, especially if the decision-making body has jurisdiction over a wide range of issues.

1 The United Nations Security Council is one decision-making body which includes some members with veto rights. Can you provide an explanation for this current structure and the implications for global peace and security?

2 What other examples of consensus voting and veto rights can you provide in the international and national contexts?

3 Can you provide examples of consensus voting that exclude important stakeholders to the decision? Analyze why those stakeholders have been excluded from the decision-making.

4.2 MAJORITY VOTING

Majority voting in some form is typical in most jurisdictions, and is generally considered an essential part of democratic regimes. Nevertheless, a few important questions can be raised in relation to this accepted standard for collective decision-making:

- How reliable is majority voting in terms of yielding outcomes representative of the electorate?
- Does majority voting ensure some degree of economic efficiency in the decision-making?

4.2.1 Majority Voting and Representation (Direct vs. Representative Democracy)

Consider the following hypothetical situation with three voters, direct democracy (e.g., through a referendum), and three policy options, A, B, or C. Only one of the policy options can be chosen and implemented. The voters' preferences over the policy options are summarized in table 4.1.

Consider the voters' options by comparing the policy alternatives in pairs:

- Voter 1 prefers option A to B, B to C, and A to C
- Voter 2 prefers option B to C, C to A, and B to A
- Voter 3 prefers option C to A, A to B, and C to B

Table 4.1. Voters' preferences over policy options

Policy choice	Voter 1	Voter 2	Voter 3
Rank 1	A	B	C
Rank 2	B	C	A
Rank 3	C	A	B

Now consider these choices:

- *A* versus *B*: *A* wins over *B* by 2 votes against 1
- *B* versus *C*: *B* wins over *C* by 2 votes against 1
- *A* versus *C*: *C* wins over *A* by 2 votes against 1

So overall, for this group of three voters, *A* is preferred to *B*, *B* is preferred to *C*, and *C* is preferred to *A*, which means the collective preferences of the voters are not transitive, since *A* is not preferred to *C*. This collective outcome can occur even if individual voter preferences are transitive; this phenomenon is also known as the *Condorcet paradox*, in recognition of the work by the Marquis de Condorcet in the late eighteenth century (Condorcet, 1785).

When there is no clear, most-preferred collective choice, or *Condorcet winner*, as in this case above, the outcome of decision-making is unstable due to the cyclicality in collective preferences. There has been some debate in the literature on the likelihood of such occurrences in practice, but it is important to keep in mind that it can be difficult to collect data on such revealed preferences, and hence it should not necessarily be utilized as an argument against the applicability or importance of the phenomenon in practice. Kurrild-Klitgaard (2001) provides an overview of the issues that may prevent us from observing the Condorcet paradox in practice, along with an actual example of it in the context of Danish voters' preferences for prime minister in 1994.

Nevertheless, the application of the Condorcet paradox in the context of sequential or multi-stage decision-making is clearer. Consider the following, for example:

- If the first question we pose to voters is to choose between *A* or *C*, then *C* wins, and then in the second round comparing *C* and *B*, *B* becomes the final outcome.

- If the first question we pose to voters is to choose between *A* or *B*, then *A* wins, and then in the second round comparing *A* and *C*, *C* becomes the final outcome.
- If the first question we pose to voters is to choose between *B* or *C*, then *B* wins, and then in the second round comparing *B* and *A*, *A* becomes the final outcome.

Consequently, the order in which we pose the questions for comparing the policy alternatives matters for determining the outcome. In political terms, this means the power to set the voting agenda and the order of voting over policy alternatives can determine the outcome.

Iterative consideration of options is present in negotiations over new laws or amendments in the legislature, or in the context of party leadership or primary elections, with the second round being the national runoff. Internal party rules, election rules, and the rules for proposing and approving legislation and amendments can therefore have a material impact on the legislative or policy outcome. It is typically the winning party in government that has such agenda-setting powers, and it is therefore not surprising that different groups vie for such positions.

Under representative democracy, when voters elect their representatives among political candidates, the approximation between the voters' preferences and those of the political candidates also needs to be taken into consideration. As individual voters, we are unlikely to agree with any political candidate on every issue. Hence, we choose the "second-best" or closest match candidate with whom we can agree on the majority of issues. Consider, for example, in table 4.2 the following hypothetical situation with two political candidates – candidate *L*, who is in favour of public projects, and thus announces to vote in favour of each of the projects under consideration, and candidate *R*, who is fiscally conservative and principally opposed to government involvement in the economy and society, and who thus pledges to reject each project.

The result is that voters 1 and 2 choose candidate *L* since they agree with this candidate on two issues out of three, while voter 3 chooses candidate *R*. Candidate *L* wins with a 2:1 majority vote, and under representative democracy approves the implementation of all three projects, *A*, *B*, and *C*. This stands in contrast to the result under direct

Table 4.2. Outcomes under direct democracy and representative democracy

Type	Voter 1	Voter 2	Voter 3	Direct democracy result	Representative democracy result
Project A	Yes	No	No	No*	Yes*
Project B	Yes	Yes	No	Yes	Yes
Project C	No	Yes	No	No*	Yes*
Candidate	L[†]	L	R	Candidate L	N/A

* Results with an asterisk indicate where there is an inconsistency in outcomes under direct democracy versus representative democracy.

[†] L = Yes; R = No.

democracy because if a referendum were to take place on each project, projects *A* and *C* would be rejected. The last two columns of table 4.2 demonstrate that, in this case, the outcomes under direct democracy and representative democracy match up only in the case of one of the three projects, for project *B* specifically. This inconsistency in outcomes under direct and representative democracy is called *Ostrogorki's paradox* (Ostrogorski, 1902).

4.2.2 Majority Voting and Economic Efficiency

Can we rely on majority voting or democracy more broadly to ensure at least some degree of economic efficiency in policy-making?

Consider the following example of a hypothetical distribution of costs and benefits (no specific denomination is assumed for the sake of simplicity in this case) across different voters for a given policy option, as seen in table 4.3.

Under simple majority voting with self-interested voters, the policy gets approved by the majority of two votes against one, but the overall societal impact is negative given the aggregate loss to society at −70. From an economic point of view, this is an inefficient outcome, but it is driven by the unequal distribution of costs and benefits on different parts of the electorate. It is noteworthy that the decision is approved despite the significantly negative impact on voter 1, while voters 2 and 3 benefit relatively little. Therefore, it is clear that majority voting or democracy on one hand, and economic efficiency on the other, are two independent, unrelated concepts.

Table 4.3. Distribution of costs and benefits

Type	Voter 1	Voter 2	Voter 3	Total impact on society
Costs	160	70	100	330
Benefits	40	100	120	260
Net benefit	−120	30	20	−70
Vote	No	Yes	Yes	Negative

When decisions on policies are bundled due to elected representatives voting along political party affiliation lines or exchanging favours to form coalitions, the lines between economic benefit and voting are further blurred. The practice of vote trading is also called *logrolling*.

QUESTIONS FOR DISCUSSION AND FURTHER RESEARCH

Identify an example of minority government in a certain jurisdiction.

1 What are the main policy issues they face at the given time?
2 What is the likelihood of a deal on these issues across political parties and what are the factors driving it?

4.2.3 Majoritarian versus Proportional Voting Systems

While majority rule is at the core of most political systems, there can be differences in terms of its application. The most basic distinction is between *majoritarian* and *proportional representation*. Under majoritarian systems, one member of parliament represents a given constituency or geographic area after securing the largest number of votes in that constituency. Under proportional representation, political parties are assigned seats in proportion to the share of votes secured.

The two voting systems are systematically more or less conducive to certain outcomes. For example, the number of political parties securing a seat in parliament is likely to be larger under proportional representation, hence more diversity in political options. At the same time, majority government is less likely under proportional representation and because smaller parties are more likely to secure seats, they can hold the balance of power in their hands despite their size.

Majoritarian systems, on the other hand, put the emphasis on geographic diversity in political preferences and often lead to voters in smaller, more remote communities having a relatively stronger voice than those in more populated, urban areas. Under majoritarian systems, the number of votes assigned to electoral districts can also vary based on historical conventions or political bargaining, which makes it more difficult to predict the aggregate outcome of voting, rather than just relying on a general survey of the population. Majoritarian systems can result in elections being won based on the particular weighing of electoral votes, rather than the total number of votes or popular majority. Clearly, this fact creates incentives to manipulate the electoral districts and their assigned weight. Since the assigned electoral weights tend to be anchored historically and more difficult to alter, the practice of manipulating electoral district boundaries for political gain is more widespread and is referred to as *gerrymandering*.

Majoritarian versus proportional voting systems have implications for political maneuvering, the chances of winning elections, and the size and composition of the winning majority, but they also have implications for policy decisions and policy outcomes.

4.3 WHY DO POLITICAL PARTIES EXIST?

Political candidates tend to form groups or, more specifically, political parties. Independent candidates without a party affiliation tend to be rare across jurisdictions. How can we explain this trend?

There are several factors at play. First of all, political campaigning is costly. If some fixed costs of campaigning are involved that can be shared among candidates, then it will be cost-effective if political candidates for elected office pool their resources. In other words, economies of scale are at play that drive down the average cost of campaigning per candidate if the fixed costs of campaigning can be spread across several candidates.

Another consideration is that as the number of candidates running for office increases, it also becomes costly for voters to seek out the relevant information on the individual candidates and their proposed policies. The costs will be both explicit and implicit, including the opportunity cost of time spent on researching individual candidates that could be spent on more productive activities. The media reporting on candidates helps reduce these costs by absorbing most of the explicit costs of research and disseminating the information, which ultimately becomes a public good as the word spreads. Nevertheless, there can be a prohibitive amount of information out there for voters to follow (often conflicting), interfering with their work and family obligations. Therefore, voters may decide to cut their losses and limit the investment they make in becoming informed voters. This phenomenon is referred to as *rational ignorance* (following the works of Downs, 1957; Schumpeter, 1950), since it is a conscious decision weighing the costs and benefits associated with acquiring relevant information in the face of limited resources such as time and money. The result is that we have an asymmetric information problem: Voters do not know much about individual candidates and have very few incentives to find out more about them. Martinelli (2007), through his theoretical work, shows that in so-called large elections – with a large number of voters, who thus each have a negligible impact on the outcome of the election – the share of voters acquiring costly information declines to zero. In other contexts, if the number of voters is small and the probability of being a decisive voter increases, so does the incentive to acquire relevant information, but it will be still subject to the cost of information acquisition, which also tends to vary across different voters.

The formation of political parties helps deal with the issue of acquiring information about individual candidates because political parties form common platforms. Thus, for individual voters, just finding out a candidate's party affiliation conveys a great deal of information to them about where roughly the candidate stands on common issues of public policy. Party affiliation then becomes a key information signal that is very cost-effective. At the same time, political candidates commit to uphold the party's principles, which helps parties maximize votes on policy issues. Political parties thus require commitment, aim to instil party discipline, and frown upon dissenting votes within their ranks.

QUESTIONS FOR DISCUSSION AND FURTHER RESEARCH

1 Can you think of factors that may lead to differentiated costs of acquiring information for different groups of voters?

2 What common practices do political parties employ to instil party discipline and voting along party platforms?

3 How do campaign financing rules shape the formation of political parties? Are the rules conducive to the creation of new parties or not?

BOX 4.1. UNCONSCIOUS PREFERENCES, BIAS, AND VOTING

The next frontier in predicting voting behaviour is going beyond the rational self-interest, other-regarding preferences or even the lies we may tell ourselves. From a psychological point of view, we may think of ourselves as free from biases or having all the "right" values and acting or voting accordingly, but do we actually?

Svoboda (2018) ventures into the world of political consultants to report on the latest methods and technology they have adopted to test voter preferences. The old concept of utilizing focus groups remains at the centre of the methods, but with some important differences. For example, the value of the focus group lies not in the answers directly provided by the participants (who are traditionally asked to rate or describe the performance of political candidates on ads or at debates), but in the biometric data collected and analyzed from one's facial expressions and the reaction time when forming a response. The assumption is that we may not be able to perfectly control our emotions and expressions, especially the most immediate reactions, and they become involuntarily revealing. It is also noteworthy that a longer reaction time is interpreted as hesitation, therefore revealing doubts and the potential to sway particular voters.

The methods and frameworks are borrowed and adapted from psychology, neuroscience, behavioural economics, and so-called neuromarketing to current political contexts. They build on the work of Daniel Kahneman and Vernon L. Smith, the 2002 winners of the Sveriges Riksbank (Sweden's central bank) Prize in Economic Sciences in Memory of Alfred Nobel.[1] Notably, Kahneman, as a psychologist, partnered with economist Amos Tversky to bring new elements beyond pure rationality to economic decision-making under uncertainty (see, e.g., Tversky & Kahneman, 1974, 1986). Smith pioneered the integration of laboratory experiments into economics (see, e.g., Smith, 1962, 1982, 1991a, 1991b). In combination, these streams of research led the development of behavioural economics as a new subfield in economics, which has interesting applications in the context of voting and political economy.

Technological advances have also helped the adoption of psychology and neuroscience to decision-making, as facial video analysis can replace the physical need to attach electrodes to one's head to complete an electroencephalography, or EEG. Now the focus group subjects can participate long-distance in the privacy of their home with only a computer, camera, and Internet access, while the political consultants run the relevant software for analysis on their end. As a result, the biometric data gathered in this type of focus group may become more objective (assuming the theories and algorithms are able to account for cultural and other aspects of diversity across populations), as opposed to the purely subjective self-reported data in conventional focus groups and surveys.

QUESTIONS FOR DISCUSSION AND FURTHER RESEARCH

Discuss the impact of technological development, access to information, and information quality on voting behaviour.

1 What is the scope for influencing voter behaviour and why does it vary across different groups?
2 Which groups are most susceptible to being influenced and why?
3 Which groups are most stable in their assessments and values, and therefore least influenceable, and why?

---

1   The prize is marked by controversy, as economics was not part of the original list of fields designated for the Nobel Prizes, and some question its legitimacy as well as ideological leanings.

4.4 STRATEGIC INTERACTION AND DECISION-MAKING

Another aspect of decision-making is strategy – that is, considering what the likely choice of our opponents is, how they might react to our actions, and how this interaction will affect our outcomes in terms of costs and benefits. Strategic interaction acknowledges that our outcomes and decisions are dependent on the actions of others. Contexts may range from how dominant firms engage in competition with each other (oligopoly models in economics) to how international treaties on anything (trade, nuclear proliferation, environmental protection, etc.) are negotiated, or how dictators interact with opposing groups domestically and abroad. But they are also present in everyday interactions among political representatives in governing bodies (legislatures, councils, committees) and in their statements to the public. When you walk into a meeting to present an idea and/or to ask questions, you are engaging in strategic interaction with the audience.

The number of parties to the decision-making also matters for the outcomes, but in general it is easier to draw conclusions and come up with more stable outcomes if the number of parties is low. At the same time, people also have incentives to form groups under certain conditions, so it is not that unrealistic to assume a low number of parties in strategic interaction.

Austen-Smith and Banks (1998) also argue that in complex environments (such as elections, for example), direct preference aggregation models are not equipped to make predictions about outcomes, while non-cooperative game-theoretical models are more likely to generate pragmatic projections.

Another consideration for analysis is whether there is scope for repeated interactions, sequential decision-making, or if the decision-making is simultaneous and finite by the relevant parties (so-called ultimatum games).

In strategic interaction, the parties have an incentive to keep their information private and try to acquire information on their opponents. In order to analyze a given strategic interaction, it is important to try to shed light on the information sets of the participants. For now, assume that the relevant information on possible payoffs is public and known with certainty.

Consider the interaction of two agents that each have the option to co-operate with each other or not. The corresponding possible outcomes are given in table 4.4, with the first number always denoting the payoff to group 1 and the second number denoting the payoff to group 2.

Table 4.4. Possible outcomes under strategic interaction

Probability of action	for group 2	p_2	$1 - p_2$
for group 1	Group 1 / Group 2	Co-operate	Reject co-operation
p_1	Co-operate	20, 25*	4, 10
$1 - p_1$	Reject co-operation	10, 6	10, 10

* This cell represents the socially optimal outcome.

If group 1 chooses to co-operate, their payoff will be 20 or 4, depending on the choice of action by group 2. If group 1 chooses to reject co-operation, their payoff will be 10 either way. Since 20 is better than 10, but 4 is inferior to 10, there is no clear choice or *dominant strategy* for group 1. The same holds for group 2 if you compare the payoffs. The socially optimal outcome among the four possibilities is when both groups co-operate with each other because that yields the highest aggregate payoff $(20 + 25 = 45)$, while both groups also happen to be better off individually under this scenario. But how likely are we to end up with the socially optimal outcome of co-operation by both parties? Well, there is uncertainty about that, as denoted by the interaction of probabilities p_1 and p_2, corresponding to group 1 and group 2 choosing to co-operate, respectively. Nevertheless, it is also interesting to consider what happens if we have an initial starting point: Is the outcome likely to change or not?

Consider, for example, that our starting point is that both groups have rejected co-operation and each have a payoff of 10 (i.e., the lower right-hand corner of table 4.4). Do any of the parties have an incentive to change their position?

- Assuming that group 2 has chosen to reject co-operation (last column of table 4.4), group 1 has the choice of receiving 4 if they decide to co-operate unilaterally, or 10 if they remain in the non-cooperative state. Clearly, it remains the best option for group 1 to stick with non-cooperation.
- Similarly, assuming group 1 has chosen to reject co-operation (last row of table 4.4), group 2 has the option of receiving 6 if they chose to co-operate unilaterally, or 10 if they continue to reject co-operation. Rejecting co-operation thus remains the best option for group 2.

In summary then, if our starting outcome is non-cooperation by both groups (the lower right-hand quadrant in table 4.4), then it is a stable outcome because none of the parties has an incentive to change their position. This is also known as a pure strategy (discreet choice) *Nash equilibrium*. While this outcome is superior to the other two possible outcomes with unilateral co-operation, it falls significantly short of the socially optimal outcome that involves co-cooperation by both parties in the upper left quadrant.

Hence, it is interesting to explore what the probability is that we will end up with co-operation by both parties. If group 1 receives 10 with certainty when rejecting co-operation, then the expected payoff from co-operation has to match that (assuming risk-neutral behaviour by group 1).

The expected payoff to group 1 from co-operation versus non-cooperation nevertheless depends on the choice of action by group 2 (or the probability of cooperation, p_2) as follows:

Expected payoff from non-cooperation = Expected payoff from cooperation

$$10 = 20p_2 + 4(1 - p_2)$$
$$10 = 20p_2 + 4 - 4p_2 = 4 + 16p_2$$
$$6 = 16p_2$$
$$p_2 = 6/16 = 0.375 = 37.5\%$$

Similarly, the expected payoff to group 2 from co-operation versus non-cooperation depends on the choice of action by group 1 (or the probability of cooperation p_1) as follows:

Expected payoff from non-cooperation = Expected payoff from cooperation

$$10 = 25p_1 + 6(1 - p_1)$$
$$10 = 25p_1 + 6 - 6p_1 = 6 + 19p_1$$
$$4 = 19p_1$$
$$p_1 = 4/19 = 0.21 = 21\%$$

Hence, according to our analysis, group 1 chooses to co-operate with 21 per cent probability and group 2 with 37.5 per cent probability. The corresponding probabilities for the possible combinations of outcomes are given in table 4.5. The most likely outcome is non-cooperation by

Table 4.5. Probability of outcomes

Probability of action	For group 2	p_2	$1 - p_2$
For group 1 p_1	Group 1 / Group 2 Co-operate	Co-operate 0.21 × 0.375=0.07875 = 7.9%	Reject co-operation 0.21 × 0.625=0.13125 = 13.1%
$1 - p_1$	Reject co-operation	0.79 × 0.375=0.29625 = 29.6%	0.79 × 0.625=0.49375 = 49.4%

both groups, at 49.4 per cent, while mutual co-operation is the least likely outcome, with only 7.9 per cent probability. Note that the four possible outcomes add up to 100 per cent probability since this list is exhaustive.

In general, Nash equilibria can be pure or mixed-strategy (Nash, 1950a, 1950b, 1951). Mixed-strategy involves playing a strategy with a given probability, while pure strategy assumes discreet choice between strategies. In general, there can be multiple pure strategy Nash equilibria or none. To determine how many pure strategy Nash equilibria there are, you need to analyze one by one each of the four possible outcomes in table 4.4 by asking and answering the defining question: Do any of the parties have an incentive to change their position or strategy?

Analyzing Nash equilibria can help us determine likely outcomes under uncertainty and strategic interactions (mixed strategy Nash equilibria), or if a particular state of affairs (e.g., an agreement or refusal to negotiate) between strategic opponents represents a stable or unstable outcome (pure strategy Nash equilibrium or not).

Readers interested in learning more about game theory applications to public policy may consult, for example, McCain (2015).

QUESTIONS FOR DISCUSSION AND FURTHER RESEARCH

1 In the above example, if we were to start off in the position of mutual co-operation, would this be a stable, Nash equilibrium? Refer back to table 4.4 to determine your answer.

2 How many pure strategy Nash equilibria are there in the context of the example in table 4.4?

Table 4.6. An alternative scenario for cooperation

Probability of action	for group 2	p_2	$1 - p_2$
for group 1	Group 1/Group 2	Co-operate	Reject co-operation
p_1	Co-operate	18, 16	6, 10
$1 - p_1$	Reject co-operation	10, 8	10, 10

3 Can governments increase the likelihood of achieving the socially optimal outcome of mutual co-operation? If yes, how?

4 What would be the likelihood of the different outcomes if the payoffs in table 4.4 changed to the outcomes in table 4.6?

RESEARCH ADVICE: HOW TO SHED EMPIRICAL LIGHT ON STRATEGIC

INTERACTIONS

In general, it is difficult to empirically test theoretical hypotheses that involve strategic interaction, because the relevant information may not be public, there is uncertainty about the possible payoffs to parties under different scenarios, and factors other than pure rationality and self-interest may be at play and affect decision-making. Therefore, a controlled experiment that defines the information sets and possible payoffs to participants in the form of simulations and hired participants can be another option.

Behavioural economists have conducted such experiments, but they are not without threats to validity, given possible selection bias in the recruitment of volunteers, cultural and psychological factors affecting the results, or the need for the stakes to be reasonably high to be realistic. At the same time, the necessity for the stakes to be high enough to affect behaviour means that actual monetary payoffs are necessary, which increases the costs of those studies. Thus they may need to be moved to low-cost settings, utilizing university students, for example, or volunteers in lower-income countries.

Another option is historical analysis of documents. The 2010–11 WikiLeaks scandal of leaked secret government communications in the United States provides a rare glimpse at what information and uncertainty different parties had at any given time, and how those information sets would change over time. Normally, such documents would be declassified and released with a significant time lag, making the analysis truly historical. Nevertheless, while the information contained in the WikiLeaks documents is more recent, large volumes of information in its raw form provide a challenge for processing and analysis, and therefore interpretation.

CHAPTER FIVE

Interest Groups, Collective Action Problems, and Regulatory Capture

In this chapter, we focus on policies that seem to benefit a select few at the expense of many other constituents. How is that possible in democratic societies with majority voting?

To analyze such cases, a reminder is due from chapter 1, in which we utilized a definition of "public interest" provided by Levine and Forrence (1990): "general-interest policies or actions adopted or undertaken by a regulatory agent that would be ratified by the general polity according to its accepted aggregation principles if the information, organization (including exclusion costs), and transaction and monitoring costs of the general polity were zero" (p. 176). Under this framework by Levine and Forrence (1990), deviations from public interest policy outcomes included the following:

1. *private interests* prevailing or *regulatory capture by special interests*, which can effectively constitute corruption
2. the case of the Burkean regulator with other-regarding preferences, who believe themselves to be acting in the public's "best interest," although such policy would not be approved by the general polity (Burke, 1774)

In this section, we focus on the first type of scenario outlined above, and we will also spend time analyzing the impact of non-trivial information, organization, and transaction and monitoring costs to the general polity, as those contribute to deviations from public interest policies as outlined in the definition by Levine and Forrence (1990, p. 176).

After completing this chapter, you should be able to do the following:

- appreciate the importance of organized groups and their potential to influence public policy
- identify determinants of group formation and explain differences in potential for forming effective groups and deviations from public interest policies
- apply theoretical frameworks capturing interest group formation and influence to policy areas including trade and competition policy and industry-specific regulations

5.1 DETERMINANTS OF INTEREST GROUP FORMATION

The works of Olson (1965, 1982) are generally considered foundational for the development of modern political economy theories of special interest group formation and their impact. Forming groups is not easy; they require effort, which is costly to individuals, and the benefits need to outweigh the costs. Moreover, if others benefit from a group's actions, free riding on the costly group formation and policy lobbying effort will take place. These dynamics are at the centre of so-called *collective action problems*, and only those groups that can overcome them have a chance of exerting influence over policy outcomes. Successful groups then engage in purported *rent-seeking behaviour* to create *abnormal profits* or *rents* for themselves. When such behaviour is prevalent, it will serve as an impediment to innovation and lead to *institutional sclerosis* with a negative macroeconomic impact on growth.

Coates et al. (2007) empirically analyzed the determinants of interest group formation using Olson's (1982) hypotheses that interest groups build up in stable societies with freedom to organize and that they have a negative impact on income levels and economic growth as they compete for influence. In contrast to earlier studies with small sample sizes and a focus on high-income OECD countries, Coates et al. (2007) utilized a relatively large, even if unbalanced, panel dataset of 140 countries at five points in time between 1973 and 2002. The study included a range of factors as explanatory variables for possible determinants of interest group formation, including different measures of stability (or absence of institutional upheaval), socio-economic development, political system (democracy and number of parties), country size (by population and number of industries), diversity (ethnic, linguistic, and religious fractionalization), and government size (government consumption expenditure as a percentage of GDP). They generally found the empirical evidence to be consistent with the theoretical predictions: Stability, socio-economic development, size, and diversity all appear to contribute to the buildup of interest groups. Nevertheless, this research does not shed light on the potential of different interest groups to influence policy outcomes. We explore this issue in the subsequent sections.

5.2 THE LINKAGES BETWEEN POLICY TYPES AND INTEREST GROUP FORMATION

The type of policy issue at hand can have a material impact on the likelihood of success by special interests in exerting influence or being blocked by competing interests and lobbies. Lowi (1964) classified the types of issues and policies into three categories: distributive, regulatory, and redistributive. Their defining features can be summarized as follows:

- *Distributive policies* are identified by Lowi (1964) through the lens that "politics works in the short run, and in the short run certain kinds of government decisions can be made without regard to limited resources" (p. 690). In practice, this can represent increased government spending (without much regard for how it will be financed), and in that sense it can be relatively easy to secure coalition partners for such policies in a logroll-type arrangement when decision-makers trade favours or votes (i.e., distributive policies represent relatively homogenous interests).[1]

---

1   You may refer to chapter 4, section 4.2.2 for more information on logrolling.

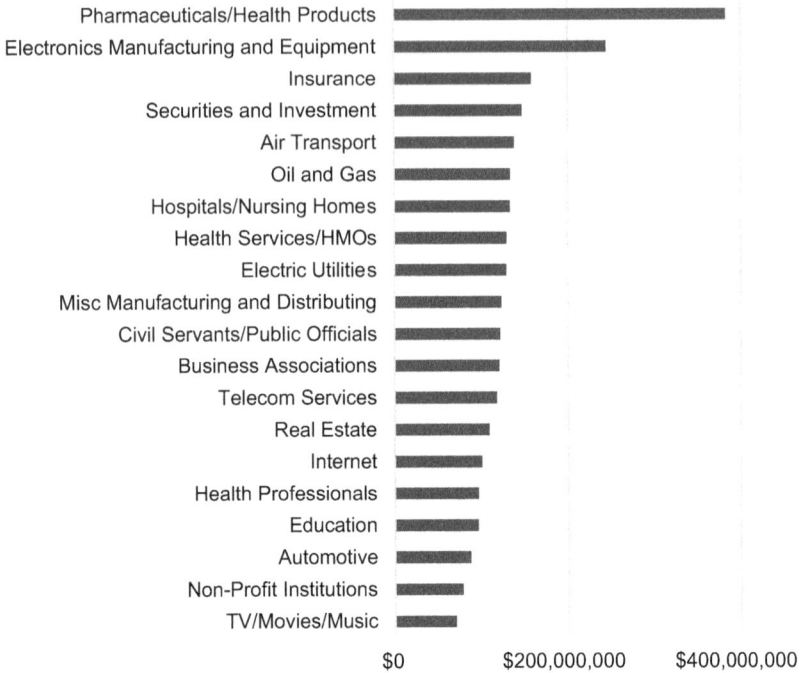

Figure 5.1. Federal government lobby spending by industry in the United States in 2023

Source: OpenSecrets

- *Regulatory policies* have a concentration of costs or benefits due to their specific impact on relatively few actors and, as such, will provide strong incentives to form well-defined, and thus effective, interest groups. As a result, large firms in regulated and/or concentrated industries tend to be relatively more effective in overcoming their collective action problems, organizing, and funding their efforts to shape public policy and regulation. Figure 5.1 illustrates this supposition using industry-level federal government lobbying expenditure data from the United States in 2023.[2] Most of the industries on the list represent those that are subject to public sector regulations, and changes to regulatory policies can have material impact on market competition and firm-level profitability.

---

2   Calculations by OpenSecrets based on data from the US Senate Office of Public Records, available at https://www.opensecrets.org/federal-lobbying/industries.

- *Redistributive policies* have broadly defined winners and losers (often according to economic class), which means incentives to organize will be relatively weaker than under regulatory policies due to the greater potential for free riding on lobbying efforts. Dür and De Bièvre (2007) characterized this set of policies by assigning them diffuse costs and small benefits to many, but this characterization is debatable. When political and economic polarization and economies of scale are involved, individual costs and benefits from redistributive policies can be significant. In this context, it is also important to reiterate that redistributive policies cannot and should not simply be interpreted as redistribution from "rich" to "poor," but can involve expropriation by certain groups at the expense of others. Colonization is one such clear explicit policy example, but other examples of more implicit redistributive policies can include policies that favour large versus small business, online versus traditional retailers, capital versus labour, skilled versus unskilled labour, urban versus rural residents, climate-safe regions versus those prone to higher risk due to extreme weather events, etc.

While the costs and benefits to such groups can be significant, the potential to overcome collective action problems may be nevertheless weak due to free riding on costly lobbying efforts and the inability to exclude non-contributors from the benefits of such policies if the lobbying effort is successful and leads to implementation. Another aspect of redistributive policies worth noting is that even a threat of such policies, or potential impact, can invoke action even if the actual degree of redistribution might be limited. In Lowi's (1964) own words, "The nature of a redistributive issue is not determined by the outcome of a battle over how redistributive a policy is going to be. Expectations about what it can be, what it threatens to be, are determinative" (p. 691).

QUESTIONS FOR DISCUSSION AND FURTHER RESEARCH

1 Can you identify other policy examples that have primarily distributive, regulatory, and redistributive characteristics?
2 Are there strong lobbies and counter-lobbies associated with them? Explain why such lobbies are present or absent.

5.3 INTEREST GROUP INFLUENCE ON POLICY FORMATION

Dür and De Bièvre (2007) conceptually define influence or power as control over political outcomes. Political outcomes can be either an official position or actual implementation, which are observable and thus can be measured. Measuring actual influence over political outcomes in a reliable manner is nevertheless very difficult because there are multiple factors that influence policy-makers' decisions and because activities aimed at inserting influence can be overt, or covert and indirect. Dür and De Bièvre assume that political actors have clear preferences over outcomes, and these preferences can also change over time. However, these preferences are hard to observe in practice due to the fact that actors may have incentives to not reveal their (true) preferences for strategic reasons.

Importantly, this line of work by Dür and De Bièvre highlights that institutions (formal or informal ones) and resources matter because they empower or disenfranchise specific interests. Pathways to influence include access to decision-makers, influencing the selection of decision-makers, strategies to shape public opinion, and employing structural coercion power, which in practice typically means market exit or entry by economic agents (e.g., threats or promises to relocate businesses and investment based on the adoption of certain policies, which may affect employment in certain jurisdictions and similar decisions).

An interesting question is whether multilayer decision-making under federal systems or supranational agreements is more or less conducive to interest group influence. Dür (2008a) explored the issue in the context of the European Union (EU) and found that the evidence is mixed across different studies. It is not clear if the differences are driven by the institutional frameworks specific to the EU, the methods utilized, or policy types involved. From a broader theoretical perspective, multilevel governance can increase veto points, thus propagating the status quo, or enhance access points for influence, thus enabling more interest group influence. Laffont (1999) argued that the separation of power among different levels and/or branches of government can increase the *transaction costs of capture* and thus diminish interest group influence. Divisions between executive powers (e.g., for inter-governmental coordination in the international arena) and the legislative branches of government (single or multi-cameral systems) can also empower executive decision-making at times at the expense of the legislative branch and thus elected officials, which in turn could diminish domestic interest group influence (Dür, 2008a). Of course, this involves the implicit assumption that somehow the executive branch is less prone to interest group influence relative to the legislative branch.

Arguably, the EU has a very unique institutional structure in many aspects,[3] but one worth highlighting is that private actors can take advantage of a supranational judicial channel, the Court of Justice of the European Union (CJEU). One of the CJEU mandates is ensuring that the EU takes action – that is, "actions for failure to act" – under certain circumstances, and this channel can counter the tendency for the status quo when multiple veto points are present under multi-level governance. The CJEU also has the power to award damages to individuals and companies who have been harmed by the actions or inaction of the EU.[4]

The European Convention on Human Rights, which came into force in 1953, has established the European Court of Human Rights (ECHR) under the judicial branch of the Council of Europe and has an even wider reach than the EU, with 46 countries as signatories as of 2024. Similar to the CJEU, individuals have the right to bring cases forward to the ECHR without interference from their governments.[5] In April 2024, the ECHR issued a landmark ruling, setting precedent for individual rights to health against the inaction of their government on climate change. The case of *Verein KlimaSeniorinnen Schweiz and others v. Switzerland* (ECHR 2024) was brought forward by a group of elderly women arguing that their health is especially susceptible to heat waves that have become more frequent due to global warming,

---

3   For an overview of the main EU institutions, please refer to European Union (n.d.-b).
4   For more information on the CJEU mandate, please refer to European Union (n.d.-a).
5   For more information, please refer to ECHR (n.d.).

which is attributable to harmful emissions in the atmosphere.[6] They argued that the Swiss government failed in its duty to comply with existing climate agreements and protect citizens' health by reducing emissions. The ECHR ruled in favour of the proponents, and the case is expected to trigger more climate rights–related litigation by citizens against their governments.

Of course, litigation is a costly and lengthy process, but the case brought to the forefront the interests of a marginalized group with limited resources and diffuse costs and benefits, thus theoretically fraught with all the collective action problems outlined by Olson (1965). It was the private right of legal action that enabled access to decision-makers, overcoming collective action problems. In this case, the multilevel governance structure enabled better access to decision-makers by marginalized special interests with limited organizational ability, compared to the conventional political process, which tends to favour larger and better-organized lobbies.

Nevertheless, the story does not end here, because it is still up to the Swiss government and elected officials (or a referendum) to design the policy response, and details of policy design and implementation do matter for effectiveness. Furthermore, such rulings, which favour marginalized private interests, can also induce special interests with more power in the national (or sub-national) political arenas to take counteraction. The withdrawal of the United Kingdom from the EU – dubbed "Brexit" – serves as a glaring example of such a response that highlighted the dissatisfaction with the erosion of national interests in favour of superseding EU policies. More recent plans in the United Kingdom to withdraw from the European Convention on Human Rights similarly reflect resistance to supranational legal accountability and the veto that the European Court of Human Rights can impose on UK government decisions (see, for example, Dickson, 2023). From an analytical point of view, this means that institutions cannot be taken as exogenous or given in the medium to long term, as they will also be shaped by the changing landscape of policy influencers in an endogenous manner.

Finally, it is worth noting that Brexit was decided in 2016 in a very narrow national referendum, and critics have argued that campaigns

---

6   For more context on the case and its proponents, see reporting by Rajvanshi (2024).

by special interests to sway public opinion played a significant role in the outcome (see, for example, Mortimer, 2017). In the next section, we turn to analyzing how special interests advance their agendas by affecting public opinion.

BOX 5.1. CAN GOOGLE/ALPHABET AND FACEBOOK/META EFFECTIVELY EXERCISE STRUCTURAL COERCION POWER IN RESPONSE TO A "LINK TAX" BY CANADIAN AND AUSTRALIAN GOVERNMENTS?

Large enterprises that dominate particular goods and services markets tend to have stronger incentives and asymmetric capacity to shape public policy outcomes. Threats of reduced investment, employment, and market exit provide large firms with some leverage to shape public policy and regulations. An illustrative example of this can be found in attempts by a number of governments to compel global tech giants such as Google/Alphabet and Facebook/Meta to pay for links and snippets of news they display on their search and social media platforms. These global platforms aggregate information from third-party sites and display them to their users, which then connects users to third-party sites and drives traffic to them. In this so-called *two-sided market*, both users and content providers depend on the global platforms to find each other, and this tends to create network effects prone to market dominance.

Displaying links and snippets benefits both users and third-party sites, as well as search/social media platforms in the middle that bring them together and sell advertising. While publishing third-party content (i.e., articles, videos, etc.) would normally require permission from and payment to rightsholders, web links and short-form text are exempt from copyright law.

Pointing to the importance of local news production, a number of national governments have been trying to compel global tech giants to pay for displaying links and snippets of content from news outlets and publishers in their countries. An early example of this was in Spain, which in 2015 introduced a copyright fee on online information aggregators to be paid for linking and displaying content snippets from Spanish newspapers and pub-lishers. Google responded to the law by shutting down Google News in Spain and links to Spanish publishers on Google News.[1] Research on the impact of this law suggests that it did not reduce overall news consumption in Spain, but the introduction of the law was associated with increased fragmentation of news con-tent people consumed (Majó-Vázquez et al., 2017). Recognizing the ineffectual nature of the tax in generating subsidies for local news production and its negative impacts on consumers, the Spanish government ultimately reversed course and repealed the law in 2021. Google subsequently relaunched its Google News services in Spain (Hazard Owen, 2022).

In contrast to the direct tax used in the Spanish experiment, Australia and Canada have opted to achieve the same objective using a different approach in which the tech giants are mandated to bargain with local news publishers to determine the amount they will have to pay. In both cases, coalitions of large national news and media companies that would ultimately benefit most from such regulations were able to overcome their collective action problems and were the primary interest groups driving the adop-tion of the measures. In Australia, for example, Rupert Murdoch's News Corp. was a primary proponent of the mandated bargaining regulations (Masnick, 2021). Small independent news organiza-tions that rely on global tech giants for reaching local and global customers, as well as consumer advocacy groups, opposed the new measures due to the potentially adverse impacts that poten-tial blocking/delinking of Canadian news content could have on distribution and access to news (Hatfield, 2020).

Meta started blocking news sites following the introduction of Australian regulations in 2021, but its approach led to blocking a wide range of non-news sites as well (i.e., false positive errors). Examples of essential sites that were blocked included domes-tic violence charities, government departments, and meteorol-ogy services, which forced Meta to abandon blocking after a few days and enter into private agreements to pay certain Australian media publishers. In early 2024, Meta indicated that it will not renew the agreement to pay $70 million per year to Australian news media organizations and shut down certain Facebook news features (Morris-Grant, 2024; Roberts & Doran, 2024).

Canada's 2023 *Online News Act* (Bill C-18)[2] essentially replicates the Australian model that tries to indirectly tax the tech giants by mandating them to bargain with and pay certain local news providers for the publication of links and snippets.[3] Meta similarly threatened to start blocking Canadian news and has followed through on this threat by permanently blocking Canadian news on its Facebook and Instagram platforms (Geist, 2023).[4] Under this outcome, the tech giant avoids paying the Canadian news industry for links and snippets, but ultimately it is a lose-lose situation for both the Canadian media industry and consumers of locally relevant information produced by local news organizations, now excluded from the platform. Research on the impacts of Canada's *Online News Act* suggests that it has limited impact on the overall behaviour of Canadian Facebook users, but has led to a significant decrease in engagement with Canadian news outlets (Parker et al., 2024). The consequent fragmentation of news associated with Meta's exit from the Canadian news aggregation market has material impacts in terms of access to essential local news, including those relating to fast-evolving local events such as wildfires (The Canadian Press, 2024).

In June 2024, Google announced that they had reached an agreement with a coalition of Canadian news organizations to pay $100 million annually (indexed for inflation) (Zaidi, 2024). The tentative deal still requires approval by the Canadian Radio Television and Telecommunications Commission (CRTC). There are also disputes between media organizations as to the administration of the fund, even though under Bill C-18 all the news media outlets that applied for funding are to be awarded their share, irrespective of who makes the deal with Google or another tech company (see, e.g., Geist, 2024). This suggests that the transactions costs of any arrangement under this legislation are likely to be non-negligible.

Attempts to adopt similar mechanisms at the sub-national level have led to analogous responses by the tech giants. In response to the proposed *California Journalism Preservation Act* (CJPA), Google started to block links to California-based news outlets and publishers in April 2024, and stopped entering into news content distribution agreements with California news entities that the law intends to benefit (see, e.g., Allyn, 2024).

---

1 To view Google's official statement and arguments for making Google News unavailable to users in Spain, please visit https://support .google.com/news/publisher-center/answer/6140047?hl=es&visit _id=638519079209598068-2278800767&rd=1.

2 Bill C-18, *An Act respecting online communications platforms that make news content available to persons in Canada*, is available at https://www.parl.ca/legisinfo/en /bill/44-1/c-18.

3 The *Online News Act* is part of the Canadian government's digital agenda, along with the *Online Streaming Act*. For more information and the government's rationale for the legislation, please visit https://www.canada.ca/en /canadian-heritage/services/online-news.html.

4 For a selection of articles on the evolving responses to Bill C-18, please see Michael Geist's blog, at https://www.michaelgeist.ca/tag/online-news-act/.

5.4 INTEREST GROUP INFLUENCE THROUGH SHAPING PUBLIC OPINION

Shaping public opinion is a costly endeavour in which access to resources – financial, human, and information – matters. As a result, political campaign finance rules can have a significant impact on how special interests can influence policy-makers and their selection process. Some interest groups – for example, those representing persons with disabilities and other marginalized groups – may also depend on state resources to be able to participate in official policy-making proceedings.

The degree of complexity of policy issues and asymmetric information problems between special interests, policy-makers, and the general public creates a fertile field for influencing public opinion. Voters are presented with a large volume of often contradictory information, and it is costly for them to analyze and verify such information. The rise of social media and proliferation of misinformation have further exacerbated the problem.

The *salience* of issues – whether issues capture public attention at any point in time or fade over time as fatigue prevails or other issues emerge and appear more pressing or interesting to the public – also plays a significant role in determining the potential for special interests to influence political agendas and policy outcomes. Erbring et al. (1980) highlighted the agenda-setting power of media organizations and their utilization in shaping public policy, as well as a variety of mechanisms through which media-induced salience of issues dissipates. The development of the world wide web and Internet information aggregation platforms (e.g., Google, Meta, TikTok) have reduced the gatekeeper and agenda-setting powers of traditional media in shaping public opinion and policy. Empirical research on traditional versus digital social media issues and agenda-setting suggests that they tend to replicate each other, with the notable exception that the social media agenda of political parties is more predictive of policies than the traditional media agenda (Gilardi et al., 2022).

In light of the strong impact of issue *salience*, some jurisdictions explicitly forbid political advertisement in the immediate run-up to elections or may limit corporations from participating in such communication campaigns. The rationale is that corporations are more likely to have accumulated resources relative to individuals and may thus distort the information landscape and disenfranchise voters. For similar reasons, some jurisdictions also limit how much individuals can donate to political campaigns to remain close to the democratic principle of equal voice for each citizen regardless of their wealth. Other jurisdictions may also provide state resources to political parties based on their attained votes in elections to counter the influence of wealthy individuals.

BOX 5.2. THE ROLE OF SPECIAL INTERESTS IN POLITICAL COMMUNICATIONS IN THE UNITED STATES

In 2010, the US Supreme Court overturned an earlier decision in *Austin v. Michigan Chamber of Commerce* (1990) that allowed restrictions on corporate expenditures related to elections. The decision in the case of *Citizens United v. Federal Election Commission (FEC)* (2010) rejected the earlier rationale for limiting corporate electioneering communications, based on corporate resources possibly distorting the elections and the government's interest in preventing the threat or appearance of corruption. Instead, in 2010 the Supreme Court emphasized the free speech rights of corporations and allowed electioneering communications by corporations, labour unions, and other private interests, as long as they do not directly coordinate with political candidates or political parties. This provision has been generally considered very weak protection, which created a loophole for corporate interests and wealthy individuals to weigh in heavily in public communications related to political campaigns and electoral candidates.

The *Citizens United v. FEC* decision has led to a proliferation of so-called Super PACs – independent expenditure-only political action committees – that allow unlimited funds to be raised from corporations, unions, other groups, or individuals and spent on political messaging for and against candidates running for office. The erosion of disclosure requirements and limits on political expenditures under this decision has led to rapid growth in the development of opaque organizations shaping public opinion, interest group formation, and coordination of activities via relatively untransparent Super PACs (Bauerly & Hallstrom, 2012). According to FEC data, there were 1,616 Independent Expenditure-Only Political Committees/Super PACs registered in 2019 with $432.6 million in receipts and $229.7 million in disbursements, and another 346 political committees with non-contribution accounts, which also allow unlimited contributions from individuals, corporations, labour organizations, and other political committees, with $1.121 billion in receipts and $1.074 billion in disbursements.[1]

For comparison, table 5.1 provides a snapshot of PAC contributions, which are subject to donation limits, for the 2019–20 US federal elections campaign. Interestingly, the data indicate little difference in the contributions to candidates from the two

Table 5.1. Summary of PAC contributions to all federal races

$	2019	2020	2-year total
Incumbent	190,904,015	150,408,326	341,312,341
Challenger	10,283,364	5,324,159	15,607,524
Open seat	3,048,357	4,331,920	7,380,278
Democrat	100,636,905	84,877,995	185,514,900
Republican	103,389,815	74,954,661	178,344,476
Other	209,017	16,000	225,017
Total	204,235,737	159,848,655	364,084,392

Source: Federal Election Commission (2019–20).

major political parties that dominate US politics. The vast majority of PAC contributions supported incumbent candidates from the major parties, with very limited support for challengers or third-party candidates. This is not surprising, since incumbents have a higher likelihood of winning.

Finally, it should be noted that special interest influence and channelling of resources are not limited to PACs and Super PACs. Special interests can also masquerade as non-profit organizations. They have multiple benefits, including tax-exempt status, unlimited donations, and limited transparency. Irvin (2023) explores this landscape of so-called "dark money" in the United States as part of its political ecosystem, specifically in the "ideas industry," and concludes by arguing for enhanced transparency by requiring public disclosure of largest donors in non-profit organizations.

---

1 For more information, please see Federal Election Commission (2020).

5.5 APPLICATION OF INTEREST GROUP POLITICS TO INTERNATIONAL TRADE POLICY

Trade protectionism is a classic example under which tariffs and/or quotas imposed on imports from other countries benefit a select few in the specific industries shielded from foreign competition at the expense of the many consumers (and possibly some producers who utilize such imports in their production processes[7]) who pay higher prices. As a result, consumers (and affected producers who utilize imported inputs) should favour free-trade policies rather than protectionism, even if their costs increase only marginally. Given that consumers and negatively affected producers very likely outnumber the limited number of owners and workers in the protected industries, free-trade policies rather than protectionism should prevail under majority voting. In reality, deviations from free trade are present in most countries and specifically built into so-called free trade agreements and even the multilateral World Trade Organization (WTO) framework.

Grossman and Helpman's (1996) work sheds light on such seeming contradictions by providing a theoretical framework for analyzing incentives for lobbying and the ability to form effective interest groups in certain industries over others. They divide industries into so-called *sunrise* and *sunset industries*:

- Sunrise industries are growing, and they often export but receive no protectionism from the state.
- Sunset industries are underperforming relative to foreign competition and in decline, with little promise of recovery, yet are much more likely to receive protectionism from the state.

Sunrise industries enjoy, even if temporarily, higher than average rates of return, which invites entry into the industry. The opposite holds for sunset industries: There is no entry given the bleak prospects and below average or negative rates of return on investment. Nevertheless, this dynamic creates the perfect incentives for organizing and lobbying, because if successful, a well-defined and limited number of actors will be able to reap all the benefits of protectionism

---

7 It is important to differentiate between intermediate and final consumption goods in trade policy and protectionism. Tariffs on final goods are less likely to affect other sectors of the economy beyond consumers. On the other hand, tariffs on intermediate goods, such as raw materials and product components, will have broader economic impact and cause collateral damage. The methodological implication is that general equilibrium analysis should be employed to uncover unintended consequences of policy in other areas of the economy rather than just partial equilibrium analysis limited to the industry or sector directly affected by the policy. In practice, this means that you should include "general equilibrium" in your keyword search for relevant literature on a given policy issue.

through higher prices in the domestic market. Sunrise industries, on the other hand, face new entry, and even if their lobbying efforts were successful, the new entrants could reap the benefits, dissipating the rents from lobbying without contributing to the costly lobbying effort. Under such conditions, firms in the sunrise industries have little incentive to organize.

You might also wonder why the sunset industries do not just change their businesses and divest from the declining industries. The answer lies in the *specificity of factors of production* – capital, labour, and land are often highly specialized in certain sectors and unable to switch to other production processes or uses. Their investments are long-term and immobile across industries, and as such they have a lot to lose and a lot to gain if protection is granted by the state. In other words, the costs and benefits of lobbying efforts are concentrated rather than diffuse in this case, and that is crucial for overcoming the free-riding problem in collective action.

Recognizing and extending applications of factor specificity beyond international trade is also important. Building a nuclear power plant and investing in becoming a neurosurgeon are examples of long-term specific physical and human capital investments, respectively, with limited alternative uses for such investments and difficult entry into the business area. As a result, incentives to protect such investments with lobbying efforts will be strong.

QUESTIONS FOR DISCUSSION AND FURTHER RESEARCH

1 Can you identify other industries with high factor specificity?
2 Are they sunset or sunrise industries?
3 What is their market structure and degree of competition?
4 Do they have a strong ability to organize and lobby effectively?

BOX 5.3. ONLINE PRIVACY PROTECTION IN THE EUROPEAN UNION VERSUS THE UNITED STATES

Growth in online engagement and the diffusion of mobile devices generates rich data about individuals and groups, which are collected, aggregated, and distributed via a complex and fast evolving global data market ecosystem. This market includes a diverse range of actors from global tech giants such as Google, Meta, and TikTok, which utilize their users' data to sell targeted advertising, to specialized data collectors, aggregators, and brokers focusing on specific sectors/applications (business strategy development, training artificial intelligence (AI) algorithms, etc.). Individual consumers typically have limited information about what data is collected and when, for what purposes it might be used, or the consequences of its use (Acquisti et al., 2016). In terms of impacting public policy in this space, consumers face substantive collection action problems relative to large global and local corporations that monetize their personal data.

Although the basic economic challenges in balancing demand for data and privacy are broadly similar, privacy policy outcomes have diverged across jurisdictions. A notable example of this is associated with the rights-based approach adopted in the EU under the 2016 *General Data Protection Regulation* (GDPR) versus the sector-specific and decentralized model in the United States (Bakare et al., 2024). The GDPR codifies a set of rights of "data subjects" (i.e., individuals), which include the right of access, the right to rectification, the right to erasure, the right to restrict processing, the right to data portability, the right to object, and the right not to be subject to a decision based solely on automated processing.[1] It is also relatively comprehensive in its scope and it applies to all organizations that collect, store, or hold personal data of EU residents within EU member states. GDPR compliance emphasizes a set of key principles of practice for the governance of data markets, including minimization in data collection, storage limitation, and accountability. Importantly, the GDPR also includes substantive penalties for non-compliance (up to €10 million or 2 per cent of annual global turnover for standard violations, and up to €20 million or 4 per cent of annual turnover for severe violations).

In contrast, the United States lacks a comprehensive data privacy law that applies to all types of data and all companies. Instead, various regulations govern different sectors and data types. Examples include the regulations that apply to sensitive medical patient and personal information held by financial institutions under the *Health Insurance Portability and Accountability Act* (HIPAA) and the *Gramm-Leach-Bliley Act* (GLBA), respectively. This suggests that interest groups representing data economy players with demand for personal data and more relaxed standards of privacy have been relatively more successful in shaping privacy policy outcomes at the federal level in the United States. Demand for higher standards of privacy protection than those under federal law have led to successful collective action by consumer privacy interests at the state level. As of early 2024, nearly 20 of the 50 U.S. states had adopted their own privacy laws and a number of other states were in the process of debating privacy bills.[2] However, as state-level bills have become law, tech industry lobbyists have been increasingly successful in influencing the legislative outcomes and minimizing adverse impacts of emerging state privacy laws on their capacity to collect, use, and resell data (see, e.g., Bordelon, 2023).

In general, state privacy laws adopted or under discussion in the United States fall substantially short of the GDPR in protecting the online privacy of individuals and potential penalties for breaches of privacy regulations by data market actors. While providing a higher level of protection, it is relevant to note that the adoption of GDPR appears to be associated with some reduction in competition and increasing structural dominance of global tech giants such as Google and Meta in the European data markets (Johnson et al., 2023). This suggests the global tech giants that opposed GDPR adoption may have been too focused on potential compliance costs with the new law and underestimated the strategic advantages that higher privacy standards may afford them relative to their smaller rivals.

---

1   Regulation (EU) 2016/679 (General Data Protection Regulation), available at https://gdpr.eu/what-is-gdpr/.

2   See, for example, the US State Privacy Legislation Tracker, provided by the International Association of Privacy Professionals (IAPP), at https://iapp.org /resources/article/us-state-privacy-legislation-tracker/.

QUESTIONS FOR DISCUSSION AND FURTHER RESEARCH

1 Based on what you have learned about interest group
   formation and regulatory capture so far, how can you explain
   the divergent policy outcomes with respect to online data
   protection in the EU versus the United States?
2 What further research would you conduct to answer the
   above question?

5.6 TRANSACTION COSTS, GROUP FORMATION, AND COMPETITIVE LOBBYING

The ability of individuals and organizations to engage in effective collective action varies across issues, industries, and jurisdictions. There are a number of basic economic factors that shape the incentives to engage in collective action, build interest group coalitions, and invest in shaping public policy. These factors can be viewed in terms of the *transaction costs* associated with decentralized bargaining (i.e., per the Coase Theorem;[8] see Coase, 1960; Acemoglu, 2003; Holcombe, 2018). In settings with low transaction costs of bargaining, for example, when there is one or a few players in an industry, it is usually easier to coordinate activities and make a return on joint investments in policy shaping. In contrast, in more competitive industries where there are many firms with differentiated products and interests, it can be challenging to build a coordinated approach. Furthermore, when there are many players, the potential for free riding limits the incentives of those with resources to invest in collective action, compared to coalitions of a few, where coalition members can more readily monitor joint contributions required to achieve a group's policy objectives.

The scope for competitive lobbying can exist when the transaction costs of collective action are relatively low for different groups

---

8 For more information and a refresher on the applications of the Coase Theorem in practice, please see chapter 2, section 2.6.

with competing interests around a particular policy issue or proposed adjustments/non-adjustment to current rules and regulations. An example of this is when narrow interest groups of domestic producers seek import tariffs, which would lead to an increase in prices consumers have to pay. If there are a small number of large importers and distributors of that product/service that face low transaction cost of collective action, they may have incentives to organize and invest in countering efforts by the import tax lobby of local producers. If they can do so effectively, their investments would benefit both the coalition of importers as well as consumers/users through lower prices. When no viable counter-lobby emerges, diffuse groups of buyers face significant and typically insurmountable transaction costs of collective action to build a viable counter-lobby. Due to such asymmetries in collective action capacity and incentives, public policies and laws that benefit the few and impose costs on the many can emerge and persist in both democratic and authoritarian societies alike. Table 5.2 outlines some of the common factors that determine transaction costs, and therefore the feasibility and effectiveness of collective action, lobby, and counter-lobby formation.

Table 5.2. Transaction costs and collective action incentives

Cost factor	Implication/example
Homogeneity/ heterogeneity of goods and preferences	Individuals and groups with diverse interests and preferences tend to face high transaction costs in forming coalitions. Examples of this include building industrial alliances among firms producing differentiated goods, or coalitions of people with diverse disabilities and therefore needs. Building coalitions among people with shared preferences and objectives requires less bargaining and is therefore less costly to implement.
Number of group members	Building and sustaining a coalition made up of a small number of like-minded entities is less costly than organizing many individuals and/or firms. Industries with significant economies of scale and scope where there are only a few large players face relatively low transaction costs of organizing and tend to be successful in forming effective interest groups. Costs facing small and medium-sized enterprises (SME) operating in competitive markets, or individuals as consumers, tend to be relatively high, undermining their capacity to form effective interest groups.

(Continued)

Table 5.2. Continued

Cost factor	Implication/example
Familiarity/affinity within groups	Previous interactions that help build trust and social as well as cultural affinity with other potential members in a coalition reduce transaction costs of collective action compared to unfamiliar parties. Political interest groups that claim to represent the interests of people affiliated with a religion or race are common and are relatively easier to build. Organizing groups of people and organizations that are unfamiliar with each other requires building trust, which is costly and undermines the feasibility of collective action.
Coalition monitoring and enforcement costs	When coalition members can take actions or negotiate with other parties covertly, monitoring costs will be high and enforcement of discipline may be ineffective. This will limit the group's overall effectiveness.
Level of cost/benefits	When the potential costs/benefits of a particular policy are low, individuals and organizations that might be impacted have limited incentives to invest in collective action. As the potential costs/benefits increase, so do incentives to engage in collective action. An example of this is enhanced interest group formation and advocacy over the past decades regarding global warming and climate change.
Distribution of costs/benefits	When the costs or benefits stemming from a policy or regulation are concentrated, the incentives to invest in collective action are strong. Conversely, when costs and benefits are diffused among a large number of actors (and especially when they cannot be excluded from the benefits of successful lobbying efforts), free riding on costly lobbying tends to limit organizational endeavours.

5.7 CORRUPTION-MINIMIZING INSTITUTIONS AND POLICIES

Corruption is typically defined as the abuse of public office for private gain, which can cover a wide range of behaviour, from bribery to obtain a favor or avoid punishment to theft of public funds.[9] In practice, corruption involves a bargain between public and private actors, which may involve tangible benefits such as cash, or less concrete benefits such as implicit promises of future employment, contracts, etc. Large differences in economic development and quality of life that we observe around the world today are to a large extent a function of

9   See, for example, the World Bank's (2020) *Anticorruption Fact Sheet*.

institutions that have evolved to counteract the asymmetric power of the few to shape public policy and fight corruption (Acemoglu et al., 2001; Akkoyunlu & Ramella, 2020).

Developing and sustaining institutions and mechanisms that help deter corruption remains a challenge in both advanced and developing countries. Although corruption can be viewed as a way of "greasing the wheel" of economic transactions, perceived corruption has particularly pernicious economic implications, as it undermines trust and produces even more corruption, with the potential for a race to the bottom. To counteract actual and perceived corruption, a variety of institutions have evolved to constrain incentives to engage in corrupt public-private bargains and minimize undue private influence on public sector decisions:

- Audit institutions: Internal and external auditing play a central role in identifying financial and other irregularities in government agencies and deterring corruption. Beyond the usual accounting compliance functions, ex post examinations and audits are used to establish facts about a wide range of other decisions by public office holders (e.g., use of force by the police, or procurement decisions by a government agency).
- Independent judiciary: Public servants operating in corrupt environments may have incentives to protect each other. The presence of independent prosecutors and a judicial system enhance the credibility of punishments for violating formal rules and regulations against corrupt practices and public-private bargains that are, or appear to be, corrupt.
- Disclosure and transparency requirements: Interests involved in illegal corrupt bargains have strong incentives to keep their arrangements secret from both their own management and the public. Rules that require the disclosure of information about lobbying, political financing, and government agency activities help counteract this secrecy and deter corruption and/or systematic biases in the application of law and regulations.
- Independent academia and journalism: Disclosure of information about public sector activities and market conditions provides researchers and the press opportunities to investigate and identify incidences of corruption and anomalies in the application of public policy and law.

QUESTIONS FOR DISCUSSION AND FURTHER RESEARCH

1 Can you name special interest groups that have difficulty
   organizing and influencing public policy?
2 Can you explain why they face challenges organizing?
3 The National Rifle Association (NRA) is a powerful organized group
   in the United States. Can you explain their power and influence
   on public policy despite the high rate of mass casualties to gun
   violence in the United States?

RESEARCH ADVICE: GATHERING INFORMATION ON LOBBYING

EFFORTS AND INFLUENCE

Dür (2008b) summarized the methodological challenges of measuring interest group influence in the context of the European Union, but
the main issues characterized are broadly applicable to this area of
research.

Dür (2008b) identified three main methods for measuring interest
group influence: process tracing, the "attributed influence" method,
and assessing the degree of preference attainment.

Process tracing aims to identify a causal chain of events that led to a
certain policy outcome. This process typically includes tracing interest
group access to decision-makers, analysis of their views being reflected
in comments by decision-makers, and conducting semi-structured interviews with relevant staffers and other sources. The challenge is to verify
the information provided in interviews in a credible manner.

The "attributed influence" method involves surveys of various groups,
including self-assessment of decision-makers, and assessment by
peers, observers, and experts. Obviously, a major weakness of this
method is the subjective nature of the responses, possible bias, and
strategic incentives to mislead.

Assessing the degree of preference attainment compares the distance between a policy outcome and interest groups' ideal point. The
smaller the distance between the policy outcome and an interest
group's ideal position, the greater the degree of influence inferred.
This method clearly involves a qualitative assessment but has the
advantage of being able to identify influence even if other visible

actions of coordination were not detected or proven, which is a strict requirement for the process tracing method. While process tracing is likely to underestimate influence due to its high information requirements, assessing the degree of preference attainment is likely to overestimate influence.

To minimize the weaknesses of the above outlined methods, Dür (2008b) recommends triangulation – that is, employing multiple methods to cross-check and verify information and assessments and more data collection in general.[10] Nevertheless, the information requirements for research in this area are very high even for single case studies, let alone more systematic measurement of influence by a multitude of interest groups on complex policy issues. It is therefore not surprising that empirical research in this area is rather limited.

Other practical tips for research in this area include the following:

- Determine if there is a legal requirement in the relevant jurisdiction to register as a lobbyist and if such a registry is public.
- Determine if there is a legal option to request access to information under the control of government or other decision-makers. For example, in Canada the *Access to Information Act* (RSC, 1985, c. A-1), last amended on January 22, 2024,[11] provides such an option under certain conditions and may provide internal documents and communications, including electronic searches by keywords. Individual privacy and security provisions will in general limit the scope of available information.
- Determine if campaign finance data are publicly available in a given jurisdiction. For example, in Canada political financing data are available through Elections Canada[12] and US federal campaign finance data are available from the Federal Election Commission.[13] Both databases allow searches by individual recipients and contributors.

---

10 For a more comprehensive review of methods including so-called method-shopping and large-scale data collection, please refer to Dür (2008b).

11 The full text of the *Access to Information Act* (RSC, 1985, c. A-1) with amendments is available at https://laws-lois.justice.gc.ca/eng/acts/a-1/.

12 Explore data at Elections Canada (2025).

13 Explore data at Federal Election Commission (n.d.).

- Be mindful that sometimes interest groups masquerade as independent non-profit organizations or independent experts, and their credentials and funding linkages should therefore be vetted.
- Scan for reports of ethics violations and see if there are official processes for investigating ethics violations by policy-makers. Moreover, are penalties for ethics violations significant enough to serve as a deterrent?
- Assess the scope for investigative journalism in the relevant jurisdiction.
- Assess if there are effective ways for marginalized groups/ counter-lobbies to engage in the policy process through public consultations or other means, and if there is state support to cover the associated costs for such groups in an effective manner.
- Differentiate carefully between *de jure* and *de facto* preference attainment in enacted policies because broad proclamations often fail to deliver effective implementation. The language or rhetoric utilized in legislation or policy proclamations can also be deliberately chosen to mislead the public, which generally suffers from an information overload.
- Similarly, significant resources available to certain groups and heightened levels of activity should not be equated with influence. Influence can be measured only in terms of outcomes, not by the inputs into the policy-making process.

CHAPTER SIX

Fiscal Policy

The ability of governments to provide public and private goods to their citizens and to engage in redistribution depends on their revenue-generating capacity. The main source of government revenue is taxation, but in general nobody likes to pay taxes. So how do we decide who gets to pay and how much? Does who bears the burden of taxation change over time? If yes, what political and economic factors drive the incidence of taxation? And how do we decide what to spend the raised revenue on? Who benefits from government spending?

Another major issue in terms of fiscal policy is the accumulation of public debt. When does the public debt burden become excessive and cause economic and political instability? Why do governments so often delay fiscal consolidations even when the fiscal stance appears unsustainable?

Upon reviewing this chapter, you should be able to do the following:

- differentiate between the legal obligation to pay tax and the economic incidence of taxation
- utilize elasticity measures to determine the incidence of taxation for different types of taxes
- understand redistributive considerations involved in taxation and determine if tax systems are progressive or regressive in nature
- analyze how economic growth, development, globalization, technological change, political trends, and regulatory policy changes affect the tax capacity of governments

- understand the determinants of differential tax capacity and transfers across different levels of government
- recognize variance in budgetary spending priorities over time and across jurisdictions
- appreciate strategic political considerations in fiscal policy and debt accumulation
- determine the government's inter-temporal budget constraint and its implications for economic (in)stability
- understand the concept of fiscal dominance of monetary policy and its implications

While governments can have multiple sources of revenue (e.g., proceeds generated by state-owned enterprises and other assets), taxes are generally the dominant revenue source and therefore the focal point of this chapter. Major trends in government expenditure are also included, along with an analysis of the factors driving fiscal (in)stability and the implications for monetary policy independence.

This chapter is filled with interesting applied questions in fiscal policy analysis, ranging from environmental taxes and positive fiscal incentives to the impact of globalization, population aging, and political stability on the fiscal stance. The chapter concludes with suggestions for a critical look at fiscal accounts and threats to their stability.

6.1 WHO BEARS THE BURDEN OF TAXATION?

6.1.1 The Role of Elasticity in Determining the Incidence of Taxation and Taxable Capacity

The first lesson to note when trying to determine who assumes the cost of any given tax is that the legal obligation to transmit the payment to the government does not necessarily (or typically) coincide with the real burden of the duty, which we refer to as the *incidence of taxation*. In general, the party that is less able to adjust to the presence of the tax is the one that bears more of the burden of the tax. In economic terms, we measure the responsiveness of different economic agents who might be affected by a tax (e.g., consumers, producers, workers, owners of capital, etc.) utilizing the concept of *elasticity*.

There can be many types of elasticities; hence a general definition is in order first. The responsiveness of variable Y to changes in variable X is its elasticity (E):

$$E = \frac{\% \Delta Y}{\% \Delta X} = \frac{\dfrac{Y_1 - Y_0}{Y_0}}{\dfrac{X_1 - X_0}{X_0}} = \frac{Y_1 - Y_0}{X_1 - X_0} \times \frac{X_0}{Y_0} = \frac{\Delta Y}{\Delta X} \times \frac{X_0}{Y_0} \tag{6.1}$$

The variables with the subscript 0 (X_0, Y_0) denote the initial values of the variable, while the variables with the subscript 1 (X_1, Y_1) represent those observed after the change in X. The symbol Δ denotes change in a variable, specifically the difference between the new observed value with subscript 1 and the old value with subscript 0. Elasticity is a unitless number, positive or negative.

In order to develop a fundamental understanding of the concept of elasticity, it is helpful to verbalize equation (6.1) as follows:

> The elasticity of variable Y with respect to changes in variable X is the percentage change in Y relative to the percentage change in X.

The last part of equation (6.1) lends further insight into the concept of elasticity by showing it as a function of two components: the slope of the function relating Y to X (i.e., the change in Y relative to the change in X) and the initial values of X and Y. This means that even if there is a straightforward linear relationship between the variables Y and X, the value of the elasticity E changes depending on where the starting position on that line is.

Consider the following example: As the price p of a good (variable X in equation [6.1]) increases (e.g., as a result of a tax imposed on the good), consumers respond by demanding a lower quantity of that good, denoted by q_d (variable Y in equation [6.1]). Hence, there is a typical inverse relationship between price p and quantity demanded q_d, and the price elasticity of demand E_d is a negative number. When we start off on the demand curve at a high price (high X_0/Y_0 in the last portion of equation [6.1]), the price elasticity of demand will be greater than at a place on the demand curve where the price is lower. This makes sense intuitively since a higher price has a more significant

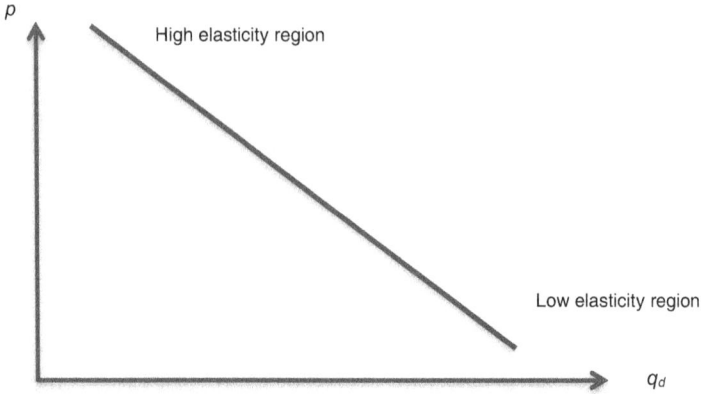

Figure 6.1. Variation in elasticity value along a linear demand curve

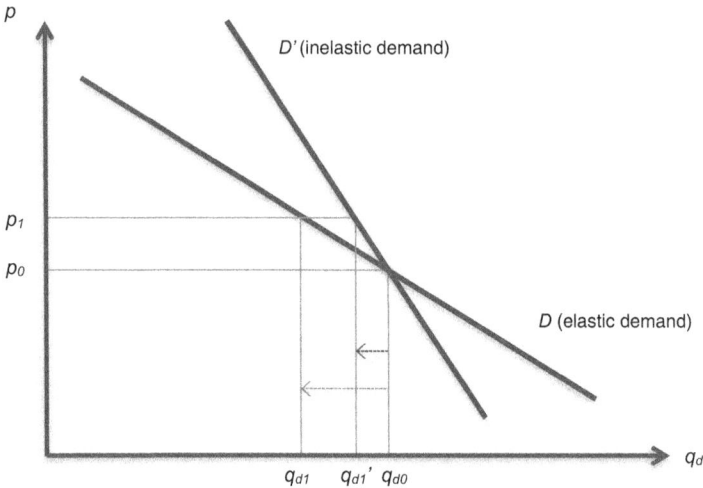

Figure 6.2. Variation in elasticity at a single price point due to differences in the slope of the demand curve

impact on a consumer's budget and is therefore likely to induce a greater response than when the price is at the lower end of the spectrum. See figure 6.1 for a graphical representation of this phenomenon utilizing a linear demand curve for a normal good.

Figure 6.2 further illustrates how elasticity at any given point also depends on the slope of the demand curve. The D demand curve exhibits greater responsiveness in quantity demanded q_d for any given price change relative to the D' demand curve and therefore, D is in general more elastic than D'. More specifically, elasticity nomenclature is defined as follows:

- If the % change in Y exceeds the % change in X (the elasticity value in absolute terms exceeds one: $|E| > 1$), the relationship between Y and X is *elastic*.
- If the % change in Y equals the % change in X (the elasticity value in absolute terms equals one: $|E| = 1$), the relationship between Y and X is *unit elastic*.
- If the % change in Y is lower than the % change in X (the elasticity value in absolute terms falls below one: $|E| < 1$), the relationship between Y and X is *inelastic*.

How does this all relate to the incidence of taxation? As mentioned in the introduction to this section, the party with the relatively greater degree of responsiveness or ability to adjust to the presence of the tax – that is, higher elasticity – will have an advantage and bear the smaller share of the burden of taxation.

For example, if an excise tax is imposed on the purchase of a good and consumer demand is relatively less elastic than producer supply, then consumers will pay for a larger share of the tax than producers. On the other hand, if consumer demand is relatively more elastic (e.g., because consumers can substitute the good subject to the tax with an alternative), then producers will have to absorb a greater share of the cost of the tax. Swinton and Thomas (2001, pp. 360–1) provide useful illustrations of this occurrence (see figures 6.3 and 6.4).

We can calculate the share of the excise tax burden borne by consumers versus producers based on the following assumptions and formulas:

- Assume that a tax of t dollars per unit of output of the good in question is up for consideration by policy makers.
- Assume that (inverse) demand and supply functions are linear:

$$p = a - bq_d \qquad\qquad (6.2)$$

$$p = c + dq_s \qquad\qquad (6.3)$$

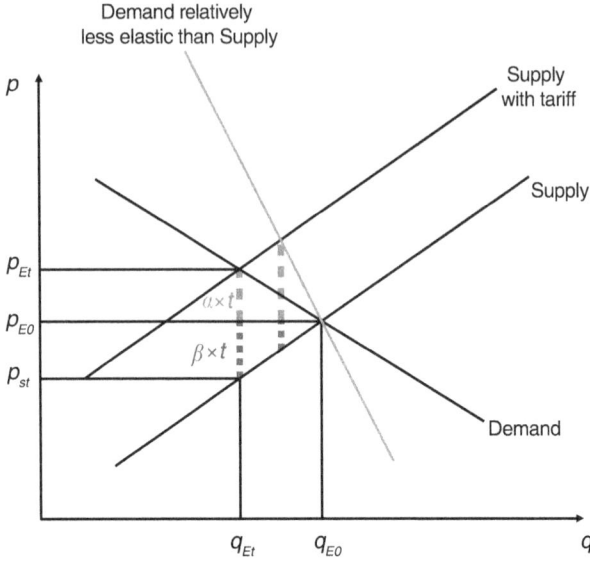

Figure 6.3. Relating tax burdens to point elasticities and slopes: demand less elastic and steeper than supply

Source: Adapted from Swinton and Thomas (2001, 360).

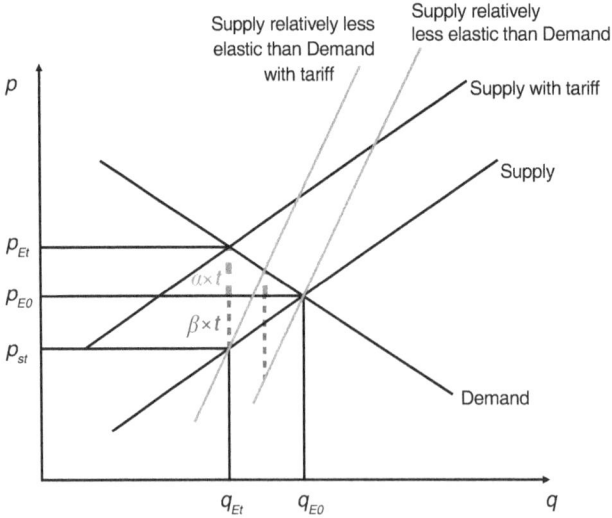

Figure 6.4. Relating tax burdens to point elasticities and slopes: supply less elastic and steeper than demand

Source: Adapted from Swinton and Thomas (2001, 361).

where q_d and q_s denote respectively quantity demanded by consumers and quantity supplied by producers, and parameters a, b, and d are greater than zero and c is a constant that can be positive, negative, or zero.

Arguably, most demand and supply curves are not likely to be linear in practice. Nevertheless, Swinton and Thomas (2001) argue in favour of utilizing this assumption in order to be able to employ empirical estimates of point elasticities to teach and calculate the incidence of taxation. We follow their approach here.

- Assume that empirical estimates of elasticity values correspond to the before-tax market equilibrium. Research the literature for relevant estimates of elasticity of demand and elasticity of supply values. Alternatively, if the supply and demand functions are specified, one can calculate the elasticities of demand and supply based on the following formulas:

$$E_d = \frac{p}{p-a} \tag{6.4}$$

$$E_s = \frac{p}{p-c} \tag{6.5}$$

- The consumers' share of the burden of the excise tax (denoted by α) can be then calculated as

$$\alpha = \frac{p_{Et} - p_{E0}}{t} = \frac{b}{b+d} = \frac{E_s}{|E_d| + E_s} \tag{6.6}$$

- Similarly, the producers' share of the burden of the excise tax (denoted by β) corresponds to

$$\beta = \frac{p_{E0} - p_{st}}{t} = \frac{d}{b+d} = \frac{|E_d|}{|E_d| + E_s} \tag{6.7}$$

- The excise tax then affects the price for consumers by

$$\Delta p = \frac{bt}{b+d} = \frac{E_s t}{|E_d| + E_s} \tag{6.8}$$

- The impact on the equilibrium quantity supplied is

$$\Delta q = \frac{-t}{b+d} = \frac{E_d E_s}{|E_d| + E_s} \times \frac{q_{E0}}{p_{E0}} \times t \qquad (6.9)$$

- Tax revenue T generated equals to $T = tq_{Et}$ \qquad (6.10)

It is important to note that the above presented framework by Swinton and Thomas (2001) for analyzing the incidence of taxation can be applied to different settings. For example, in the context of taxation on labour, the relevant supply and demand schedules become the hours of labour supplied by workers and demanded by producers.

In general, the empirical estimates of elasticities that the above formulas rely on can vary significantly in the literature. We can differentiate between short-run and long-run elasticity estimates, and estimates can vary depending on the specific jurisdiction, market, or time period analyzed or the estimation method utilized. Therefore, in practice, analysts should employ averages of different estimates in the literature or conduct a sensitivity analysis by comparing results under the extreme values of the elasticity estimates to develop an understanding of the range of the expected outcomes.

QUESTIONS FOR DISCUSSION AND FURTHER RESEARCH

In July 2016, the Government of British Columbia made a surprise announcement to launch, just eight days later, a 15 per cent real estate transfer tax on foreign nationals buying property in the Metro Vancouver area. The stated motivation for this new tax was to curb the ever-increasing real estate price rises in the area and to protect residents against them.

1 Was this mission accomplished?
2 Were there any unintended consequences of this policy?
3 Analyze the incidence of this tax and its impact on Vancouver real estate prices and other areas in British Columbia and Canada more broadly.

6.1.2 Taxable Capacity and Its Determinants

A government's taxable capacity – the ability to raise tax revenue – will be negatively affected if those subject to the tax can avoid it by relocating to another jurisdiction or by changing their behaviour. For example, you can avoid the excise tax on cigarettes if you stop smoking, or you can pay lower property taxes if you decide to buy a house in a municipality where the tax rate is relatively low.[1] But what if the property tax rate used to be low and now it suddenly jumps? Well, you may decide to stay in your house or move depending on a number of factors – for example, how much you like your house and neighbourhood and what it has to offer (amenities, closeness to work and/or school, etc.), the cost of moving, and how alternative neighbourhoods compare in terms of property prices and municipal property tax rates. In other words, the decision to stay or move – and hence your property tax burden – depends on your responsiveness (elasticity) and tax competition by nearby municipalities. It follows that highly sought-after municipalities will have relatively higher taxable capacity due to higher property values (higher tax base) and higher property tax rates due to the lower elasticity of demand for the desirable location by residents.

In Canada, the authority of municipalities to impose taxes stems from provincial legislation. This means that provinces can grant, alter, or abolish municipal taxing powers. Meloche and Vaillancourt (2021) document the limited revenue-generating capacity of municipal governments and reliance on property taxes and user fees.

Because there is free movement of people between states or provinces, there exists tax competition between them. People consider job prospects (probability of employment and expected salary) as well as property and state/provincial income tax rates across regions in their location decision. However, due to restrictions on the movement of labour internationally, the decision to emigrate is more complex and costly. It follows that, in general, national governments will have higher taxable capacity than sub-national governments such as states or provinces. National governments will also have better enforcement capacity to crack down on tax evaders and tax fraud than sub-national governments.

Since national governments tend to have higher taxable capacity, they often transfer part of their revenue to lower levels of government. Whether lower levels of government have the authority to allocate

---

1   Such a change in behaviour aimed at preventing being subject to a tax is called *tax avoidance* and should not be confused with *tax evasion*, which refers to unlawful conduct – that is, being subject to the tax, but not paying it as a result of engaging in illegal activity.

that revenue as they wish or if the national government conditions those choices depends on the relative bargaining powers between the sub-national governments and the national/central government.

Countries also vary in their taxable capacity. The most significant determinant of such variation is the income level of the population. If people are very poor, they spend most or all of their income on necessities, thus leaving little scope for taxation. If income and wealth inequality across households is great, it also tends to impede taxation, because only a small minority of rich households have the ability to pay taxes. In addition, those households likely have the means to avoid or evade taxation, or to exert political influence to limit tax rates. It is therefore not surprising that income taxes as a proportion of total revenue and as a proportion of GDP rise with per capita income – historically over time and in cross-country comparisons. Poor countries with low per capita GDP and high income inequality have limited scope for income taxation and thus low overall taxable capacity. Tax enforcement is likely to be difficult as well, given weak administrative capacity and the often informal nature of the economy (small businesses, cash transactions, and incomplete records of transactions). Given these limitations, developing countries tend to resort to taxing what they have relatively most control over – the goods flowing through their borders. Taxes on international trade typically make up a significant proportion of government revenue in poor countries, thus limiting the scope for trade liberalization, and with the side effect of raising costs for consumers and producers who rely on imports for consumption or production inputs, including capital goods for investment.

In addition to income per capita and the share of international trade in economic activity, another empirically significant determinant of taxable capacity is natural resources. If a jurisdiction is well-endowed with natural resources, that increases its taxable capacity – provided that there is the prerequisite political and economic stability.

When natural resources are unequally distributed around the world, control over them can entail monopoly or near-monopoly powers, and thus abnormal rates of profit. Abnormal profits in turn invite political competition for them, which can yield to conflict, exploitation, or even armed conflict. This phenomenon has been commonly dubbed as the *natural resource curse*.

QUESTIONS FOR DISCUSSION AND FURTHER RESEARCH

1 Can you name countries or sub-national jurisdictions (states, provinces, regions, municipalities) for which government revenue is significantly linked to natural resource endowments?
2 Are there any risks associated with a large share of government revenue from natural resources? Identify those risk factors and their channels of impact on government revenue, and the economy and politics more broadly.

BOX 6.1. GLOBALIZATION AND THE RELATIVE BURDEN OF TAXATION ON LABOUR AND CAPITAL

The end of the Cold War era in 1989 marked the end of most restrictions on international capital flows. The world has seen an unprecedented wave of financial liberalizations and the resulting surge in cross-border capital flows. This time, lower-income developing countries were included in the movement and became destinations for foreign direct investment (FDI), not just for the purpose of natural resource extraction, but also manufacturing. Financial and trade liberalizations as well as technological advances have made it easier for corporations to take advantage of significantly lower labour costs in developing countries, especially in the production of goods that utilize low-skilled labour. Arguably, this has increased the elasticity of supply of capital. While international restrictions on the movement of labour remain quite stringent, this raises the following questions: Is there competition among jurisdictions to attract mobile capital? And has the burden of taxation now shifted more towards labour relative to capital?

It turns out these questions are not easy to answer. Several methodological approaches can be taken to try to address these questions. First, we can look at nominal (statutory) tax rates for personal income and corporate income taxation. While there has been some downward movement in both compared to the high marginal tax rates in the post–Second World War era, in many jurisdictions the statutory corporate tax rates still remain high, thus putting in doubt claims of a race-to-the-bottom scenario for corporate taxation. Nevertheless, statutory corporate income tax rates can be misleading when governments offer special tax holidays, introduce new and elaborate tax credit schemes, transfer pricing is an option for multinational corporations with overseas subsidiaries, or direct corporate subsidies are also available. Costs can be artificially inflated or revenue deflected through such schemes, thus reducing accounting profits based on which corporate income tax liabilities are calculated. To determine the real burden of taxation, we should aim to calculate effective tax rates. Even with effective tax rates, different methodological challenges emerge depending on whether we look at macroeconomic tax data (national accounts) or microeconomic data at the firm and individual/household level. The problems stem from aggregation in macro-data: Firms can receive differential tax treatment based on their sector, location, or size, but all this information is lost in aggregate accounts. Arguably, some sectors may employ capital that is relatively mobile, while in other sectors capital is very specific and immobile. For example, one cannot relocate a power plant from North America to China, but it is easy to do so for a garment factory.

The Organization for Economic Cooperation and Development (OECD) provided both macro- and micro-data-based estimates of average effective tax rates (AETR) – the percentage of income that is payable in tax, on average – in two reports in the early 2000s:

- Carey and Tchilinguirian (2000) provided the macro/national accounts-based estimates for the periods 1980–5, 1986–90, and 1991–6. They were careful to differentiate between labour and non-labour income for households (income from financial assets, pensions, etc.) and their differential tax treatment, along with consumption taxation, which also falls on households. Their data (which are somewhat outdated at this point) show that while AETR on capital remained roughly steady during the period under investigation, the AETR both on labour income and consumption has increased in OECD countries. Nevertheless, it should be noted that the methodology adopted in this study abstracts from "tax-shifting," as described in section 6.1.1, with the implicit assumption that the tax burden remains with the party with the legal obligation to pay (i.e., only primary tax burden is considered).[1]

- OECD (2003) supplied an overview of a few micro-data based analyses of AETR. Because the micro-data require in-depth processing of large datasets, they are typically country studies. Austria, Belgium, Canada, Denmark, and Norway were included in this meta-analysis by OECD (2003). Accounting for business losses and carry-over across periods is a key feature of the analyses that is enabled by micro-, firm-level data that is simply lost in aggregation in previous macro-based studies. OECD (2003) highlights that effective tax rates can vary significantly from nominal (statutory) tax rates and by industry and firm size, and by income level for households. Relying on aggregate AETRs can be therefore misleading and inappropriate for drawing policy conclusions. Nevertheless, micro-data based estimates of AETR are limited to government agencies due to privacy and data protection provisions, and thus still largely unavailable.

To overcome the challenges of accessing micro-level data, Hourani et al. (2023) look at the features of the tax systems in OECD countries and simulate the tax burden on hypothetical high-income earners under different scenarios. The scenarios involve individuals earning wage income only, a combination of wages and dividends, wages and capital gains on shares, and capital gains only. Their results show that the differential treatment of labour income (wages) and capital income (dividends, capital gains) leads to lower effective tax rates (ETR) for capital income.

Egger et al. (2019) take a closer look at the evolution of the tax burden of labour in OECD countries due to globalization from an empirical point of view. They find that prior to 1994, greater economic openness (more international trade at that time) meant that high-income earners were taxed progressively more. After 1994, the tax burden on the labour income of middle-class earners increased while the top 1 per cent of employees saw a reduction in their tax burden, leading to increased inequality. The findings are consistent with the hypothesis that the very high-income earners likely have greater international mobility (similar to that of capital) under globalization than the middle class, thus improving their implicit bargaining position with respect to governments and their tax powers.

Bachas et al. (2022) examine a large historical dataset of 154 countries between 1965 and 2018 and find that while ETRs on capital have declined in high-income countries, they have actually increased in developing countries since 1990. This finding is very interesting because it seems to reject the race-to-the-bottom hypothesis for developing countries, at least on average, and reflects the shifting bargaining position of developing versus developed countries and private businesses due to globalization. The off-shoring of manufacturing jobs to developing countries has increased competition for their services, thus improving the bargaining position of their governments with respect to internationally mobile capital.

You likely wonder: Given all these data and methodological caveats, imperfections and limitations, what is the main take-away for policy analysts? Aim to disaggregate your data for industry-specific analyses as much as possible, using micro-level data. This is not unusual in economics. For example, analyses of outcomes related to international trade necessitate the same approach as different industries, and/or factors of production and consumer groups are differentially affected.

---

1   The only exception to this rule is the treatment of tax-exempt goods. In those cases, it is assumed that producers are able to pass on the cost of VAT on inputs to consumers through higher output prices.

6.1.3 Progressive and Regressive Taxation

A key question in the analysis of tax systems is whether relatively poor or rich households or individuals are taxed at a higher rate relative to their income. *Progressive tax systems* tax the rich relatively more heavily, while *regressive tax systems* place more burden on the poor. A tax is proportional when it collects the same proportion of income from all income groups.

When income taxation is divided into different income brackets with higher-income earners facing increasingly higher marginal tax rates, such income taxation is progressive because the average effective tax rate (AETR) on the rich is higher than the AETR on the poor.

We also know that consumption taxes (such as excise taxes on specific goods, services, or activities; tariffs on imported goods; sales taxes or value added taxes) are significant and/or on the rise, so into which category do they fall? In general, household income can be divided into consumption and saving. Since poor households tend to spend a larger proportion of their income on consumption, they pay more consumption taxes as a proportion of their income compared to rich households. Therefore, consumption taxes tend to be regressive and this theoretical prediction is also confirmed by the estimates provided by Blasco et al. (2023) using cross-country micro-level data on income and consumption.

An exception to the rule that consumption taxes are regressive is taxes on luxury goods. If a luxury good is simply beyond the reach of poor households, then the burden of this tax falls exclusively on the rich and thus increases the degree of progressivity of the given tax system.

Another form of taxation is the so-called head tax because it is levied per person ("per head") or per property, but without taking into consideration the person's income or the value of the underlying property. In other words, whether rich or poor, one would be required to pay the same amount of tax, and this can pose significant hardship for the poor.

Head taxes have been utilized throughout history in pre-modern and modern states despite, or arguably because of, their extremely regressive nature.[2] A head tax is often also referred to as a poll tax, because historically head taxes have been linked to the right to vote and disenfranchised specific groups of people politically and/or economically. McRae (2017) offers an overview of the Chinese head tax in

---

2   For a general overview of the evolution of tax systems from pre-modern to modern taxes, see Kiser and Karceski (2017).

the context of Canada, while Bearer-Friend (2024) provides examples of discriminatory race-based head taxes in the United States.

Head taxes have political or ideological drivers and tend to be very unpopular due to their regressive nature. In 1989, the British government under Conservative Prime Minister Margaret Thatcher attempted to replace municipal property taxes by a poll tax. This clearly benefited rich property owners, but public opposition was so strong that a repeal of the legislation was announced in 1991. For more detail on this experiment, see Smith (1991).

In Canada, there exist provincial legal restrictions on municipal poll taxes. The last province to outlaw poll taxes by municipalities was Newfoundland and Labrador. Their *Towns and Local Service Districts Act* (the "Towns Act") came into effect on January 1, 2025, stipulating that all towns must charge a property tax and no towns may charge a poll tax.[3]

QUESTIONS FOR DISCUSSION AND FURTHER RESEARCH

1 Is corporate income taxation progressive or regressive? What are the factors that the answer to this question likely depends on?
2 Is taxation of cigarettes progressive or regressive? Why?
3 Consider a tax on meals served by so-called "fast food restaurants," justified on the grounds that their meals are not healthy and therefore their consumption should be discouraged. Would such a tax be progressive or regressive?
4 Are municipal pet licences/taxes progressive or regressive?

BOX 6.2. ENVIRONMENTAL TAXES VERSUS POSITIVE FISCAL INCENTIVES

Environmental taxes aim to correct undesirable conduct that inflicts harm on nature and threatens environmental and economic sustainability in the longer term. Many natural resources – including, for example, clean water, clean air, or ecosystem stability to name a few – have no market value or a market price that is significantly lower than their inherent existential and economic

---

3   The legislation allows a transition period for towns that have not been charging property taxes.

value. In many cases, it is the cumulative effects of harm over time that threaten long-term survival, and when the public discounts the future heavily, individuals and firms behave in an irresponsible manner and overuse those natural resources.

Political movements that focus on bringing attention to the problems of environmental sustainability have gained momentum, and so have environmental taxes that aim to increase the prices of the natural resources and/or the cost of environmentally harmful activities in order to reduce their consumption/utilization. Is this good news for environmental protection? Who bears the burden of this taxation?

Environmental taxes in the form of carbon taxes – for example, taxes on gasoline, or on emissions by coal-burning power plants – tend to be by themselves regressive. This is because energy, transportation, and related products tend to be necessities that poor households spend a larger share of their income on than rich households. Moreover, if the demand for these goods is inelastic – for example, because public transit is an inadequate substitute for driving one's car to work – then the tax will generate revenue, but make little progress towards deterring undesirable, environmentally harmful conduct.

This leads us to a second question: Can governments mitigate the regressive character of environmental taxes through rebates to poor households or using the raised revenue to lower taxes on labour income? Fullerton and Monti (2013) analyze this question with a general equilibrium model with low- and high-skilled labour. Their simulation shows that even if the environmental tax revenue is used to reduce the taxes on low-skilled, low-income labour, low-skilled workers can be worse off if the "dirty sector" employs low-skilled labour intensively. This is because as demand for and output in the "dirty sector" decline due to the tax and resulting higher prices, the demand for low-skilled labour employed in this sector also declines. As a result, low-skilled wages decline. This effect is exacerbated if high-skilled labour is the better substitute for pollution than low-skilled labour, and thus the demand for and wages of high-skilled labour increase relative to low-skilled labour.

Rausch and Schwarz (2016) utilize a different model and set of assumptions about consumer and production heterogeneity to analyze the distributional impacts of environmental taxes. They echo the emphasis by Fullerton and Monti (2013) on the use of general equilibrium analysis to determine the impact of the taxes on returns to factors of production (specifically, low-skilled labour income) rather than just aggregate output, consumption, and the first-order tax effect.

The experience with carbon taxes and rebates to taxpayers in Canada is consistent with the predictions of Fullerton and Monti (2013) and Rausch and Schwarz (2016). Carbon taxes became increasingly unpopular among the electorate in the early 2020s, despite the distribution of carbon rebates to eligible individuals and small businesses. Ahead of looming federal elections, Prime Minister Mark Carney eliminated the federal fuel surcharge (and requirement that provinces and territories have a consumer-facing carbon price) on March 15, 2025, just one day after being sworn in as prime minister. The governing Liberal Party thus fully reversed its own policy on carbon taxes due to their regressive character and unpopularity, which could not be mitigated with the carbon rebate cheques.

Costa Rica also employed fiscal policy to address an environmental challenge, specifically deforestation. Konyn (2021) reported that by 1987, it was estimated that between a third to half of the forest cover was lost in the country. By the early 2020s, approximately 60 per cent of all the land was covered by forests again and is home to a diverse ecosystem. How was this dramatic reversal possible? In 1996 the Costa Rica government made unauthorized logging illegal, and a year later they also introduced the Payments for Environmental Services (PES) program. The PES program provides fiscal payments to landowners (typically farmers) to reward environmental conservation. The payments directly incentivized environmental protection and made landowners active stakeholders in the process. Powlen and Jones (2019) conducted surveys and in-depth interviews with farmers and confirmed that the financial supports played a critical role in overcoming the initial barriers to reforestation efforts.

The government disbursed a total of $500 million to landowners over 20 years (Konyn, 2021) and funded the PES program largely by taxing fossil fuels, thus utilizing a similar instrument as the carbon tax in Canada. However, the payments targeted a specific group (landowners) who were able to respond to the incentives by changing farming practices (rather than the inelastic demand for fossil fuels in most of Canada) and the incentives were large enough to be impactful and induce change.

6.2 WHO BENEFITS FROM GOVERNMENT SPENDING?

The biggest difference in government spending across countries with different income levels, and in the same jurisdiction over time as the economy grows and develops, is social spending. Social spending includes, for example, spending on health, education, pensions, unemployment insurance, and income support for the poor. We will explore the different types of social spending in detail in chapter 8, but in aggregate, this pattern is not just facilitated by the fact that taxable capacity increases with income, but demand by voters for social supports also grows with economic development and the accompanying social, demographic, and structural changes in the economy.

Social spending as percentage of GDP typically peaks in times of recession when GDP declines and social security claims increase simultaneously. Given the nature of so-called *automatic stabilizers* such as unemployment support and others, social spending fluctuates over time, but there are other trends in social spending that are related to factors other than the economic cycle. Shifting political ideologies or deeply rooted cultural and political preferences also have a material impact on the level of spending on social services, direct income supports for the elderly and the working age population, and the distribution of these supports across different income groups. One should not assume that social spending simply means transfers from the rich to the poor through a progressive tax system. OECD (2014) in fact highlights that the highest quintile – the richest 20 per cent of the population based on disposable income – receives a significantly higher share of public social benefits paid in cash than the lowest quintile in a number of OECD member countries, including Mexico, Portugal, Turkey, Italy, Greece, Spain, France, and Austria, for example.

How is this possible? At least in part this pattern can be attributed to the fact that social benefits in these countries are determined by one's work history in the formal sector – that is, public pension systems. The redistributive aspects of social policy appear much more dominant in Australia and the United Kingdom, where income or means-tested benefits dominate entitlements and there is relatively less reliance on public pensions. Nordic European countries such as Norway, Denmark, and, to a lesser extent, Sweden also redistribute relatively more to the working-age population in the lowest quintile. This large variation in the distribution of social benefits across OECD countries shows that social spending does not necessarily coincide with redistribution from the rich to the poor.

BOX 6.3. POPULATION AGING AND ITS IMPLICATIONS FOR FISCAL POLICY

It is a well-documented demographic phenomenon that over time, especially in high-income countries, people live longer and have fewer children. The combination of these two factors lowers the ratio of the labour force to the elderly, retired segment of the population. If retirement benefits are funded at least in part by transfers from the working population through taxation, fiscal revenue is declining while fiscal liabilities are on the rise. Under such circumstances, immigration can help foster the labour force and thus the tax base, but there needs to be the political will to be open to immigration, and the labour market absorption of immigrants also has to be strong. If there exists discrimination against immigrants or if there is a mismatch between their skill sets and labour market demand, immigration might be a less productive substitute to raising domestic fertility rates. All in all, population aging in high-income countries raises an interesting question: How do these demographic changes affect the incidence of taxation?

Kudrna et al. (2015) analyze the above question in the context of Australia and aim to quantify the effects using an overlapping generations computable model to simulate the impact over the next 100 years. Importantly, their dynamic model allows for behavioural changes to adjust for the evolving demographic and economic situation – including, for example, households working and saving more for retirement, discounting the future less, and lower pension benefits in response to more private saving for retirement. Despite all this, their simulation results show a shift in the tax base from labour income towards consumption taxes mainly, while asset/capital income taxes increase initially and then decline as the capital stock declines. Interestingly, they also find that the decline in fertility is not the main driving force behind the results and that increasing immigration and/or fertility would not be effective solutions to the problem of population aging because it is the fiscal costs of longer time spans that dominate.

QUESTIONS FOR DISCUSSION AND FURTHER RESEARCH

1 Find other examples of countries in demographic transition. How do their macroeconomic and fiscal data compare to the projections provided by the simulations of Kudrna et al. (2015)?
2 How do countries with relatively high rates of immigration (e.g., Canada, the United States, and the United Kingdom) compare to those with low immigration rates (e.g., Japan, China, and northern European countries)? Are there any significant differences between them?

6.3 THE GOVERNMENT'S INTER-TEMPORAL BUDGET CONSTRAINT AND ITS IMPLICATIONS FOR ECONOMIC (IN)STABILITY

Government revenue and spending are typically mismatched in terms of their timing. For example, government spending commitments are more or less stable, while revenue may fluctuate seasonally. Automatic stabilizers in the form of social assistance to the unemployed, or bailouts to companies in distress, surge precisely at the time when government revenue drops during an economic downturn. Capital expenditures like investment in infrastructure, for example, tend to be large layouts concentrated over a relatively short period of time, while their benefits span over the medium to long term, potentially even to future generations of taxpayers. All of this implies that governments regularly run budget deficits and finance a part of their current expenditure by borrowed funds. They also have to allocate funds to cover the costs of borrowing (interest on outstanding debt) and repayment of principal due.

Successive budget deficits lead to the accumulation of public debt, which raises the question: When is the amount of accumulated public debt excessive, leading to widespread financial panic?

Conceptually, any government needs to maintain and/or be perceived to be maintaining solvency in the long term. This can be summarized by the government's inter-temporal budget constraint:

$$D_0 + \sum_{t=0}^{\infty} \frac{G_t}{(1+i)^t} = \sum_{t=0}^{\infty} \frac{T_t}{(1+i)^t} \tag{6.11}$$

where D_0 denotes the current outstanding government debt liabilities (including interest on debt due at present), G_t and T_t correspond to government spending and tax revenue in period t respectively, and i is the rate of interest on government debt (assumed to be constant over time for ease of exposition).

Equation (6.11) can be summarized as follows:

The present value of current and future tax revenue (the right-hand side of the equation) has to cover the present value of government debt liabilities and current and future government spending (the left-hand side of the equation).

In practice, there is a great deal of political and economic uncertainty about these future expenditure and revenue streams. Unexpected events can sharply increase government expenditure, or there may be political or economic obstacles to raising taxes.

When the right-hand side of equation (6.11) starts falling short of the left-hand side, which represents liabilities, a financial crisis ultimately unfolds. Government bonds are supposed to be the safest low-risk assets in the economy, and if they cannot fulfil this function, investors panic, sell off financial assets, and recall debts, which leads to shortage of liquidity and falling financial asset prices. Accumulated wealth dissipates (both household and corporate wealth) and companies resort to employee layoffs. Nevertheless, the timing of a fiscal crisis is a challenge to determine because it depends on several factors:

- *Is the economy growing and/or expected to grow?* Economic growth in general increases taxable capacity / tax revenue and improves the fiscal outlook (right-hand side of equation [6.11]). Just like in the case of an individual, when income grows, it becomes easier to repay a given amount of debt. Therefore, one indicator to watch for when determining fiscal stability is the ratio of debt to GDP. There is no single number when the debt to GDP is deemed unsustainable; some countries manage to maintain economic stability with very high debt to GDP ratios, while others unravel into panic at moderate levels of the ratio.
- *Does the government enjoy credibility among financial market investors to implement "sound" economic policies?* While there are certainly forward-looking and political elements to this question (e.g., is it politically feasible to implement policies that are called for from a purely economic growth and efficiency point of view?), history also matters in this context. For example, if a country has a history of hyperinflation or chronic inflation, credibility, and thus a stable investor base, is likely to be lacking. This implies that even relatively low levels of public debt to GDP can trigger financial panic in certain jurisdictions.
- *Is public debt denominated in domestic or foreign currency?* If foreign currency debt is significant, take into consideration the potential for major exchange rate fluctuations (due to changes in export prices, export volume, capital flows, etc.) and their impact on the burden of debt.
- *What is the maturity structure of public debt?* If the share of short-term debt is high relative to long-term debt, it is an indicator of vulnerability.
- *What is the relative standing of the jurisdiction in terms of its attractiveness to investors?* If a given jurisdiction offers a stable regulatory environment, and well-developed, liquid financial

markets compared to other alternatives, it will remain relatively inexpensive for the government to borrow, and thus maintain high debt levels.

- *How independent and credible are the private rating agencies?*
  The 2007–9 financial crisis in the United States and the Greek government debt crisis in 2009 were widely attributed, at least in part, to the failure of rating agencies to adequately assess and downgrade corporate, household (mortgage), and sovereign debt as the underlying vulnerabilities accumulated.

We will explore the above questions and financial crises broadly in more detail in chapter 7.

QUESTIONS FOR DISCUSSION AND FURTHER RESEARCH

1 Can legal debt limits actually prevent the rise of government debt? What has been the experience in the United States with its debt ceiling regulations? What economic and political factors come into play when debt ceiling regulations are in place?
2 Suppose a country suffers from chronic unemployment, suggesting that structural imbalances are present in the economy. How will this affect the government's inter-temporal budget constraint and investors' reactions?
3 Prior to the terrorist attacks on the United States on September 11, 2001, the US debt to GDP ratio was low at levels slightly over 30 per cent.[4] At this time, the US Federal Reserve Chairman Alan Greenspan recommended a tax cut to prevent the debt to GDP ratio from falling further. Can you explain why?

6.4 GOVERNMENT DEBT DEFAULT

Both unilateral government debt default and debt forgiveness by investors are very rare. Even in instances of *debt overhang*, when the burden of public debt is so high that it impedes investment, and

---

4 The US fiscal situation changed dramatically after the events of September 11, 2001, but analyze the question from the perspective of decision-makers prior to this unexpected shock.

therefore reduces growth and the probability of debt repayment, there is fundamental reluctance by all parties involved to declare default.

The debtor countries fear loss of credibility and thus the ability to borrow at any rate of interest, leading to a catastrophic shortfall in liquidity and the inability of the government to pay its most immediate bills, including public servants' salaries, pensions, etc. The lenders, on the other hand, are concerned about setting precedent and propagating the problem of *moral hazard*, under which those who let the fiscal situation spiral out of control would be the ones rewarded, or perceived to be rewarded, with debt forgiveness.

Of course, there is the disconnect between the decision-making elites of a country and the public, especially the most economically vulnerable segments of the society, who disproportionately bear the burden of economic hardship, whether in the form of servicing the high cost of debt or of a government in default that cannot honour its bills.

As a result, even the poorest countries of the world have received very little, if any, debt forgiveness, even by organizations with a broad mandate for economic development and stability, such as the International Monetary Fund (IMF) or the World Bank. Instead, a more common scenario unfolds under which a country in serious financial distress is loaned more funds on a Friday ahead of the Monday payment due date for a major loan repayment instalment. Such arrangements help avoid formal default by providing liquidity, but any analyst should consider such jurisdictions to be de facto in default.

QUESTIONS FOR DISCUSSION AND FURTHER RESEARCH

1 Are there any successful examples of unilateral sovereign debt default? What were the factors that helped avoid protracted credibility, liquidity, and other economic and political problems in those cases?

2 Consider a country with a history of decades of political dictatorship, horrific oppression, and corruption leading to a large accumulation of public debt. Following the downfall of the dictatorship and a period of political unrest with violent episodes, a fragile, but democratically elected government

is emerging. There are calls to dishonour the sovereign debt accumulated by the dictator. As a policy analyst, would you recommend default or not? Explain your answer, the factors it depends on, and the strategy for execution, including the timing of the steps to be taken.

6.5 FISCAL DOMINANCE OF MONETARY POLICY

Aside from the long-term perspective on government finances given by equation (6.11), we also need to examine the short-term period-to-period cash flow viewpoint. This is important because, given the term limits of their office, many governments can be opportunistic, driven by short-term goals rather than maintaining long-term solvency under the government's inter-temporal budget constraint.

Consider a government's cash flow constraint in period t:

$$\Delta D_t = D_t - D_{t-1} = iD_{t-1} + G_t - T_t \tag{6.12}$$

where the change in government debt level from period $t - 1$ to period t is determined by the interest due on outstanding debt (iD_{t-1}) and current government budget deficit, the excess of government expenditure over tax revenue ($G_t - T_t$).

Because economic agents are incentivized by the real burden of these factors, we need to convert equation (6.12) into real terms. We accomplish this by dividing each nominal variable X_t by the current price level p_t to arrive at real variable x_t:

$$x_t = \frac{X_t}{p_t} \tag{6.13}$$

Hence, after some re-arranging and dividing both sides of equation (6.12) by p_t, this yields the following:

$$d_t = \frac{d_{t-1}p_{t-1}}{p_t}(1+i) + g_t - t_t \tag{6.14}$$

Given that the rate of inflation π_t is defined as the percentage change in price level between periods t and $t - 1$,

$$\pi_t = \frac{p_t - p_{t-1}}{p_{t-1}} = \frac{p_t}{p_{t-1}} - 1 \tag{6.15}$$

rearranging equation (6.15) and substituting it into equation (6.14) yields the following:

$$d_t = d_{t-1} \frac{(1+i)}{(1+\pi_t)} + g_t - t_t \tag{6.16}$$

Equation (6.16) shows that the real debt burden in period t is negatively related to the rate of inflation π_t. This creates incentives for governments to create inflation, at least in the short run, to lower the real burden of outstanding debt. You may relate to this from personal experience: When you have a fixed liability to repay $1,000 of the debt you owe on your credit card, it will be easier to accomplish that if your income has grown by 10 per cent over the past year due to inflation. The $1,000 due will now be a smaller percentage of your income.

Equation (6.16) shows crucially that a high level of public debt can create perverse incentives for governments to create inflation. This implies that low inflation can be a credible monetary policy target only if public debt levels are manageable – hence, the concept of *fiscal dominance of monetary policy* is derived. The argument also lays the foundation for institutional safeguards for avoiding high inflation, including central bank independence from politically elected governments and long-term, singular policy targets rather than conflicting objectives. We explore these issues in detail in chapter 7.

6.6 WHY ARE FISCAL STABILIZATIONS SO OFTEN DELAYED?

Alesina and Perotti (1995) ask the above question, motivated by the burgeoning budget deficit and public debt figures among the high-income OECD member countries in the 1980s and early 1990s. As fiscal indicators deteriorate, calls for action to bring them under control abound among policy analysts. However, the willingness to act may be lacking on the part of governments, or political and economic constraints may limit the effectiveness of any initiatives for fiscal consolidation. Alesina and Perotti (1995) provide an interesting, and still relevant, overview of the literature on the possible theoretical explanations for the phenomenon of delayed fiscal stabilizations. These include the following:

- *Fiscal illusion* – This framework is based on the key assumptions that policy-makers behave in an opportunistic manner (e.g., are motivated to be re-elected) and that voters are naive. Voters do not understand the government's inter-temporal budget constraint: They overestimate the benefits of government expenditure and underestimate the future tax burden. In practice, this translates into running budget deficits in recessions to stimulate the economy and limit the social impact of recessions, but these periods are not offset with budget surpluses in times of economic growth.
- *Intergenerational redistribution of the tax burden* – Incentives may exist by current taxpayers to run deficits, accumulate debt, and leave the burden of higher taxes to future generations. Under this scenario, the usual assumption of inter-generational altruism in overlapping generation models does not hold. If we take into consideration the demographic trend of childless households, one could argue that it is feasible that voters aim to leave negative bequests to future generations.
- *Debt as a strategic instrument* – Political polarization and re-election uncertainty can lead even ideological fiscal conservatives to overspend in order to limit the ability of successor governments to increase funding for their preferred causes and constituents.
- *Distribution conflicts and wars of attrition* – Even if decision-makers can agree on the necessity of aggregate spending cuts, their allocation to different programs is likely to be problematic. Cuts to different programs affect different groups and individuals in society in diverse ways and to varying degrees. For example, cuts to corporate subsidies, education, or health care have disparate impacts and require a micro-level analysis of the distribution of costs on different stakeholder groups/constituents and their organizational ability. When political powers are dispersed (e.g., due to coalition governments), it is more difficult to transfer

the cost of fiscal consolidation onto rival constituencies, and therefore inaction tends to persist. The optimal concession time is arrived at when the marginal costs of waiting (i.e., a lack of fiscal consolidation) equal the marginal benefit of waiting. Therefore, fiscal imbalances often have to deteriorate further, reaching dramatic crisis levels, and only then does action to implement unpopular fiscal cuts become politically more feasible. This is because in a crisis, the marginal cost of waiting exceeds the marginal benefit of inaction.

- *Budgetary institutions* – The laws, rules, and regulations governing the drafting and approval of budgets can have a material impact on fiscal outcomes. Agenda-setting powers, transparency in the budget process (or lack thereof), veto points, rules on universalism, and reciprocity affect the likelihood of exercising fiscal restraint.

A key underlying question that arises under the above hypotheses is if political leaders can get away with disregarding the government's inter-temporal budget constraint or not. And even if they do get away with it for some time, will the voters ultimately punish them at the end?

In terms of economic theory, the question is this: Does Ricardian equivalence hold in practice or not? *Ricardian equivalence* requires that consumers/voters internalize the government's inter-temporal budget constraint, and if governments resort to deficit financing rather than raising taxes for a given level of government spending, consumers/ voters will compensate for this by saving more today in anticipation of future tax increases. For Ricardian equivalence to hold, a few more assumptions have to be satisfied, including intergenerational altruism to maintain the indefinite horizon of the inter-temporal budget con- straint, perfect capital markets for consumers to be able to borrow and lend at the same interest rate as governments, and fixed government expenditures.

Arguably, these assumptions are unlikely to hold in practice, but the question of at least partial Ricardian equivalence, or the ten- dency of households to internalize the government's inter-temporal budget constraint over the long term, is interesting from an empiri- cal point of view. Economically, the empirical validity of the

Ricardian equivalence would limit the efficacy of government stimulus to the economy during a downturn through increased spending or through tax cuts because private saving behaviour would adjust to offset these changes. From a political point of view, the question that arises indirectly is whether fiscal illusion or strategic fiscal policy can persist, or if voters will punish opportunistic politicians who promise fiscal spending or tax cuts at levels that clearly violate the government's inter-temporal budget constraint by not voting for them in elections. This question is posed in elections at different levels of government and across jurisdictions around the world repeatedly.

QUESTIONS FOR DISCUSSION AND FURTHER RESEARCH

1 Which one of the above theoretical hypotheses best explains, in your opinion, the following fiscal outcomes?
   - the increase in government budget deficits and debt during the two consecutive George W. Bush administrations in the United States between 2000 and 2008 (Was there a qualitative difference in the drivers of fiscal policy between the first and second Bush administrations?)
   - the fiscal stance of the Italian government in the second half of the twentieth century
   - the developments in the Greek debt crisis unfolding since 2009
   - Japan's persistent escalation of the debt to GDP ratio in the 2000s

2 Find examples of the following:
   - voters endorsing excessive deficit financing that could be considered a violation of the government's inter-temporal budget constraint
   - voters rejecting politicians running on pro-deficit financing platforms in times of financial distress

3 Can you identify factors that can explain the different scenarios for voters upholding fiscal discipline or failing to do so?

BOX 6.4. WHY DID CANADA MANAGE TO GET GOVERNMENT FINANCES UNDER CONTROL IN THE 1990S WHEN OTHER OECD COUNTRIES DID NOT?

Canadian Liberal Prime Minister Chrétien started his office with a $38.5 billion federal government deficit (5.3 per cent of GDP) in the 1993–4 fiscal year. Bleak fiscal data were generally not uncommon during this period for counterparts among high-income OECD countries either. Nevertheless, just four years later in 1997–8, the federal government recorded a slight budget surplus of $2.9 billion, or 0.3 per cent of GDP. The fiscal stance continued to improve and reached the peak of $19.9 billion surplus, or 1.8 per cent of GDP, in 2000–1.[1]

Although somewhat smaller, a budget surplus was nevertheless maintained in each subsequent year of the Chrétien administration until 2004. Liberal Prime Minister Paul Martin, who previously served as Chrétien's minister of finance, maintained the positive fiscal outcomes in the subsequent two years of his minority government until 2006 when the Conservatives won a minority government.

If we look at the disaggregate data for government spending and revenue during this time, it is evident that spending cuts were implemented in the mid-1990s by the Liberal government, and they were crucial to achieving the turnaround in fiscal figures. Spending cuts are never popular or easy to implement, which leads us to the following question: Why were the federal Liberals in Canada in the mid-1990s willing and able to achieve them?

First of all, it helps if one is able to make decisions without political compromise or forming coalitions with other parties. Canadian Liberals won a majority in federal elections in 1993, 1997, and 2000, and thus did not face major institutional obstacles to making unilateral decisions without the need to compensate political partners (and their constituents) for their support.

Furthermore, the Liberals enjoyed a relatively lengthy period of political stability and high probability of re-election. This induced them to look at the fiscal problem from a long-term point of view: If they did not start dealing with the problem in the mid-1990s, a further deteriorated fiscal situation would likely still be the problem of a future Liberal government. In economic terms, this means that the Liberals had the right incentives to internalize the government's inter-temporal budget constraint as their own, which induced them to behave in a fiscally responsible manner to maintain this constraint. A political party less confident in prospects for re-election would likely not have behaved in such a fiscally responsible, and potentially socially unpopular, manner.

---

1   Data here are taken from an interactive fiscal data presentation compiled by CBC News based on Finance Canada, Statistics Canada, Bank of Canada, Parliament of Canada, and IMF data. They can be found at https://www.cbc.ca /news/multimedia/canada-s-deficits-and-surpluses-1963-to-2015-1.3042571 (select Chrétien as Prime Minister).

RESEARCH ADVICE: HOW TO CRITICALLY ANALYZE FISCAL DATA

To avoid drawing faulty conclusions about the state of fiscal affairs in any jurisdiction, one should be mindful of a few common problems in the data and their interpretation or analysis:

- Differentiate between central government and overall public sector fiscal stance, as those can differ significantly. For example, public pension funds or public utilities can be a source of vulnerability even if central government finances are in order.
- Sub-national government spending may not reflect the true degree of political and fiscal decentralization when sub-national governments rely to a significant extent on transfers from higher levels of government as those often come with stipulated conditions.
- Determine if sub-national governments can borrow, what their fiscal stance is, and if upper-level governments are guarantors for such debt.
- Account for the share of revenue linked to external factors such as foreign aid and proceeds from commodity exports (e.g., oil, coffee) and analyze the uncertainties involved in their determination (political factors and world commodity price fluctuations). Consider

the likely magnitude of the impact from a sudden change in the trend.

- Explore if there are contingency funds set aside for natural and human-made disasters.
- Explore the financial stability of key private sector industries, as they may become a contingent liability for the government if they fall into distress and governments are compelled to bail them out for political and/or economic reasons.
- Determine who holds government bonds and treasury bills. Are they domestic or foreign investors?
- Is public debt denominated in domestic or foreign currency? If the latter, take into consideration the potential for major fluctuations in the exchange rate and export volume, and their impact on the burden of debt and debt-servicing obligations.
- Consider the economy's growth prospects and the implications for the debt to GDP ratio.
- Conduct sensitivity analyses by considering different scenarios for future developments, including unexpected shocks.
- While many different debt sustainability and risk indicators can be computed or simulated, fiscal analysis should never be a purely quantitative exercise. Any quantitative model is inherently vulnerable to its assumptions and omissions, and a qualitative assessment of political risks, structural changes, and data quality is called for.

CHAPTER SEVEN

Monetary and Exchange Rate Policy and International Policy Coordination

Analysts around the globe spend a great deal of time analyzing daily monetary policy decisions, monitoring key indicators, and trying to predict the next policy moves. This is because the smallest adjustments in monetary policy stance can have a widespread impact on financial and economic outcomes for everyone in the economy. Mortgage and car lease holders monitor the costs of borrowing, pensioners the return on their savings, and companies are affected through both their liabilities and investments.

We ended chapter 6 with the concept of *fiscal dominance of monetary policy*, and the framework and tools of analysis introduced in section 6.5 should be kept in mind when reading through the current chapter on monetary and exchange rate policy. Since the topic of exchange rate policy takes us into the realm of international policy, we will also discuss more broadly the prospects of policy coordination in the international arena.

Specifically, the chapter should enable you to do the following:

- have a basic understanding of key monetary variables and policy tools and their linkages
- appreciate the impact of monetary policy and monetary outcomes on different components of the economy, including distributional effects

- differentiate between short- and long-term policy responses and outcomes and the linkages between them
- appreciate the importance of credibility and reputation-building in monetary policy, and international policy more broadly
- understand how institutional design can enhance or inhibit credibility of policy making
- analyze the scope for international policy coordination in various contexts, along with its inherent constraints and limitations

7.1 INFLATION AND ITS IMPACT

Inflation is defined as a sustained increase in the general price level. Key components of this definition are "sustained increase" and "general price level." In other words, a one-time increase, no matter how significant, in the price of a certain good would *not* qualify as inflation. It would likely be either a temporary price shock or a relative price change brought about by a change in technology, tastes, or another reason.

Inflation is a key economic variable that is monitored closely by policy-makers, analysts, businesses, and the general public alike due to its far-reaching implications. Throughout history, some of the most severe examples of economic hardship are closely linked to episodes of extreme inflation, or *hyperinflation*.[1]

The negative effects of inflation include the following:

- *The erosion of the purchasing power of people*, especially those on fixed incomes, such as pensioners or welfare recipients, which implies that inflation hurts the poor the most.
- *The erosion of the function of money as a store of value*, thus reducing the incentive to save, redistributing money from savers to borrowers by reducing the real burden of repaying nominal debt. For example, it is easier to repay $1,000 dollars if your income rises with inflation and the lender ends up getting less in real terms (in terms of purchasing power) than expected.

---

1 Hyperinflation is a situation with very high and accelerating inflation. Quantitative definitions of hyperinflation can vary. Following Cagan (1956), economists usually define hyperinflation as inflation rates higher than 50 per cent per month.

- *A reduction in the productivity of investment*, by making it more difficult to predict which investments are likely to be profitable. Given inflation uncertainty, especially over the longer term, this results in favouring short-term, less risky, and thus likely less productive investments by investors.
- *A persistence over the long term*, as once high inflation or hyperinflation takes place, it is very difficult to eliminate it, and inflationary expectations (and thus a lack of credibility of policy-makers) tend to persist long after inflation has been reduced and brought under control.
- In extreme cases, *a refusal of the public to hold any of the domestic currency*, and a retreat to holding foreign currency, both for making transactions in the economy and for saving. Historically, the US dollar has been utilized for this purpose, as it has been widely regarded as a safe, credible choice of alternative currency, given its strong low-inflation track record. Consequently, this phenomenon of switching to a foreign currency by the public in the face of hyperinflation is called *dollarization*.

7.2 MONETARY POLICY FUNDAMENTALS

Barro and Gordon (1983) provided a seminal piece of economic litera-ture that students of political economy should be familiar with. They defined the policy-maker's dilemma through an optimization prob-lem that involved balancing the costs of inflation against the benefits of surprise inflation that would create unexpected profit for producers and thus growth and presumably more employment in the economy. Specifically, Barro and Gordon minimize the costs of inflation through the following objective function facing policy-makers (p. 104):

$$\left(\frac{a}{2}\right)\left(\pi_t\right)^2 - b_t\left(\pi_t - \pi_t^e\right) \tag{7.1}$$

where a, $b_t > 0$. The first part of equation (7.1) captures the costs of inflation in period t (denoted by π_t) as an abstract aggregation of all the negative effects of inflation outlined above in section 7.1. It is notable that the costs of inflation involve a quadratic term to reflect that the negative impact of inflation rises at an increasing rate.

The second part of the objective function is the benefit from surprise inflation: When actual inflation in period t exceeds expected inflation (denoted with the superscript e), it will subtract from the costs of inflation by aiding employment and growth. This latter part of the equation is more broadly referred to by economists as a type of *Phillips curve*, based on the work of Phillips (1958), who found that inflation and wages tend to move together, and when unemployment is low, wages tend to be high, and thus (moderate) inflation is associated with low unemployment and vice versa.

However, it is important to note that only surprise inflation can stimulate the economy. Inflation that is expected by the public (i.e., not a surprise because it is already built into contracts, and thus the cost of production) will do nothing or harm the growth of the economy. When expected inflation exceeds actual inflation, wages will be too high and will cut into profits and economic growth.

The public form expectations rationally, and therefore it is not possible to sustain inflation surprises in the medium to longer term. This implies that the potential benefits from surprise inflation disappear (the Phillips curve with a negative relationship between inflation and unemployment no longer holds), and only the longer-term costs of inflation remain.

As a result, Barro and Gordon (1983) reach the conclusion that the no-inflation policy as a rule is the superior solution to the government's optimization problem. Nevertheless, short-sighted governments have the temptation to cheat on the no-inflation rule, thus leading to the *dynamic inconsistency problem* (also referred to as *time inconsistency of optimal policy* in the literature) between what the best solution is for the policy-maker in the short versus long term (cheat vs. respect the no-inflation rule, respectively).

Barro and Gordon also show that fighting inflation when inflation is expected by the public is very costly to decision-makers: With inflation set to zero, the first part of equation (7.1) becomes zero, but the second part becomes positive due to expected inflation exceeding actual inflation. This, in practice, leads to economic contraction and unemployment, and incumbent policy-makers tend not to be popular or re-elected under such conditions.

7.3 MONETARY POLICY TARGETS AND INSTITUTIONS

Barro and Gordon (1983) showed that policy-makers can have perverse incentives when it comes to inflation because they have the temptation to cheat by delivering higher than expected inflation in the short run to stimulate the economy. However, this backfires, as the public cannot be fooled – they will expect inflation in return and build it into wage and other contracts. Once inflation is high, the government has no credibility and fighting inflation will be very costly because it shrinks the economy in the process. This theoretical framework lays the foundation for the following kinds of policies:

- *setting explicit low inflation targets as a rule,*[2] rather than allowing discretionary monetary policy
- *setting low inflation as a sole policy objective*, rather than balancing multiple policy objectives like stimulating the economy or lowering unemployment at the same time
- *institutional safeguards for central bank independence* from elected political officeholders to ensure the rule is followed

Each of these policy components also warrants further exploration. First, what is low inflation? How do we define it? How do we measure it? On one hand, the public is always concerned with all-encompassing headline inflation because it impacts their everyday reality. However, certain price developments are actually beyond the control of monetary policy and reacting to those price changes could harm the economy rather than do any good. For example, supply shocks or imperfect competition in the oil, gas, or agricultural sectors can lead to product price increases, but these are unlikely to translate into wage growth, and therefore tightening monetary policy in response to them would be inappropriate, as it would contract

---

2   Many developed economies, including Canada and the EU, for example, target 2 per cent inflation per year as a rule rather than the theoretical zero inflation rule, because inflation targeting is always imperfect, and a zero inflation target could lead to contracting the economy.

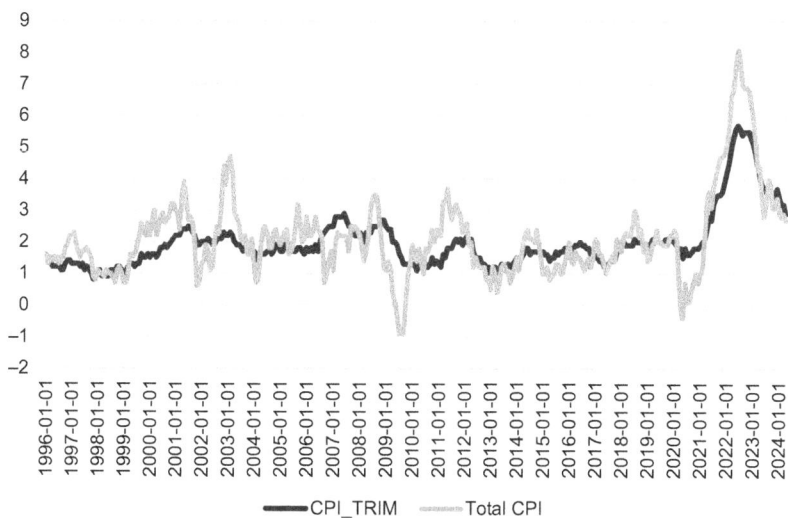

Figure 7.1. Inflation in Canada (% change year-on-year, 1996–2023)

Source: Bank of Canada

the economy. For such reasons, most central banks monitor several measures of inflation:

- *headline/total inflation*, through a measure that involves a consumer price index (CPI) of major household consumption items
- *core inflation measures*, which exclude price movements that are short-lived and/or beyond the control of monetary policy

Figure 7.1 illustrates this point for Canada by looking at the total CPI and CPI TRIM as one of the two core inflation measures that the Bank of Canada utilizes when setting monetary policy.[3] As the figure shows, headline/total CPI tends to fluctuate more than core inflation (CPI TRIM in the case), and occasionally they may even move in opposite directions. This can put the central bank in a difficult position: There might be calls to act against inflation, but when inflation is driven by external factors beyond the reach of monetary policy, an

---

3   For more details on the two core inflation measures the Bank of Canada utilizes, please see Bank of Canada (n.d.).

undue response by the central bank may exacerbate the economic situation. At the same time, if the central bank is seen as unresponsive, inflationary expectations may emerge along with the usual negative repercussions outlined above.

The COVID-19 pandemic and the economic recovery that followed brought on major price fluctuations and inflation levels that have not been experienced in countries around the world, including developed economies, for quite some time. Price increases of necessities affect the lower-income segments of society in significant ways, but monetary policy is unlikely to be able to tackle the high prices of gasoline or food driven by factors other than wage inflation. This leads to public dissatisfaction with government, but competition policy and expanding the supply of the given products and their substitutes is likely to be a more effective response than monetary policy affecting aggregate demand.

It is also noteworthy that Canada has been targeting 2 per cent annual inflation with an explicit target band of +/− 1 per cent. Both headline inflation and core inflation have exceeded the upper bound of 3 per cent annual inflation between 2021 and 2024. While inflation reaching levels outside an explicit target band diminishes monetary policy credibility, enforcing the target band as a strict limit rather than a desired range is typically not deemed appropriate due to some inflation being outside the reach of monetary policy and because extraordinary circumstances may render a risk of recession greater than the harm from inflation.

This leads us to the second element of the common monetary policy framework outlined above, which emphasizes setting low inflation as a *sole* policy objective rather than balancing multiple policy objectives at the same time. You might be wondering: Why would a central bank mandate not ask the central bank governor to balance the economy overall, taking into consideration unemployment, economic growth, and perhaps even real estate prices or stock market performance rather than just a concern to keep inflation low? After-all, unemployment, economic growth, and stock market performance will affect the income and wealth of citizens. The answer is that the different objectives are likely to be at odds with each other, and a balancing act would open the door to discretion and different interpretations of the mandate, which could lead to compromising the objective of keeping inflation low because it often entails taking unpopular and economically costly steps. In other words, balancing multiple objectives would lead us back to the original problem of incentives to stimulate the economy winning over and inflation rising, as shown in the Barro and Gordon (1983) model. Countries with a history of high inflation would be especially weary of the threat of rising inflationary expectations and are likely to opt for a singular, simple, and explicit low-inflation policy target and nothing else.

Finally, separating the control of monetary policy from the government/elected officials is an important hallmark of monetary policy credibility and is typically established in legislation that requires the head of the central bank (typically a governor) to be appointed for a period of five to seven years (i.e., longer than the usual political/election cycle of four years), making it very difficult to fire the central bank governor by typically requiring a qualified majority in parliament (e.g., two-thirds or more of parliament) rather than just a simple majority (50+ per cent), or based on a discretionary decision by the head of state (prime minister or president).

Besides the public and economic actors, the International Monetary Fund (IMF) is an international institution that monitors closely central bank independence around the world and publishes relevant assessments. Adrian et al. (2024) outline the methodology for the IMF's new index for measuring de jure or official central bank independence. The new index is being introduced after 30 years of work in this area, and the paper also outlines the limitations of the previous indices utilized until now.

7.4 MONETARY POLICY TOOLS

How does a central bank (CB) actually achieve an inflation target? Before proceeding with an outline of the relevant policy tools, it is important to explore what causes inflation in the first place. Monetary economist Milton Friedman became famous for stating in a 1963 speech that "Inflation is always and everywhere a monetary phenomenon." In other words, prices rise, and thus inflation prevails, if the money supply expands too much relative to the economy.

What constitutes the money supply? It turns out that the answer to this question is somewhat complicated as well because different

Table 7.1. Monetary aggregates

MO – Monetary base	M1 – Narrow money	M2 – Narrow money	M3 – Broad money
Currency in circulation	MO	M1	M2
Bank reserves held at the central bank	Demand deposits (checking accounts) at banks, credit unions, etc.	Small time deposits (savings up to a certain amount)	Large time deposits, money market funds, repurchase agreements, short-term debt securities
More liquid			Less liquid

Table 7.2. Key monetary policy tools

Tool	Explanation	Expected impact
Reserve requirements	The CB requires commercial banks to set aside a % of funds in demand deposits (chequing accounts) as cash reserves.	Reserve requirements limit loanable funds and thus an increase in reserve requirements is expected to decrease the money supply.
Discount rate	Interest rate at which commercial banks can borrow short-term from the CB.	Increasing the interest rate, i.e., the cost of borrowing, is expected to reduce the amount of loanable funds and thus the money supply. Banks will also pass on the higher interest rates to their customers, which will curb demand and thus inflation.
Open market operations	The purchase and sale of securities by a CB in the open market.	When a CB purchases securities (typically from banks), banks receive cash and that increases loanable funds and thus the money supply. Alternatively, when a CB sells securities, it reduces the money supply.

monetary aggregates can be utilized as money supply measures based on their degree of liquidity – that is, the ease or efficiency by which these assets are converted into cash without affecting their value. Table 7.1 provides a broad summary of different monetary aggregates. In general, higher monetary aggregates include the lower-level monetary aggregate plus less liquid financial assets. The most commonly used measure of money supply is so-called *broad money*, or M3. CBs in general have several policy tools at their disposal to affect the money supply and, indirectly, target inflation. These are outlined in table 7.2.

Table 7.3. Commercial bank balance sheet

Assets	Liabilities
Loans to customers	Demand deposits (funds in chequing accounts)
Mortgages issued	Time deposits (savings accounts)
Securities bought	Loaned funds from the CB and other financial institutions
Cash reserves	Expenses

Not all policy tools may be a viable option to all central banks because some of these depend on a certain level of economic and financial development. For example, when securities markets are underdeveloped, open market operations are unlikely to have a significant impact. It is also clear from tables 7.1 and 7.2 that commercial banks and other financial institutions play a significant role in monetary policy implementation. It is therefore not surprising that CBs are often given the task of overseeing the health of the banking sector by enforcing financial regulations.

Table 7.3 illustrates why commercial banks, no matter their size, are inherently very fragile institutions. Banks accept funds from individuals and companies in chequing accounts primarily for transaction purposes, but these are demand deposits and the account holders can withdraw their funds at any time (i.e., on demand). At the same time, banks do not simply hold all these funds ready to be dispersed, but lend their customers' funds to individuals and companies with productive opportunities and charge a rate of interest on such loans. Banks perform an important financial intermediary function in this way. However, the loans that banks issue are often medium- to long-term, and consequently, banks have a maturity mismatch in their balance sheets with the majority of their assets having a long repayment time, while their liabilities tend to be short-term and can be called in at any time.[4]

If all account holders were to withdraw their funds at the same time (called a *bank run*), even the best-managed bank would become

---

4   Time deposits offer more predictability to banks, as customers agree to keep their funds in their accounts for certain periods of time and banks pay interest to customers in return. If customers withdraw their funds early, prior to maturity, they incur a loss as a penalty. Such penalties aim to induce customers to keep their funds in savings accounts to full maturity and provide banks with more predictability in their liabilities compared to demand deposits.

insolvent due to the lack of liquid assets to cover such a surge in demand for cash funds. As precautionary measures, banks are required to hold some reserves in cash, publish their balance sheets, submit to regulatory audits, and put up their own capital. Many governments around the world also provide *deposit insurance* to small bank account holders, with two objectives: to protect lower- to middle-income individuals against financial loss in the event of a bank run; and to provide incentives to account holders to stay calm if rumours of a bank failure were to emerge, and thus to prevent a bank run before it starts.

Deposit insurance is typically capped at relatively low amounts of savings for fiscal reasons and in order to prevent moral hazard by inducing large-account holders to monitor the health of the financial institutions they trust with their funds.

It is noteworthy that bank runs are not just a historical phenomenon or theoretical possibility, but a realistic prospect, and governments are likely to act swiftly to guarantee all, or the overwhelming majority of, bank liabilities in order to prevent panic and a run on other banks. When public trust is in the financial system is shaken, even sound banks can collapse due to the inherent vulnerability in bank balance sheets, as captured in table 7.3. When banks or other financial institutions collapse, they impact payment systems and solvency, and the economic viability of businesses and households is threatened. For this reason, moral hazard cannot be entirely eliminated from the financial system, as financial institutions are most likely to be bailed out or restructured/purchased by other financial institutions thanks to the swift actions of governments. For example, in the United States alone there have been 567 bank failures between 2001 and early 2024, according to the Federal Deposit Insurance Corporation.[5] Most of the bank failures occurred in the context of the 2007–9 financial crisis and its aftermath. For more detail on the crisis, please see box 7.1.

To recap, central banks do not simply choose a rate of inflation as in Barro and Gordon (1983) or other theoretical models. Central banks can only hope to target a certain level of inflation taking into consideration factors that impact inflation including the money supply,

---

5   For more information, please visit FDIC (n.d.).

demand for money stemming from economic activity, and other considerations such as financial structures, political and economic risks in a given economy, and in comparison to the rest of the world, because financial flows are mobile internationally in a globalized world.

BOX 7.1. THE FINANCIAL CRISIS OF 2007–9

The early 2000s were a period of economic prosperity in the United States, with low inflation, low interest rates, and rising real estate prices. Since the value of one's home typically represents the bulk of household wealth, demand for housing was strong under such conditions. Combined with low interest rates and banks eager to lend money under increasingly lax conditions – including low down payments and low income thresholds to qualify for a mortgage – this strong demand arguably led to a so-called bubble in the housing market. *Price bubbles* occur when prices grow so much that they no longer accurately reflect the underlying value of the assets but are simply fueled by market demand driven by the expectation of continued capital gains. Under such conditions, it is rational for investors to continue to invest in assets exhibiting a price bubble because it is uncertain when the bubble will burst and prices will start to decline, and they believe they can get out of the given market before the turnaround in prices (Blanchard & Watson, 1982).

As figure 7.2 shows, the annual rate of growth for residential property prices in the United States reached double-digit levels in the period from 2003 to 2005 before prices started to decline in 2006.[1] In the meantime, commercial banks started to sell off the mortgages they issued by securitizing them and selling them in bulk to other financial institutions and investors. *Securitization* is in general seen as a positive phenomenon in terms of financial development, because the standardization of assets that occurs under securitization helps increase their liquidity by having clear prices and the ability to buy and sell securities quickly and with ease. The mortgage loans on bank balance sheets depicted in table 7.3 are important bank assets that contain a great deal of information about individual borrowers (their incomes, credit history, etc.) and about the underlying collateral assets. But

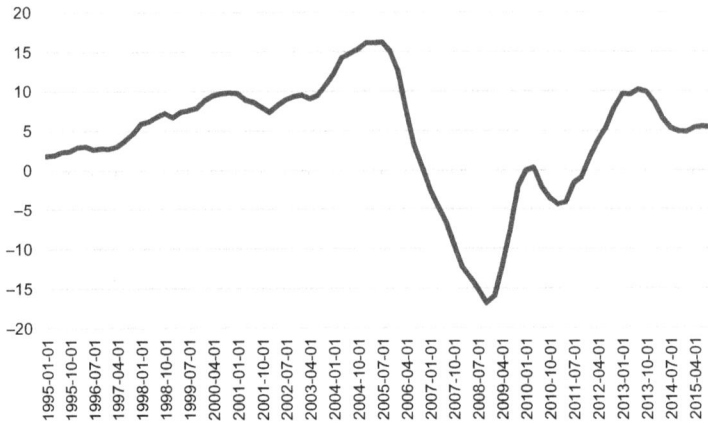

Figure 7.2. Residential property prices (% change year-on-year, 1995–2015)

Source: Federal Reserve Economic Data, Federal Reserve Bank of St. Louis.

transferring/selling those assets to another bank would likely involve a great deal of analysis and scrutiny by the purchasing bank, and selling those assets to other investors would likely be too costly because of the time, expertise, and information costs required in assessing those mortgage loans for their risk and quality. Securitization seemingly eliminated all those complications and information requirements based on the assumption that by pooling different mortgages together, the portfolio would be well-diversified with some predictable overall risk level. Nevertheless, one could also argue that systemic risk was present in the pool of mortgages that could not be diversified away because of the extent of the practice of lax lending and the price bubble.

In general, mortgage loans have been considered relatively safe assets for banks because they are backed by collateral – that is, the houses that were acquired with the help of the mortgage loans. However, this only holds as long as the price of the house/collateral is greater than the amount owed to the bank. If home prices represent a price bubble rather than fundamental value, then the mortgages lack adequate collateral. And with the pooling of different mortgages into mortgage-backed securities, important information was lost in the aggregation process about the quality of the underlying mortgages. In other words, mortgage-backed securities violated the *informational efficiency of markets*.

As housing prices started to decline in 2006 and it became clear that affected mortgage loans and mortgage-backed securities were not as safe as originally thought, the financial institutions and investors who held them faced financial peril. This was not simply a liquidity issue, as captured in table 7.3, that banks can face at any time; this was a solvency issue. When banks and other financial institutions (including insurance companies, pension funds, etc.) become insolvent, the rest of the economy is likely to follow very quickly. In recognition of this fundamental threat, the US government acted swiftly to intervene, providing liquidity and bailing out the majority of the affected financial institutions except for a few, including Lehman Brothers, an investment bank at the heart of the financial scandal.

The main reasons for not bailing out everyone included the problem of moral hazard – that is, the worry that the bailout would have rewarded rather than deterred risky behaviour. Maintaining some uncertainty about a bailout helps, at least theoretically, limit moral hazard. The other reason is that investment banks do not hold deposits by average citizens, so an investment bank failure hurts select wealthy individuals rather than the public at large.[2] The Lehman Brothers failure in 2008 was the largest corporate failure in US history at that time, with $613 billion in debt (see, e.g., Mamudi, 2008). The financial panic and fallout spread quickly, not just in the United States, but around the world, given the interconnectedness of financial institutions and economies in a globalized world. A worldwide recession followed. The US Government Accountability Office (2013) estimated that $10 trillion was lost in global economic output due to this financial crisis.

---

1   See the Federal Reserve Bank of St. Louis's information on residential property prices for the United States at https://fred.stlouisfed.org/series /QUSN368BIS.

2   In general, investment banks facilitate bringing together large investors with funds with entrepreneurs with business opportunities rather than taking on the risks of a financial intermediary on their balance sheets like commercial banks.

QUESTIONS FOR DISCUSSION

1 In March 2024, after a period of interest rate hikes, the premier of Ontario, Doug Ford, called on the Bank of Canada to lower interest rates.[6] Do you think this statement by the premier made an interest rate cut by the Bank of Canada more or less likely? Explain why.

2 Suppose that news outlets report that a former minister of finance is likely to be the next central bank governor in a certain country. How are financial markets likely to react to this news?

3 Suppose the central bank governor receives a lunch invitation from the minister of finance. Would you advise the governor to accept such an invitation?

4 Suppose the central bank and analysts expect bad economic news in the form of rising unemployment and economic contraction. When the statistical office releases the data, the numbers indeed confirm that the economy is contracting, but nowhere near the expected gloomy scenario that was projected by analysts. What is the likely reaction by the central bank and the stock markets?

7.5 EXCHANGE RATE POLICY

In this section, we integrate exchange rate policy into the discussion of monetary policy and how they affect each other.

The price of the local currency relative to other currencies – that is, the nominal exchange rate – determines how much revenue exporters receive for their products and how much imported goods a country can afford. Exporting increases the demand for local currency, and thus strengthens it, while importing does the opposite by bolstering the demand for foreign currencies. If a country has liabilities in a foreign currency, exchange rate movements can also make it more expensive to repay the debt and therefore may increase the chances of default. Investors and rating agencies closely monitor such developments, and the exchange rate regime plays a role in that as well. Table 7.4 provides a summary of official (*de jure*) exchange rate regimes from the most rigid to most flexible ones.

---

6   For more detail, see, for example, Arsenych (2024).

Table 7.4. Official (de jure) exchange rate regime types

Regime	Explanation
Currency union	Abandoning a currency and adopting another currency as a legal tender. This decision is equivalent to "irrevocably"* fixing the exchange rate and giving up monetary policy as a policy tool.
Currency board	A currency board regime is also known as a "hard peg," because the exchange rate is fixed (to another currency or basket of currencies) by law and the central bank is prohibited from affecting the money supply. The money supply expands and contracts with international capital inflows and outflows, respectively.
Fixed exchange rate	The central bank is committed to defending a declared exchange rate, but a fixed exchange rate regime is a "soft peg" because the government/central bank can abandon the peg at any time.
Crawling peg	The fixed exchange rate is set to depreciate or appreciate at a pre-announced rate to help anchor inflationary expectations by the public.
Exchange rate band	An exchange rate band is a form of a peg, but allows for fluctuations within a target band.
Managed float	Under a managed float regime, there is no exchange rate target, but the central bank may intervene at their discretion to limit fluctuations in the exchange rate.
Float	There is no expectation for the central bank to interfere with exchange rate movements.

* The exchange rate fix is "irrevocable" to the extent that that it can only be changed by separating from a monetary union.

It is also important to note that the appropriate terms for describing exchange rate movements are *depreciation* and *appreciation* (or *devaluation* and *revaluation* in the context of fixed exchange rate regimes). One should never use the terms "going up" or "going down," because that is not informative, clear, or well defined, since "up" or "down" movements depend on how the relative exchange rate is defined by convention, which varies across different markets. Economists typically define exchange rates as units of domestic currency per USD $1 (or other foreign currency). Under this definition, an increase in the exchange rate corresponds to a depreciation (or devaluation under a peg) and a decrease in the exchange rate represents an appreciation (or revaluation under a peg). We will follow this convention in this text.

Why do countries choose a certain exchange rate regime? Before we can attempt to answer this question, it is noteworthy that table 7.4 captures only de jure – that is, official – exchange rate regime declarations, while the empirical literature on exchange rates has detected several trends since the 1990s. These include fewer officially declared fixed exchange rate regimes, as well as more *de jure* floating regimes (with central banks often intervening to limit exchange rate movements, thus with exchange rates exhibiting more stability than expected of a truly floating regime). There are several possible explanations for these trends. First, the end of the Cold War in 1989, and the resulting wave of economic and capital account liberalizations in the 1990s, led to a surge in private capital flows across countries. This was a major structural change since it implied that central banks with their reserves are no longer large players in foreign exchange markets and that their powers fade in comparison to large private capital flows, thus making it impossible to maintain formally pegged exchange rate regimes. The formal commitment to a peg (i.e., the promise by the central bank to buy and sell one's currency at the given rate) only invites speculative attacks against such a declaration, leading to the depletion of the foreign exchange reserves of the central bank and the rapid depreciation of the currency, thus resulting in a crisis. This rise in private cross-border capital flows explains why most countries have abandoned pegged exchange rate regimes (i.e., soft pegs) in favour of floating regimes or hard pegs such as joining a monetary/currency union or unilaterally adopting another currency (dollarization).

The second trend documented in the literature is that even if countries formally declare a floating exchange rate regime, many of them still have a tendency to implement measures that limit exchange rate fluctuations. This trend has led to differentiating between de jure and de facto regimes based on the actual behaviour of exchange rates (Levy-Yeyati & Sturzenegger, 2003, 2005; Reinhart & Rogoff, 2004). The phenomenon has been labelled as *fear of floating*, based on the work of Calvo and Reinhart (2002).

The empirical findings on exchange regimes and the documented divergence between de jure and de facto regimes have challenged the theoretical literature on exchange rate regime choice, which typically treated the choice as a binary decision between fix or float. The literature was also largely normative – that is, in search of the optimal regime or so-called *optimal currency areas* (or *currency unions* in the terminology of table 7.4) based on factors such as the degree of correlation of economic activity across regions, trade links, and labour mobility (Mundell, 1961, 1963; Fleming, 1962; McKinnon, 1963; Frankel & Rose, 1998). The main policy recommendations on regime choice included the following:

- adopting a floating regime if real shocks to the economy prevail (e.g., supply shocks, technological changes) to allow the exchange rate to adjust and avoid over- or under-valuation of the currency and the associated trade imbalances
- a fixed regime being preferable under nominal shocks to the money supply or money demand

When we add free capital mobility as a factor affecting regime choice, there is also a recognition that maintaining a peg under such conditions is incompatible with maintaining independent monetary policy because the central bank will simply take action to keep the exchange rate fixed. In other words, under conditions of capital account liberalization (which became the norm for most countries in the 1990s), choosing a fixed exchange rate regime would imply giving up monetary policy as a tool for macroeconomic stabilization. And why would any government give up a policy tool? You may recall from section 7.2 and the Barro and Gordon (1983) framework that only surprise inflation can stimulate the economy, while a history of inflation leads to inflationary expectations by the public and the costs of inflation prevail. Under such conditions, the government has already lost the ability to stimulate the economy through monetary policy. The fixed exchange rate, on the other hand, offers predictability and a means to anchor inflationary expectations of the public by giving up the ability to affect the money supply.

Kimakova (2008) provides a more updated look at exchange rate regime choice from a theoretical perspective and allows for exchange rate regime choice as a continuous variable – that is, a regime with a certain degree of de facto flexibility, rather than a binary or de jure choice between a peg or float. Building on the Barro and Gordon (1983) framework with increasing costs from inflation, the model incorporates short-term horizons for governments facing political re-election uncertainty in a two-period model, taking into consideration the government's inter-temporal budget constraint and the structure of financial markets as key factors affecting regime choice.

Specifically, the model by Kimakova (2008) takes into consideration different classes of investors holding government debt:

- domestic investors holding government debt denominated in domestic currency, which the government has an incentive to inflate away[7]
- foreign investors holding government debt denominated in foreign currency
- foreign investors holding government debt denominated in domestic currency

It turns out that, in practice, the last option of foreign investors holding government debt denominated in domestic currency is rather limited. This is because most countries, especially developing economies, do not have sufficient monetary and exchange rate credibility to induce non-resident investors to hold their debt in domestic currency due to the fear that domestic currency debt can be inflated away by the government. This phenomenon – the inability to borrow from non-resident/foreign investors in one's own domestic currency – is called *original sin* in the literature (Eichengreen & Hausmann, 1999; Hausmann, 1999).

It is important to note that the government can inflate away the real burden of domestic currency debt (if you recall, it is easier to repay $1,000 owed if inflation takes place and earnings increase with inflation), but not the debt denominated in foreign currency, because inflation ultimately leads to depreciation of the currency, at least in the medium to long term, even if a peg can sustain an imbalance in the currency's value in the short term. In other words, the concept of *fiscal dominance* that was introduced in section 6.5 of chapter 6 on fiscal policy plays an important role here because the amount of government debt and its currency composition determine the government's incentives to inflate or not. If the government chooses inflation, that affects the de facto regime choice, as inflation inevitably leads to a

---

7   The model assumes the domestic investors cannot invest abroad or in foreign currency; they are limited to the domestic market by legislation. In other words, the model does not allow for capital flight.

depreciation, and thus a more flexible de facto regime (either a float or frequent devaluations under a peg or a crawling peg).

This framework provides an explanation for both the fear of floating and de facto exchange rate pegs through the importance of government debt held by non-resident investors being denominated in foreign currency, and thus providing the incentive to keep the exchange rate fixed or prevent depreciation under de jure floating because that would only make it harder to pay back a given amount of debt in foreign currency and increase the risk of default. The experiences of many developing countries match this theoretical proposition, as they would have historically experienced high inflation or even hyperinflation, which has led to losing monetary policy credibility, persistence in inflationary expectations, and the inability to issue government debt in domestic currency. This would lead to dollarization and/or maintaining some form of a hard peg, such as the currency board regime in Argentina between 1991 and 2000, to anchor inflationary expectations and maintain the ability to repay foreign currency debt.

Among more developed economies, the creation of the European Monetary Union (EMU) in 1992 and the introduction of the euro as its common currency in 1999 stand as a relatively recent example of a currency union formation. A total of 20 of the 27 EU member countries have adopted the euro as their currency and thus given up monetary policy as an economic stabilization tool. If you are wondering why developed European economies would do that, it is relevant to remember that many European countries have had a history of inflation, high government debt, and currency crises that plunged their economies into financial and economic turmoil. Hence, giving up monetary policy in favour of a credible central bank arguably means that the gains outweigh the losses.

The European Central Bank (ECB) is located in Frankfurt, Germany, and has a single monetary policy target of 2 per cent inflation per year in the medium term to anchor inflationary expectations. It is no coincidence that the ECB is located in Germany: The German central bank – the Deutsche Bundesbank – had developed a reputation for a strong anti-inflationary stance prior to the creation of the EMU, given the country's traumatic experience with hyperinflation in the early 1920s. Credibility and reputation are crucial for monetary policy conduct, as shown by Barro and Gordon (1983), and the countries adopting the euro have in essence decided to import such credibility and leverage it for their benefit. That said, the EMU and the euro come with strings attached due to the fiscal dominance of monetary policy, as discussed earlier. Under the Maastricht Treaty of 1992,[8] the member states are required to maintain fiscal targets to ensure the credibility of monetary policy and its low inflation target by limiting the accumulation of government debt to 60 per cent of GDP and limiting annual budget deficits to 3 per cent of GDP.

It should be noted that the above debt and budget deficit targets were chosen by European leaders based on economic and political considerations, along with the specific circumstances of EU member states, and should not be interpreted as universal standards. The reason is that some developing countries may see a crisis emerge, even with healthier fiscal indicators, while other countries with significantly worse fiscal performance may not experience a crisis. Confidence in a country's institutions and economic performance will play a role in risk assessment by investors, which also takes place in relative terms to other alternatives.

Finally, the model in Kimakova (2008) also explains why Great Britain chose not to join the EMU (while being an EU member state at the time) and adopt the euro. The British pound has a strong history of credibility, and there is a well-developed financial market in assets denominated in the British pound, along with a significant pool of British investors as well as foreign investors who are willing to hold debt denominated in the British pound. Hence, Great Britain has had no incentive to maintain a de facto peg and instead can reap the benefits of having a flexible/floating exchange rate regime that helps stabilize the economy.

QUESTIONS FOR DISCUSSION AND SUGGESTIONS FOR FURTHER RESEARCH

1 Notable historical examples of hyperinflation include Germany in the 1920s, other European and Latin American countries from the 1940s to the 1990s, and more recently Zimbabwe in the 2000s

---

8 Treaty on European Union (OJ C 191, 29.7.1992, pp. 1–112). For the full text and summaries, see European Parliament (n.d.).

and Venezuela since the 2010s. Research their experiences and the economic contexts that led to their respective crises and explain why the IMF typically insists on bringing both inflation and fiscal deficits/debt under control at the same time.

2 Pick a country and investigate its central bank independence status. How does the assessed de jure independence stack up against inflation performance?

3 Do the member countries of the EMU meet the Maastricht criteria for government debt and deficit at this time? If not, what are the legal, political, and economic implications of such violations?

4 It is notable that the EMU member countries have not issued debt jointly in euros. The eurozone member countries continue to issue government bonds separately as individual sovereigns. Can you explain why?

7.6 CURRENCY CRISES

The combination of fixed exchange rate regimes and foreign currency debt has led to numerous economic crises, often labelled as *currency crises* due to the associated plummeting of the currency's value through a devaluation or sharp depreciation when a country is forced to abandon fixed exchange rates altogether.

At the heart of a currency crisis is a balance of payments (BOP) crisis. Table 7.5 outlines the structure and key components of the BOP. The main components are the current account, financial account, and foreign currency reserves. The current account is made up primarily of the trade balance, that is, the value of exports minus the value of imports, and primary income on foreign assets, secondary income from remittances (significant for countries whose citizens work abroad as migrant workers) minus profits repatriated to foreign owners of factors of production, which can be sizeable when foreign direct investment (FDI) is present in an economy.

For a typical developing country, the current account is often negative, and in order to equalize the BOP, the financial account has to be positive – that is, capital inflows need to outweigh capital outflows. The expected patterns for the current and financial accounts to balance each other out are highlighted in table 7.5.

Table 7.5. Balance of payments structure

Current Account: (–/+)	Financial Account: (+/–)
Trade balance: exports – imports Primary income: e.g., interest earned on foreign assets (+), repatriated profits to non-resident investors (–) Secondary income (e.g., remittances, grants)	Capital inflows (liabilities) – capital outflows (assets, investment abroad) (e.g., foreign direct investment, portfolio investment, debt instruments)
Capital Account (typically small balance, +/–):	Reserves +
Purchases and sales of intangible property rights (franchises and trademarks) Debt forgiveness, transfer of wealth	Errors and omissions +/–

Note: For more detail on balance of payments components, definitions, data, and methodology, please see IMF (2009).

Because investors search for the highest rates of return globally, developing countries have increasingly seen capital inflows since the 1990s because they can often offer higher rates of return than more developed economies. Broadly speaking, the main reason for this is the law of diminishing returns to a factor of production, capital in this case, while holding other factors of production (such as labour, for example) constant. Figure 7.3 illustrates this point by showing that the real return (r) on capital (K) (technically the marginal product of capital, denoted as MPK) declines with the accumulation of capital. Hence, less developed countries with lower capital stock (K_1) have higher rates of return (r_1) relative to higher income countries with more capital (K_2). Of course, this simple diagram does not account for political and other risks, but it explains the flow of capital from more developed to less developed economies.

However, several important caveats and empirical regularities should also be noted with respect to international capital flows:

- Capital flows can be short-term or long-term. Portfolio investment is short-term and extremely volatile, while foreign direct investment (FDI) tends to be more long-term and typically involved in mining, manufacturing, or service sectors.
- Capital tends to flow to a handful of emerging economies rather than being evenly distributed around the world.

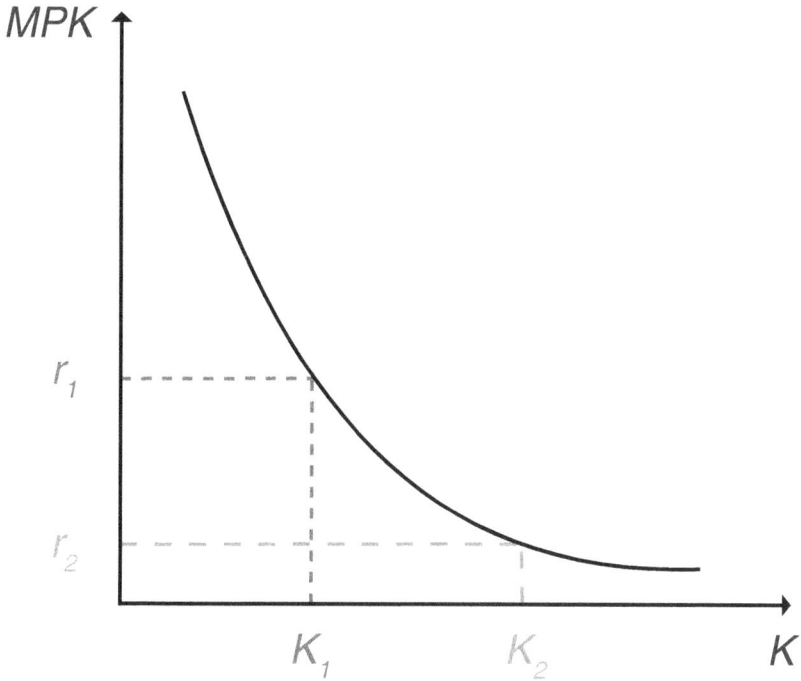

Figure 7.3. Diminishing returns to capital

- When negative news emerges about a certain economy, capital flow reversal can occur very swiftly.
- Even countries seemingly unconnected to the emerging news and affected economies can suffer sharp capital flow reversals, and this is known as *contagion*. The reason is that investors re-balance portfolios and move capital to markets that are perceived as less risky.

When foreign investors suddenly pull out of certain markets, this puts enormous pressure on the exchange rate and either the exchange rate depreciates or, under a peg, the central bank starts losing foreign exchange reserves very fast. The central banks can respond by devaluing a currency peg and/or increasing interest rates in order to make it more attractive for investors to remain in the affected market. Alternatively, the central bank can let the currency depreciate rather than defend any peg, and this has the benefit of not depleting the central bank's foreign currency reserves. In the current climate, with large private capital flows, central banks with their limited resources cannot effectively counter private flows and typically let the currency float and depreciate to achieve stabilization that way.

Besides preserving foreign exchange reserves, a depreciation has the benefit of helping exports,[9] and thus economic recovery, rather than hindering it. Of course, imports become more expensive in the short to medium term, and repayment of loans in foreign currency is more costly and less likely, raising the possibility of default. Under such circumstances, the IMF steps in to provide countries with liquidity by extending short- to medium-term loans to cover a BOP crisis and limit (at least to some extent) the immediate economic hardship on citizens and producers that would come from a dramatic contraction of the economy. The loans typically come with conditions attached to prevent a future crisis and address its root causes. This is known as *conditionality*, and the IMF has attracted a great deal of criticism as a result of these policies.

Specifically, criticism of the IMF is based on the argument that there is unequal risk-sharing between international creditors and citizens of the affected (typically developing) countries, because during a crisis, debt is typically not written off (only restructured or rescheduled) while countries are asked to cut back government spending, further exacerbating economic hardship. The lack of debt reduction serves as a form of insurance for creditors, thus creating a moral hazard problem that has been highlighted for decades (see, e.g., Vaubel, 1983) and confirmed empirically by Lipscy and Lee (2019). Stubbs et al. (2022) also confirm through their empirical analysis that IMF austerity measures deepen poverty and inequality in the affected countries while benefiting the richest segments of the economy (top 10 per cent of earners).

The criticism of the IMF is not limited to academia, as the institution is generally perceived by the public as politically and/or ideologically biased in favour of the investor class and protecting their interests. Partial debt writeoffs during financial crises could ensure a degree of risk-sharing between international creditors and the citizens of the borrowing countries. In response to the criticism, the IMF and the World Bank created the Heavily Indebted Poor Countries (HIPC)

---

9 Technically, export competitiveness is determined by the real exchange rate rather than the nominal exchange rate, but movements in the nominal exchange determine a major part of the real exchange rate, especially in the short term.

Initiative in 1996 to provide some debt forgiveness to the poorest developing countries, which suffer from a high opportunity cost of the debt burden, impeding their economic development and growth. The HIPC Initiative also relies on conditionality, and in practice it is very difficult for countries to qualify for debt forgiveness.[10]

To be able to predict future currency crises, or to prevent them, as analysts we need to understand the causes of currency crises in the first place. There is consensus in the literature that the experiences of many countries (especially in Latin America) in the 1980s and early 1990s provided ample evidence that the accumulation of excessive government debt led to inflation, resulting in loss of monetary policy credibility and a downturn in the economy. During such negative economic developments, there is typically the need for an exchange rate and fiscal adjustment, and if that does not happen, capital flight and a currency crisis will eventually unfold. In other words, there is consensus that the currency crises of the 1980s and early 1990s provide strong support for the hypothesis of fiscal dominance of monetary policy. Despite all this, the 1997 Asian crisis involving Thailand, South Korea, and Indonesia took market analysts by surprise. How is that possible?

When analysts looked at government finances and debt in Thailand, South Korea, and Indonesia in the mid-1990s, the usual warning signs of excessive spending and debt were not there (see figure 7.4).

However, with international capital flows liberalized in the early 1990s, analysts should have been taking a closer look at the BOP, as captured in table 7.5. As figure 7.5 shows, the current account balance was negative, especially in Thailand, where the crisis began in 1997, and it was important to balance the current account deficit with a financial account surplus – that is, capital inflows outweighing capital outflows. With the private sector overtaking the government in terms of the magnitude of foreign borrowing, the risks involved should not have been ignored, but they were (see, e.g., Bello, 1999). This is especially concerning when borrowing takes place by commercial banks in foreign currency and utilizing short- to medium-term loans to take advantage of lower interest rates in more developed economies, as illustrated in figure 7.3. The commercial banks then issued loans and mortgages in domestic markets, which created

---

10 For a status update on the HIPC Initiative, see, for example, World Bank (2024).

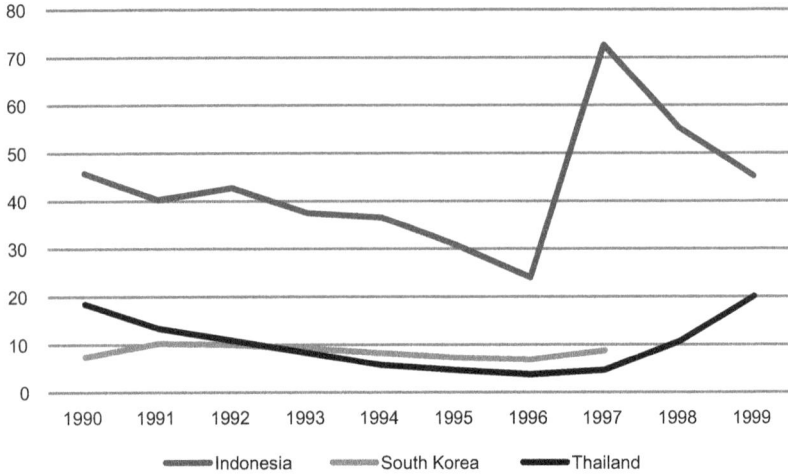

Figure 7.4. Central government debt as % of GDP
Source: World Bank (2025b).

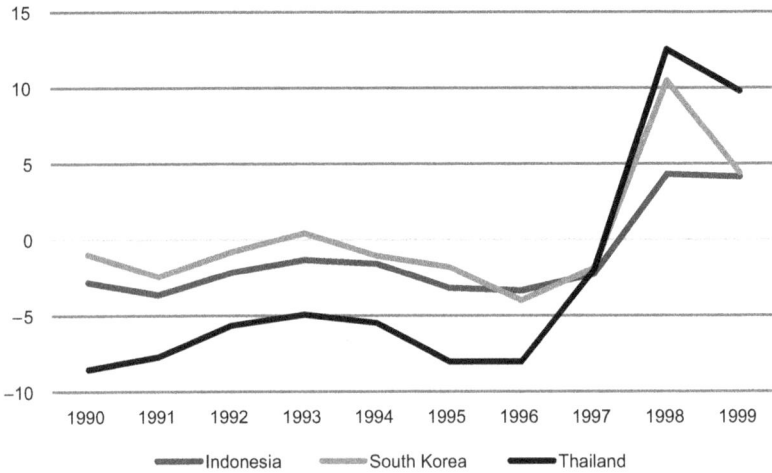

Figure 7.5. Current account balance as % of GDP
Source: World Bank (2025b).

another problem of excess liquidity, strong demand, and a real estate price bubble (Bank of Thailand, n.d.). The commercial banks thus had a major maturity mismatch between their long-term assets (mortgages and other long-term debt issued) and short-term liabilities in the form of loans from abroad in foreign currency. The scheme worked as long as short-term interest rates in developed countries – that is, borrowing costs – remained low and the exchange rate was stable. The governments contributed to this excessive risk-taking (moral hazard) by maintaining a fixed exchange rate regime that served as a free currency-hedging service to the borrowers.

Once interest rates in developed countries started increasing, the borrowing costs to commercial banks increased and/or made it impossible to refinance their loans. This exposed a major vulnerability in commercial bank balance sheets, which, combined with the real estate price bubble and low mortgage quality, led to foreign capital flight, depletion of central bank reserves, and ultimately, the need to abandon the fixed exchange rate regimes in these countries. As contagion spread in global markets, other countries had to follow suit as well, and de jure fixed exchange rate regimes (soft pegs) largely disappeared as the preferred regime choice around the world.

QUESTIONS FOR DISCUSSION AND SUGGESTIONS FOR FURTHER RESEARCH

1 Argentina's currency board regime plunged into a crisis in 2000. What were the circumstances that led to the crisis and forced the abandonment of this hard peg?
2 The US government debt to GDP ratio has ballooned and it also has a trade deficit. Are these indicators a warning of a currency crisis? What factors are likely to impact your answer to this question?

BOX 7.2. CRYPTOCURRENCIES: A VIABLE ALTERNATIVE OR ANOTHER PONZI SCHEME?[1]

Cryptocurrencies such as bitcoin have received a lot of media attention in recent years due to the rise in their prices and the associated high returns. Celebrity endorsements of cryptocurrency investments have become commonplace, and some governments have reacted by imposing a capital gains tax[2] on cryptocurrency earnings in an attempt to close the gaping tax loophole if cryptocurrencies are not recognized as investment assets.

Nevertheless, cryptocurrencies have remained controversial due to their utilization by criminal groups and other objectionable actors, the privacy associated with decentralized cryptocurrency systems, which is conducive to money laundering and other illegal activities, and the environmental impact of digital currency "mining" due to its high energy requirements. Cryptocurrencies have also fluctuated widely in price, and some cryptocurrency exchanges and investment firms have been linked to outright fraud and the laying of criminal charges (see, e.g., Sherman et al., 2024). Given that governments have no control over the supply of cryptocurrencies, they also give up monetary policy as a tool when cryptocurrencies are utilized as a legal tender.

Despite all this, it is noteworthy that many governments and central banks have not explicitly ruled out some participation in this decentralized digital currency market, which is unregulated and unpredictable.[3] In 2021, El Salvador became the first country to adopt bitcoin as a legal tender, which meant that businesses were required to accept bitcoin for payments. In this case, bitcoin is not the only legal tender, but an alternative to the US dollar, which became a legal tender in 2001. The government also provided incentives to adopt bitcoin through a free app called Chivo Wallet, which enabled users to digitally trade both bitcoin and US dollars free of transaction fees, and came with a USD $30 credit to everyone who downloaded the app. This incentive was not negligible, given that El Salvador is a poor country and USD $30 represented about 1 per cent of annual earnings for the average person.[4] The government proclaimed financial inclusion as one of its objectives with the app and the new legal tender, as a significant percentage of the country's citizens did not have a bank account and remittances from the United States play a significant role in supporting local households. Nevertheless, the IMF and the World Bank declined to support bitcoin adoption due to its risks to individual bitcoin holders as well as the government risking default on its debt liabilities, as the value of bitcoin could change in unpredictable ways. Figure 7.6 shows that the price of bitcoin,[5] and thus the value of bitcoin holdings, did in fact plummet in 2022 after

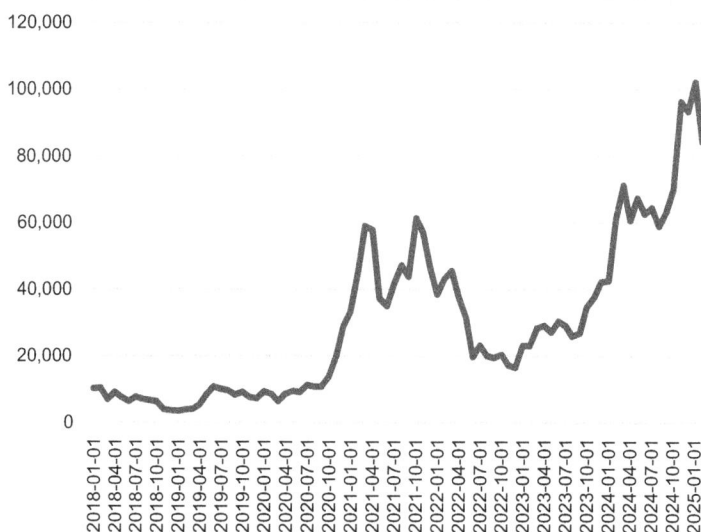

Figure 7.6. Bitcoin price in USD
Source: CoinMarketCap.

its adoption by El Salvador in 2021. The bitcoin experiment thus failed as a store of value, a primary function of money.

Alvarez et al. (2023) also found that the objective of greater financial inclusion has not been achieved, as the adoption of bitcoin and the associated app was limited largely to a specific demographic: in this case, young, educated men with bank accounts. This is despite the substantial financial incentive provided by the government and the ongoing COVID-19 pandemic making touchless payments desirable. Alvarez et al. (2023) found that the lack of transparency and privacy fears impeded uptake of the cryptocurrency, and a preference for cash remained dominant. This experiment shows that public trust plays a significant role in the government's ability to effectively utilize a legal tender.

It is also noteworthy that the government planned to issue debt in bitcoin in 2022, which would have made El Salvador the first country to do so, but this plan was abandoned, citing unfavourable market conditions due to the start of the war in Ukraine. With government debt repayment due dates looming, the country's credit rating was downgraded, as the risk of default was deemed to have increased significantly at this time. The government decided to revive the plan to issue bitcoin bonds in 2024 to fund a project for El Salvador to become a bitcoin mining hub. The experiment thus continues, and it remains to be seen whether the country at large and its citizens will benefit from it or not.

---

1   Named after Charles Ponzi, a Ponzi scheme is a fraudulent investment arrangement under which existing investors are paid from funds from new investors. Once the scheme fails to attract new investors, it collapses, as no actual investment is made or return on investment earned.
2   See, for example, the Government of Canada's (2024) tax requirements for crypto-asset users.
3   In 2013, Bitcoin was named "the year's best investment" by Forbes, followed by the title of "the year's worst investment" in 2014 according to Bloomberg. For more on this history of bitcoin, please see Pinkerton (2024).
4   For more detail on the circumstances surrounding Bitcoin adoption in El Salvador, please see Kurmanaev and Avelar (2022).
5   Data available to download from CoinMarketCap at https://coinmarketcap .com/currencies/bitcoin/.

7.7 INTERNATIONAL POLICY COORDINATION

From an economic perspective, the two major policy areas in the international context are international trade and the environment.

7.7.1 Tensions in Global Environmental Protection

Environmental damage and its consequences do not respect jurisdictional boundaries, and that is why they are commonly referred to as *trans-national externalities*. As a reminder from chapter 3, externalities can be negative or positive in general and represent the social costs and benefits that accrue to others and are therefore disregarded in private decisions. Harmful emissions from economic activity cause global warming, and the resulting consequences in terms of extreme weather events and rising sea levels might be felt the most by communities far away in another country altogether. The same goes for plastic waste that somehow ends up in the oceans far away, even when you think you did your duty and recycled your consumer waste as directed.

Combating environmental damage is typically seen as an activity involving immediate costs to producers and consumers, while the benefits are likely to be reaped in the future, which we discount to varying extents as individuals. Moreover, the benefits from environmental protection might accrue to others, and those who free ride on the costly environmental efforts will still reap the benefits because they cannot be excluded from a healthier environment and a more stable climate, as these exhibit the properties of a public good. These are the problems at the heart of attempts to commit to environmental protection in the international arena.

The Paris Agreement is an international treaty on climate change that was reached at the UN Climate Change Conference (COP21) in Paris, France, in 2015 and came into force in 2016.[11] Nominally, nearly 200 countries have ratified the agreement,[12] but notable exceptions remain:

- China (except for the territories of Hong Kong and Macau)
- the United States, which served notice of withdrawal from the Agreement in 2019,[13] which became effective in 2020, and filed again for acceptance of the Agreement, conditional on ratification by individual states, in January 2021.[14] In early 2025, President Trump signed an executive order to withdraw from the Agreement again.[15]

This is problematic from a global perspective because China and the United States are the world's largest polluters. Figure 7.7 shows their total greenhouse emissions in comparison to the EU, another significant economic bloc, and figure 7.8 shows CO_2 emissions per capita, to put total CO_2 emissions in perspective by benchmarking pollution by

---

11 For more information, please see United Nations (n.d.).
12 For the ratification status of individual signatory countries to the Paris Agreement, please visit United Nations (2015).
13 See United Nations (2019).
14 See United Nations (2021).
15 See The White House (2025).

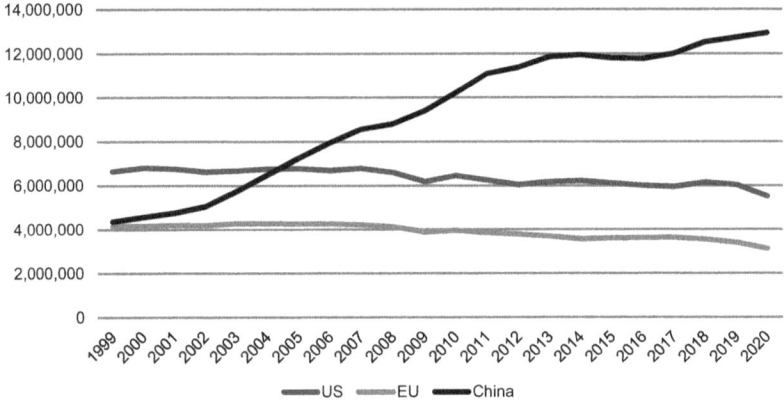

Figure 7.7. Total greenhouse emissions (kt of CO$_2$ equivalent)
Source: World Bank (2025b).

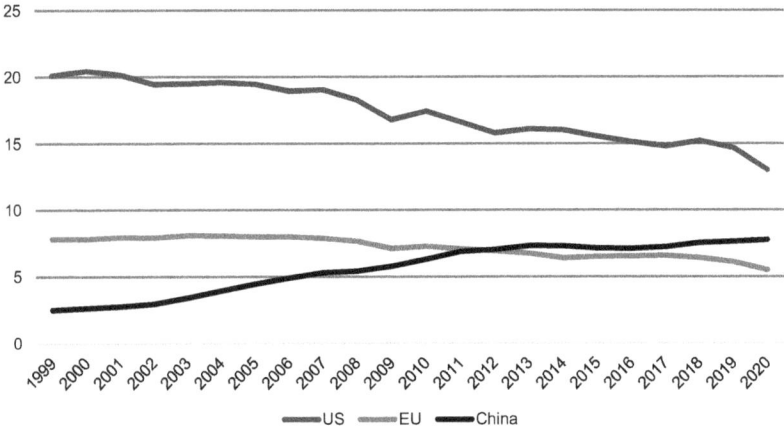

Figure 7.8. CO$_2$ emissions (metric tons) per capita
Source: World Bank (2025b).

population size. The figures show that emissions continue to increase in China, while there is a slightly declining trend in the EU and the United States. Nevertheless, the United States still stands out as the largest polluter in per capita terms.

The Paris Agreement has been widely criticized for ineffectiveness, due to countries setting voluntary targets and because non-compliance with any target is unlikely to have consequences. Research focusing on the effectiveness of the agreement has in general yielded mixed results with a slight leaning towards cautious optimism, mainly through the sharing of best practices. Nevertheless, the lack of transparency in data, the complexity of the underlying issues, the general lack of political ambition and, some would argue, public support, and free riding remain problems (Raiser et al., 2020; Tørstad, 2020). Governments are often criticized for lack of effective action to combat climate change, but right-leaning political parties, many of which even deny the scientific evidence showing the link between emissions, global warming, and extreme weather events, have been gaining popular ground in elections around the world. Some climate policies, especially those that rely on taxation, have been very unpopular because ultimately consumption taxes linked to fossil fuels (such as a tax on gasoline, for example) are regressive, as lower-income households pay a larger proportion of their income in those taxes than higher-income households. Tax rebate programs aim to counter the regressive nature of these taxes, but they tend to be perceived as imperfect attempts at mitigation.

Esty (2001) and others have argued for the inclusion of environmental protection in international trade agreements in order to enhance enforcement capabilities through economic incentives and/or penalties and to counter the free-riding problem inherent in environmental protection due to its public good nature, as outlined above.

The international trade regime under the World Trade Organization (WTO) is similarly imperfect in terms of its ability to enforce agreements and inflict punishment on violators of those agreements. However imperfect, the WTO rules and enforcement have some economic impact, and thus Esty (2001) argues that these tools should be utilized to induce environmental protection in the absence of alternative means and options.

It is important to note that under the current WTO system, individual member countries can impose product standards (e.g., regulations to ensure that the imported product is safe to consume and use). However, they cannot impose process standards – that is, how the products are produced – whether in an environmentally harmful manner or not.

Process standards are not allowed under WTO rules because they could be utilized to limit competition (especially with respect to lower-income developing countries) rather than truly just for the sake of environmental protection, thus potentially negating the mandate of the WTO to liberalize trade in a non-discriminatory manner with respect to all member countries.

An example of including environmental standards in trade integration is the EU, which imposed on its new member states the requirement to harmonize their environmental protection before allowing them to join the EU common market. Nevertheless, in the context of the "old" and "new" EU member states, one could argue that they were not that far apart economically, that the demand for stronger environmental regulations was there even in the "new" member countries, and that the benefits in terms of access to the EU market would likely outweigh the costs of environmental harmonization.

7.7.2 Political Economy Considerations in International Trade

There are two main reasons for international trade:

* *economies of scale*, that is, the average cost of production decreases with production/firm size
* because countries are different in terms of their endowments and/ or productivity

Specialization reduces costs and makes production more efficient, but given limited resources, specialization implies that no country can produce everything and will have to instead trade and import some goods and/or services. This also explains why trade is in general more important for smaller economies as opposed to larger ones: Smaller economies are unable to reach minimum efficient production scale and lower costs without relying on international demand.

It is a false narrative and oversimplification that exports are good, imports are bad, but such political rhetoric can prevail at times and is historically referred to as the theory of *mercantilism*. From an economic perspective, a trade surplus is needed if the financial account is negative (as per table 7.5). Overall balance should be the objective, not

$e = DOM/FX$

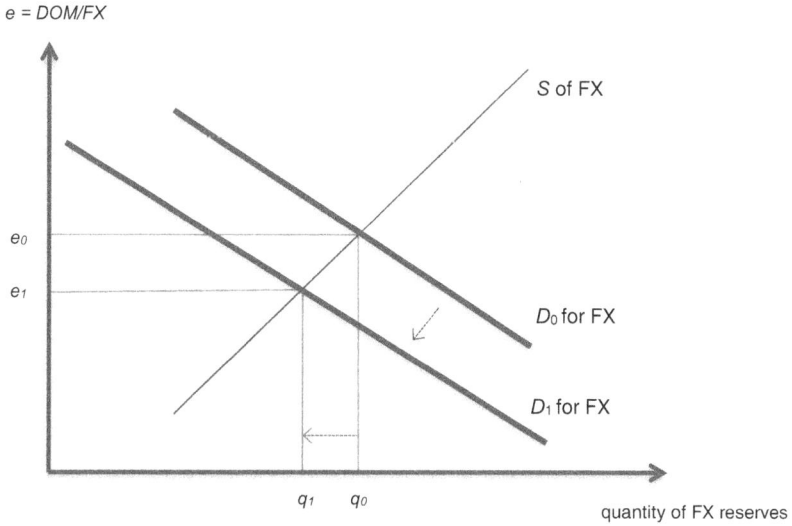

Figure 7.9. Impact of trade protectionism on the nominal exchange rate

simply maximizing exports, because limiting imports increases the cost of living for consumers and hurts industries that import intermediate products.

Trade protectionism in general hurts the objective of achieving a trade balance and can in fact exacerbate a trade deficit through its impact on the exchange rate. Trade protectionism through tariffs or quotas on imports reduces domestic demand for imports, which reduces the demand for foreign currency. Figure 7.9 depicts this dynamic with the nominal exchange rate (e) representing the price of foreign currency (FX) in terms of the domestic currency and the demand curve for foreign currency shifting in from D_0 to D_1. The result is that the foreign currency weakens, and the domestic currency strengthens or appreciates (moves from e_0 to e_1). As the nominal exchange rate appreciates, it has the same effect on the real exchange rate, which determines the competitiveness of exports. An appreciation in the real exchange reduces the competitiveness of exports and leads to a decline in export performance. As a result, the trade balance worsens further, contrary to the original policy objective of improving it.

When trade imbalances are present, the exchange rate is in general meant to adjust to restore a balance:

• When an economy is struggling, demand for domestic currency decreases, and when exchange rate movements are not restricted (by a peg, for example), the currency will depreciate and help boost exports and the economy.
• When an economy is growing, demand for domestic currency increases, the exchange rate should appreciate, consumers should benefit from importing more, and the trade balance should be restored.

China's economic growth led by exports should represent the latter scenario above, but the government has prevented the exchange rate from appreciating. The Chinese government is in a unique position to be able to implement such measures, given its size and lack of political freedoms. However, this has had significant implications for the rest of the world because China's trade surplus is persistent rather than temporary and global imbalances remain.

While mercantilism is generally considered to have been the dominant ideology with respect to trade from the sixteenth century to the mid-eighteenth century, it is clear that its underlying logic and political influence remain relevant today. International trade does have strong distributional effects – that is, winners and losers from trade arrangements and because governments can utilize trade tools strategically to pursue foreign and domestic policy objectives.

The problem with utilizing international trade tools (import tariffs, quotas, import or export bans, etc.) as instruments of foreign policy is that their reach, especially for enforcement of rules or agreements, is inaccurate: The entities or groups targeted for compliance are typically not the ones that the sanctions will be imposed on or who will bear the de facto burden of the sanctions. The first Trump administration in the United States tried to counter the long-standing trade imbalance with China in 2018–19, but it only led to a series of retaliatory actions, which are typically referred to as *trade wars*. As a result, US producers were hurt – especially the exporters who were doing well prior to the trade war, such as US farmers – and the overall trade deficit worsened. While the trade deficit with respect to China improved slightly, it came at the expense of reduced trade flows and increased costs to consumers and producers reliant on intermediate imports. The US trade deficit with respect to other countries actually widened as imports were sourced from other, more expensive, producers in other countries.[16]

When tariffs are imposed on imports, consumers face higher prices as the prices of imported products increase and competition is diminished for domestic producers. Hence, higher prices are paid not just on imported foreign goods, but also on domestically produced goods in the same industry or product category.

It is not only consumers who are harmed in this way, but also producers who utilize imported inputs. Therefore, it is not enough to look at the official/nominal tariff rates to determine the degree of protectionism in a particular industry or market; the *effective rate of protection* (ERP) needs to be calculated.

The ERP is defined as the percentage change in value added (VAD) per unit of output in the domestic market with tariffs on imported final products and intermediate inputs relative to the VAD in world prices free from trade distortions such as tariffs. VAD is the difference between the selling price (p) and the cost of intermediate inputs (c), as shown in equation (7.2), and represents the income of factors of production (labour, capital, and land). Equations (7.3) and (7.4) break down the ERP with different degrees of detail provided to show its construction:

$$VAD = p - c \tag{7.2}$$

$$ERP = \%\Delta VAD = \frac{VAD_{tariffs} - VAD_{world\ prices}}{VAD_{world\ prices}} = \frac{VAD_{tariffs}}{VAD_{world\ prices}} - 1 \tag{7.3}$$

$$ERP = \frac{p(1+t_o) - c(1+t_i)}{p - c} - 1 = \frac{pt_o - ct_i}{p - c} \tag{7.4}$$

where the symbol Δ denotes change in a variable (in this case VAD), t_o represents that tariff rate on the imported output, and t_i denotes the tariff rate on the imported input.

---

16 For a more detailed account of the events surrounding the US–China trade wars and their estimated impact, see Haas and Denmark (2020).

It is important to note that the ERP can be higher or lower than the nominal rate of protection in the given industry, and it can be also negative. A high tariff rate on intermediate inputs (t_i) can have a significant negative impact on VAD (and thus on the income of factors of production) in the affected domestic industries.

To illustrate, consider a final product with a world price per unit at $250 and the cost of intermediate inputs at $200 per unit of output. If a country imposes a 20 per cent tariff on imports of the final product (output) and a 30 per cent tariff on imports of intermediate products (inputs), what will the ERP be? Inserting the given values into equation (7.4) yields equation (7.5) with an ERP of −20 per cent as VAD declines from $50 at world prices to $40 under the given tariff structure:

$$ERP = \frac{250(1+0.2) - 200(1+0.3)}{250 - 200} - 1 =$$
$$\frac{300 - 260}{50} - 1 = \frac{40}{50} - 1 = 0.8 - 1 = -0.2 = -20\%$$

(7.5)

The example demonstrates that to limit the negative impact of tariffs on domestic industries, it is more advantageous for countries to impose lower tariffs on inputs than on final products. This is referred to as *tariff escalation*.

Equations (7.3) and (7.4) are simplified versions of the ERP to demonstrate its workings conceptually. In practice, the ERP is calculated as the per unit difference between the nominal tariff on output and the weighted average of nominal tariffs on different inputs (for more information, see, e.g., WTO, 2015).[17]

Economists typically emphasize the benefits from free international trade rather than protectionism, but a few caveats are in order:

- The benefits from trade are typically realized at the aggregate/national level, while some groups will lose within each trading country and others will gain. Typically, successful exporters gain because they benefit from increased demand in global

---

17 For data on tariff rates and other trade policy measures on goods and services in different countries, you can refer to the WTO website at https://data.wto.org/en.

markets, while the factors of production employed in import-competing sectors lose as they see the demand for their products fall. In practice, this means that unskilled labour in high-income countries loses from international trade because the demand for unskilled labour in manufacturing has shifted to developing countries due to capital investment moving there to take advantage of low labour costs. At the same time, capital and high-skilled labour dominate export industries and tend to gain from international trade in developed economies.

- If factors of production are immobile (specific) and cannot easily relocate from declining industries to growing ones, they will suffer significant losses as a result of the ever-changing competitive landscape in globalized markets.
- Economic activity also tends to cluster in certain geographic areas to take advantage of *external economies of scale* – that is, average costs decreasing with the size of the industry in a certain geographic location even when individual firms are not as large as under internal economies of scale. External economies of scale can take place due to proximity to specific infrastructure and a relevant workforce. Geographic clustering of economic activity means that factors of production, including labour, need to move. Migration, including domestic migration within national borders, entails economic and social costs.
- Economists assume that because the gains to winners from trade typically outweigh the losses to those who are hurt by trade, the winners can and will compensate the losers. But this is not what happens in reality, because even when there is scope for such *Pareto improvement* in theory, compensatory schemes would need to be approved through the political process, not by economists. Redistribution would involve heavier taxation by certain groups, but that tends to be unpopular and/or not feasible in a global economy with mobile factors of production, especially capital, as discussed in chapter 6.
- The benefits from free trade are conditional on trade being free, but so-called *free trade agreements* are not what economists refer to as "free trade." Real-world free trade agreements are exclusive agreements akin to members-only clubs with benefits to members only while discriminating against non-members and distorting

economies and economic incentives. The list of exemptions to free trade under a typical free trade agreement is much longer than the agreement itself.

- The WTO is meant to liberalize trade in a non-discriminatory manner based on the *most-favoured-nation clause*, which requires member countries to extend the same benefits to all trading partners, but exceptions to this rule have been negotiated in the creation of the WTO. Specifically, free trade agreements as outlined above are one such exception, and sector-specific exemptions include trade in agriculture and textiles, for example. These sectors tend to be especially important for low-income developing countries, but due to these exemptions, their market access to high-income countries is often limited and distributional concerns are thus present not just within countries, but also between countries.

- In response to the above outlined concerns, some *fair trade* initiatives have emerged aimed at compensating developing country producers through higher prices paid to them. Fairness is a normative concept, which means that different individuals and groups will have a different, subjective understanding of what is or is not "fair." "Fair trade" can also be a political or marketing slogan, but it lacks definition for economic analysis and should thus be avoided. Instead, assessments should focus on the analysis of market competition (e.g., whether monopsonies, or dominant buyers, are present in certain markets that hurt small producers, and gains and losses to different groups).

- Dispute resolution is costly and lengthy, even though the WTO has made some progress in an effort to cut down on the time required to reach a ruling. Nevertheless, the available remedies, such as countervailing duties, for example, often end up hurting parties others than those intended to be induced into compliance.

Akman et al. (2018) provide a very useful, non-technical summary and analysis of the tensions related to international trade in the context of domestic policies and winners and losers from trade within economies. They argue for social safety nets for workers displaced by trade (or automation having similar impact), but they do not effectively account for the political feasibility of such compensatory mechanisms and the distributional conflict involved in those. The next chapter will delve into the analysis of social policies and distributional issues in more detail.

QUESTIONS FOR DISCUSSION AND SUGGESTIONS FOR FURTHER RESEARCH

1 Explore some possible motivations by the EU and China for unilateral action on raising environmental standards (i.e., even in the absence of cooperation by the United States and other large economies).
2 International economic sanctions such as trade embargos (export and import restrictions) against so-called "rogue" regimes are typically ineffective in exerting the intended political pressure or regime change. Analyze carefully the reasons behind the lack of efficacy of trade embargos as a political tool.

RESEARCH ADVICE: FOR ANALYSTS OF FINANCIAL (MONETARY, EXCHANGE RATE, FINANCIAL REGULATIONS) POLICIES IN A GLOBALIZED WORLD

Quantitative research tends to dominate the area of monetary policy analysis, but this is how warning signs for major crises have been missed. The best advice one can provide to analysts in this area includes the following:

• Qualitative assessment is just as important as quantitative analysis of data.
• Make sure to integrate economic and market research (economists: make friends with traders in financial markets!). Economic and market research are often segregated in organizations, and this will lead to contradictions in assumptions and frameworks of analysis, as well as missing important information.
• Looking at past data and experiences is not enough to predict the future because financial innovation and structural changes are likely to drive the outcomes.

- Monetary policy analysis also needs to take into consideration the fiscal policy stance and the external liability position of private companies for a complete balance of payments analysis.
- Be aware of the political context for changes in policies, uncertainty and economic realities, and how political pressures may affect policy declarations, but also the work of private actors such as rating agencies.
- Financial markets are global markets and developments in other parts of the world will likely affect local markets and economies even if no major economic ties are apparent.

CHAPTER EIGHT

Social Policy

Social policy encompasses a wide range of government policies and programs that aim to benefit the population as a whole or support vulnerable subgroups. Policies adopted in response to the COVID-19 pandemic that transferred public funds to individuals and businesses can be viewed as social policies that aim to have broad benefit (Béland et al., 2021). Targeted programs include those that provide financial support to low-income households, the elderly, disabled, sick, unemployed, or young people. Social policies tend to involve taxation and redistribution. Some social policies may involve compulsory contributions from individual recipients or their employers (e.g., retirement benefits and health insurance fall into this category). Other programs may be financed directly from the government budget with deficit financing secured against future tax revenue (e.g., COVID-19 supports). Figure 8.1 depicts the percentage of the population covered by three broad types of social programs across countries with different income levels. Social programs are in general divided into the following categories:

- *Social insurance* includes, for example, health and disability insurance and old-age contributory pensions. Social insurance involves contributions by individuals and/or employers and is typically linked to employment status.

- *Social assistance* consists of unconditional and conditional transfers, social pensions, typically aimed at alleviating poverty and/or inequality.
- *Labour market programs* are contributory and non-contributory in nature, including unemployment insurance, wage subsidies, training programs, and employment intermediation services (World Bank, 2018).

Figure 8.1 illustrates that large segments of the population are not covered by social programs, especially in low-income countries. This is unfortunately not surprising given the limited taxable capacity of low-income countries (refer to section 6.1.2 on taxable capacity and its determinants for a refresher). Higher-income countries tend to allocate a higher proportion of GDP to social programs. In these countries, relatively efficient tax collection systems and lower government borrowing costs help finance multipronged welfare systems that offer nearly universal access to education, health care, unemployment, and retirement support. A relatively small tax base combined with higher borrowing costs make financing social programs a pervasive challenge in lower-income countries. Limited capacity to finance social programs with large positive externalities, such as education and health care, undermines the prospects for building human capital, productivity growth, and economic development. So-called *poverty traps* emerge that are nearly impossible to escape, as they may persist over generations.

To what extent are social policies driven by ideology, special interests, economic constraints, and institutional structures? In this chapter, we analyze the determinants, key design features, and impacts of a number of social policies, including health insurance, retirement benefits, education, and housing as an increasingly pressing social policy issue. This chapter adopts the broad view that all these policies affect social welfare and social mobility and are therefore integral parts of social policy beyond the more traditional concepts of social insurance, social assistance, and more narrowly defined labour market policies. Reading this chapter should enable you to do the following:

- understand and analyze distributional conflicts involved in social policy design and development in areas such as health insurance, retirement, education, housing, and other related policies

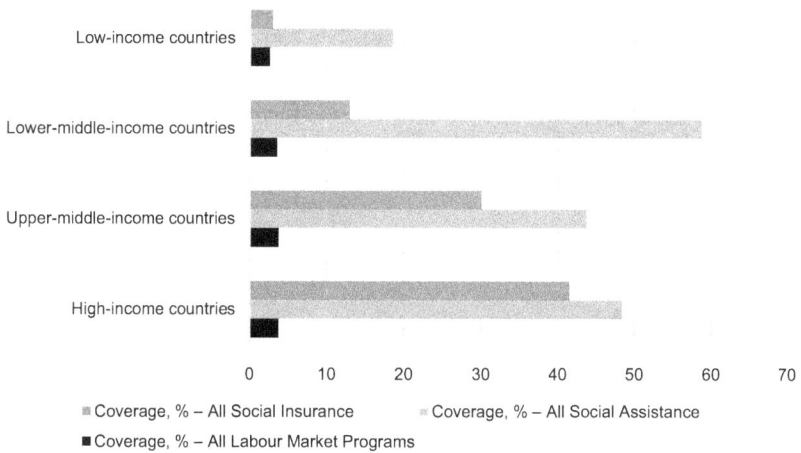

Figure 8.1. Percentage of population participating in social protection programs across countries (based on latest available data between 2010 and 2021)

Source: WDI, ASPIRE database.

- be aware of major empirical trends in the funding, risk, and outcome profiles in the areas of health, retirement, and education in a comparative setting across high-income OECD countries
- analyze the impact of health insurance, education, retirement, and housing policies on individuals, businesses, and economic structures
- appreciate and analyze the impact of institutional, political, demographic, and economic structures on social policy formation

8.1 IDEOLOGY, INCENTIVES, AND INSTRUMENTS

Social policy is usually associated with the existence of social inequality and political demand to develop a more equitable society. Ideological conceptualizations of equity can vary significantly across societies, political parties, and voters. In general, there are two basic approaches to defining equity that are relevant for explaining different classes of social programs and their impacts:

- *Equality of opportunity*: This view of social policy emphasizes the importance of programs that help expand opportunities for individuals and groups lacking access to basic services and improving their chances of success in the future. Universal access to basic education and health care are social policies that aim to promote equality of opportunity. Civil rights that aim to "level the playing field" by restricting discrimination against marginalized groups also aim to promote equality of opportunity, for instance in terms of access to public services or employment opportunities.

- *Equality of outcomes*: This view of social policy recognizes that individual outcomes do not fully depend on choices individuals make in life and that regardless of the level of initial opportunities, luck matters. The onset of health issues and disabilities, for example, can undermine all the advantages of past opportunities and skills one has gained to make a living. Disability, unemployment, housing, and old age benefit programs providing a minimum level of income for people with no or very low income reflect a desire for more equitable outcomes.

Some social programs are designed to have concentrated benefits for a targeted subgroup of the population. Other social policies can have multifaceted spillovers with social benefits beyond the particular targeted subgroup. Public investment in early education of children, for example, is critical to human capital development and associated with reductions in criminal activity and better health outcomes (Cunha & Heckman, 2007; García et al., 2022). Public expenditures on social policies such as early education can therefore lead to overall reductions in public sector spending in other areas, such as the criminal justice system, health care, and unemployment benefits. In addition to social *equity* justifications noted above, positive network effects/externalities from some social policies improve the *efficiency* of market systems and public finances.

The case of access to basic health care provides an informative example of how equity and efficiency considerations can complement each other. A health care system that provides equitable access helps promote equality of outcomes. At the same time, ensuring that people have access to basic health services reduces the risk of more serious health challenges, disability, and unemployment. Universal access to basic health care services therefore benefits both the individuals and their employers. It also may reduce demand and generate cost reductions in the delivery of other social programs where demand for benefits is negatively correlated with health outcomes (e.g., unemployment, disability). In reducing the incidence of adverse outcomes that lead to absenteeism and unemployment, universal access to basic health care promotes equality of opportunities and outcomes.

The incidence of the taxation required for delivering social benefits can generate political resistance by those who are paying more into the system than they are benefiting from it. For example, some people may find contributing to other people's retirement, health care, education, or housing to be against their self-interest. Such a group may be more open to voting for parties with ideologies that emphasize individual responsibility and propose reductions to social programs. In high-income countries with a large and aging middle class, political support for social policies that promote equality of opportunity and outcomes tends to be relatively stable and popular (Rehm, 2011). At least in part, this is because the middle class tends to benefit relatively more than the very rich or the very poor from government social policies, an empirical regularity known as *Director's law*: "Median voters or the middle class disproportionately and systematically benefit from public spending on public goods" (Hillman, 2009, p. 475).

The consequence of this empirical regularity is substantive ideological convergence of party platforms and policies relating to major social programs that benefit and are popular with the middle classes. While there might be some differences in the design and implementation of social programs that benefit the middle class, there is increasing agreement among left- or right-leaning parties about the need for such programs in middle- and high-income countries.

The tendency of social policy to disproportionately and systematically benefit the middle class has implications for people with the highest and the lowest incomes in society. Small groups of very high-income earners have incentives to organize and oppose more taxation and redistribution to the middle class. They also have incentives to build coalitions with those with low incomes who perceive that they are receiving limited benefits from social programs designed to benefit the middle class. Coalitions of very high- and low-income voters can emerge to oppose social support and redistribution to the middle class. Anti-government ideologies shared among right-leaning very high- and low-income groups in many countries partly reflect this

context of discontent with programs that are perceived to disproportionately benefit others.

Instruments used for financing social programs can further impact
how the costs of such policies are distributed within a population and the
political context shaping social policy. *Progressive taxes* on the income of
the high earners represent the most equitable approach to financing social
programs that could benefit both the middle class and the very poor. However, increasing marginal tax rates on the very rich increases tax avoidance
by people with resources to move their wealth (e.g., taking their money
"offshore"). Progressive taxation of income can become increasingly
problematic over time, as going beyond certain marginal tax thresholds
tends to undermine economic incentives of individuals to increase their
incomes and productivity growth, and they may seek to relocate to jurisdictions with lower tax rates. High-income and upper-middle-class voters
have incentives to oppose using progressive taxation regimes to finance
the provision of public goods and social programs that benefit the lower
middle class and those with little or no income.

The economic and political limits of progressive taxation create
pressure for the adoption of more regressive sources of tax revenue
that disproportionately impact those with lower income. Low-income
groups face significant collective action problems in organizing to
defend themselves against the adoption of *regressive taxes*. The result
has been growing reliance on regressive taxes to finance public goods.
In particular, consumption/sales/value-added taxes that apply to
purchases of goods and services have become an increasingly popular
complement to income taxes as instruments of redistribution. Other
examples of regressive taxes and/or mandated fees increasingly used
to finance social programs include payroll taxes on workers as their
contribution to public pension and unemployment programs. Since
lower-income people pay more of their income in sales and payroll
taxes, these methods for financing government expenditures can lead
to situations where lower-income people end up subsidizing the delivery of social policies that disproportionately benefit the middle class.

The approach to allocating social support can also provide a basis
for assessing the distribution of its impacts. *Cash payments/transfers*
that provide people with a basic income represent the most efficient
approach for targeting those most in need to ensure they have access
to essential goods and services such as housing, food, education, and

health care. On the other hand, *tax deductions/credits* disproportionately benefit the middle class with sufficient taxable income to take advantage of such deductions. For example, tax deductions related to home ownership benefit those in the upper middle class who can afford to purchase a home. People with lower incomes who rent do not benefit from such programs. People with no or very low income are particularly at risk of becoming unhoused without access to social housing and/or cash transfers that cover all or part of their rent (e.g., people with disabilities, mental health issues, older adults with limited savings, or working families with children).

Beyond housing, affordability of other essential inputs such as food and health care is a common challenge for those with no or very low income. This is particularly the case when regressive taxes that disproportionately impact people with relatively low income are used by governments to generate revenue (e.g., sales taxes, import tariffs). Some governments have attempted to control the prices of necessities by imposing a price cap. In general, this can be done in two ways: by imposing a restriction on prices, or by subsidizing consumer prices by covering the gap between market prices and the capped prices to compensate producers for their loss. The second approach has significant budgetary consequences, and any government that attempts to remove such subsidies will be extremely unpopular and risk losing re-election. As a result, consumer subsidies tend to persist for a very long time and may lead to the accumulation of government debt. Below-market prices also provide incentives to overuse such resources when they are abundant; gasoline subsidies in some oil-rich developing countries are one such example. Other examples may include putting price caps on food staples for the benefit of large urban populations, but those hurt the farmers in rural areas, who tend to be especially poor in developing countries.

While the simple price cap approach limits government expenditure and puts the onus on third parties that are presumed to be blamed for the high prices, price caps can backfire, as the suppliers may be simply unwilling to provide a good or service at a lower price, or may provide lower-quality substitutes. When that occurs, shortages will follow, ultimately hurting the target beneficiaries of a price cap. A high price is a symptom of a problem, and imposing a price cap is "dealing" only with a symptom. Instead, the root causes need to be identified: Supply shortages or lack of competition, for example, and addressing those causes of high prices will yield more effective solutions.

If affordability is the problem for certain groups, targeted cash payments to those below a certain income threshold represent a more efficient and effective approach to reaching the objective. However, the administrative burden of such means-tested programs entails significant transactions costs both for governments and for the target populations facing bottlenecks and delays. Therefore, streamlining the administration of such programs and cutting down on red tape are required for effectively reaching the target populations. In some instances, such as the COVID-19 pandemic, for example, governments may decide to forgo the administrative costs and risks of not reaching the intended beneficiaries by implementing transfers to all without a means test. The downside is that even those who do not need such transfers will receive them and the budgetary implications for governments can be significant.

BOX 8.1. UNIVERSAL BASIC INCOME

Means testing based on income can be used to exclude those in the middle class from transfers intended for the very poor and thus target available funds at those who need it most. In sharp contrast to this usual approach stand universal basic income (UBI) systems that provide unconditional cash transfers without means testing or work requirements to all individuals regardless of their income. While variants of this idea have been around for more than 200 years, it has gained increasing academic attention over the past few decades (Bidadanure, 2019). This attention has led to a number of experiments by governments around the world to explore the impacts of UBI programs (Chrisp et al., 2022). These tend to be small-scale experiments and have shown some positive impacts on UBI recipient well-being.

However, deploying large-scale UBI programs at the national level would be extremely costly and has proven to be unpopular. Lack of political support for UBI programs may seem surprising because they would benefit the middle-class median voters, but they may also see it as an increase in their tax burden, and/or it may run counter to ideological beliefs by some voters as to what constitutes social justice. For example, a 2020 Pew Research Center poll found that young adults in the United States favour UBI by roughly two-to-one, but the majority of older people oppose it (72 per cent in the 65+ category and 59 per cent in the 50–64 age group) (Gilberstadt, 2020).

QUESTIONS FOR DISCUSSION AND FURTHER RESEARCH

1 After years of rising food prices, in early June 2024 the federal New Democratic Party in Canada called for a price cap on some basic grocery staples (Djuric, 2024). Do you expect such a proposal to be approved and reach its intended outcomes? Explain why.
2 What are the similarities and differences in public attitudes towards UBI in Canada, in European countries, and other countries around the world compared to the United States?
3 Rising income inequality is well documented in high-income OECD countries. What is the public's attitude towards policies addressing inequality versus poverty?

8.2 MARKET FAILURES AND RISK AVERSION

In the case of public goods with positive network effects/externalities, such as education and health care, private actors may not adequately take into account the total private and social benefits from the good. This leads to under-supply, under-investment, and/or under-consumption compared to socially optimal levels. Public investments in education, health care, roads, and Internet infrastructure help expand supply and access to essential inputs individuals and communities need to have an opportunity to prosper. This class of policies enhances equality of opportunity ex ante, while providing a basis for generating positive network effects that come from a more educated, healthier, and connected population.

Conceptualization of social policy as a form of insurance emphasizes uncertainty in ex post outcomes, the incomplete nature of information, and the potential for under-provisioning of insurance in the market equilibrium (Akerlof, 1970; Rothschild & Stiglitz, 1976; Moene & Wallerstein, 2001; Chetty & Finkelstein, 2013). People are generally risk-averse and would purchase insurance against adverse events and outcomes as long as the insurance is available and affordable (i.e., becoming sick and disabled, unemployed, etc.). Private or public insurance companies have the capacity to pool individual risks and use the law of large numbers to develop predictable models of potential payouts. While private insurers may offer products that people can buy to pay for the costs of adverse events, insurance companies have incentives not to cover, or to charge a high price, for costly events and/or high-risk individuals. Examples of the high price and rationing in private systems include insurance companies not covering pre-existing health conditions, young drivers perceived to be risky, or entire communities vulnerable to flooding or wildfires.

One way of trying to address these market failures in the provision of insurance is through regulatory mandates that require private insurers to cover those in higher risk categories that they otherwise would not. An example is prohibiting insurance companies from refusing to provide health insurance coverage to people with pre-existing medical conditions or young drivers that recently received their licences. Doing so can have the effect of increasing potential payouts insurers have to pay over the entire pool of relatively low- and high-risk individuals in their portfolio, driving up prices, and reducing the affordability of insurance to those with relatively lower income.

There are several potential solutions to this problem. The public sector can act as an insurer itself for pre-existing conditions and high-risk individuals, but that can become cost-prohibitive. Alternatively, the public sector can pool risk across the entire population and compete with private insurers with a lower cost/risk profile, or prohibit private insurance altogether to allow for more efficient risk-pooling. National single-payer health insurance systems are one such example, and they also offer the benefit of better bargaining power with respect to pharmaceutical companies and health care providers, leading to lower per capita health care costs altogether.

However, opposition to eliminating a private insurance option can be strong both from the sector and from voters who prefer to have a choice. As a result, governments may limit their actions to mandating that individuals and/or their employers contribute to health and social insurance programs, thus enhancing the risk-pooling properties of any insurance program and avoiding the moral hazard problem of some low-risk individuals opting out of insurance when there is an option to do so. When insurance contributions are mandated as a percentage of income, they also have the properties of progressive taxation and redistribution.

When competition is limited among insurance providers, the government may regulate prices and impose caps on the price of insurance (i.e., insurance premiums). However, the economic fundamentals cannot be ignored in such cases either, and the prices have to be high enough to avoid supply shortages and ensure the financial viability of the insurance underwriters.

The insurance analogy provides a basis for explaining why the level of social expenditures and variety of other social policies tend to grow overtime and are higher in high-income countries. As traditional family supports for disabilities, unemployment, and old age become constrained with urbanization and demographic changes, the demand for government-provided insurance increases. Although private insurance in various forms (e.g., family, charities, insurance brokers) might be available for covering some risks, economic theory and the history of growth in social policies suggests that private market forces lead to a suboptimal level of insurance provision and drive social policy development.

BOX 8.2. HEALTH INSURANCE POLICY IN THE UNITED STATES

In the early 2000s, the United States was the only high-income country without universal health care coverage in the world. Since its adoption in 2010, the *Patient Protection and Affordable Care Act*,[1] commonly referred to as Obamacare, has remained controversial in the United States with multiple attempts to repeal the legislation. Kimakova (2010) aimed to explain why it is so difficult to adopt mandatory health care coverage for everyone in the United States by highlighting the redistributive elements of the policy:

- Universal health care coverage inevitably entails at least some degree of public health care coverage, and thus an increase in the burden of taxation, which falls disproportionally on labour and small businesses (as opposed to large businesses with greater mobility across jurisdictions).
- At the same time, US voter preferences in general are not in favour of higher taxes and redistribution.
- Compounding the issue is that the US political system has multiple veto points, making it easier to challenge federal Obamacare at the state level or through the courts.

---

1 H.R.3590-111th Congress (2009–10): *Patient Protection and Affordable Care Act* (2010, March 23), available at https://www.congress.gov/bill/111th-congress/house-bill/3590.

8.3 PUBLIC VERSUS PRIVATE SUPPLY OF GOODS AND SERVICES

Some public social programs are delivered by central government public sector agencies to take advantage of economies of scale, but more often the funds are transferred to lower levels of government (provincial/state, local) and non-profit organizations and delivered through their agencies and organizations. Governments may also limit their involvement to funding social services and leave the supply to the private sector, with the goods or services procured at market or regulated/negotiated prices.

There are several reasons why public funding of social services does not necessarily coincide with the direct public sector provision of those goods and services:

- Public sector employment has in general declined since the 1990s, based on both cost pressures in a strongly unionized environment and ideological shifts regarding the degree of government involvement in the economy and society.

- Lack of competition in service delivery can lead to limited incentives for maintaining quality, and introducing competition through non-profit and private sector service-delivery organizations aims to correct for that.
- When there is a great deal of diversity in communities, the heterogeneity of preferences leads to increased demands for decentralization and autonomy in the allocation of social spending. Canada in particular stands out, with a great deal of government funding for non-profit organizations for the delivery of social services in a decentralized manner.
- The need for innovation – for instance, in light of the fast pace of technological change – has necessitated public-private partnerships and/or public procurement of goods and services from private companies. The most obvious examples of this are in the health care area with the public procurement of pharmaceuticals, partnerships or subsidies for the development of vaccines (e.g., COVID-19 vaccines), or the services of health care professionals employed by private companies.

Private sector involvement in the supply of goods and services in the social policy arena has brought about benefits in terms of expanding the supply of resources for the delivery of goods and services, variety, and quality improvement. Whether it has brought about cost savings is a more difficult question to answer, and likely depends on the specific category of goods and services and market conditions. However, there have been failures as well. Notable examples include attempts to privatize the delivery of water infrastructure in developing countries advocated by the World Bank in the 1990s, or more recently emerging reports of substandard conditions in some private foster care agencies in Ontario, Canada, or private for-profit immigrant detention centres in the United States (see, e.g., Russell et al., 2002; Schwab, 2024).

Private sector incentives emphasize profit maximization and thus may not align with the social justice objectives of the public or non-profit sectors. Discipline and compliance with contract terms need to be backed with credible enforcement through public oversight and the threat of competition. When either competition or resources for public oversight are lacking, the outcomes are unlikely to be aligned with social justice objectives, and the vulnerable populations that social programs are targeting to serve are likely to be put at risk.

In the case of water infrastructure privatization attempts mentioned above, natural monopolies were handed over to private companies. Without competition or regulation, it is not surprising that they charged very high prices. In the case of private foster care homes, limited and lax oversight have arguably contributed to the problems.

Some single-payer health care systems limit the supply of health care services to public sector providers. Equity considerations are cited as the main reason for the policy stance to prevent a two-tier health care system that would prioritize the wealthy. Canada falls into this category, with only public hospitals being authorized, even though general practitioners and specialist medical practitioners can operate as private for-profit or non-profit entities. In light of the long wait times for surgeries, in 2024 the Ontario government started to experiment with allowing private clinics to offer certain types of surgeries (see, e.g., The Canadian Press, 2024). Critics argue that the move will only increase surgical wait times because it is not the shortage of surgical facilities, but shortages of qualified staff, that are driving the results. There are reports of unused MRI machines and surgical rooms, while the Ontario government's new policy does not include a plan for expanding the supply of qualified surgical staff such as doctors and nurses. The concern is that qualified staff will simply move from public hospitals to private clinics, thus further exacerbating the staffing shortage, wait times, and the financial situation of public hospitals on top of that.[1]

The Conservative Ontario government promised that patients will not see increased costs, as private clinics will simply receive the same payment from public insurance as public hospitals. Such models of public and private supply do successfully coexist in EU countries and

---

1   Health care delivery is a provincial jurisdiction in Canada, and in Ontario hospitals are typically independent crown corporations, hence public (more information can be found at https://www.ontario.ca/page/ontarios-public-hospitals).
Private hospitals are banned in Ontario with the exception of three that have been grandparented by legislation. In general, private organizations can be for-profit or non-profit, as per chapter 3.

elsewhere, but concerns remain as to whether the Conservatives will modify the original plans in the future – for instance, paying a premium to private clinics over public hospitals for the same services, perhaps utilizing the speed of service delivery as a justification for such a move.

The shortage of nurses in public institutions has been of particular concern, given the attempt by the same Conservative Ontario government to limit broader public sector employees' wage increases to 1 per cent per year for three years by legislation. Ontario Bill 124, titled *Protecting a Sustainable Public Sector for Future Generations Act*, was enacted in 2019 and affected collective bargaining during the COVID-19 pandemic and extraordinary pressures on public sector employees, especially nurses.[2] It also coincided with increases in inflation due to the pandemic, thus further eroding the real wages of public sector employees. Public sector employees challenged the constitutionality of Bill 124, and the Ontario Court of Appeal ruled in 2024 that Bill 124 violated the collective bargaining rights of public sector employees and was therefore unconstitutional.[3] The Ontario government and broader public sector institutions subsequently faced a multi-billion-dollar increase in expenditure due to retroactive pay to public sector employees (see, e.g., Jones, 2024).

BOX 8.3. THE HIV/AIDS EPIDEMIC AND THE SUPPLY OF GENERIC DRUGS

The World Health Organization (WHO, 2023) estimated that 40 million lives (mid-range of estimates) have been lost to the HIV/AIDS epidemic globally and that another 39 million people were living with the virus at the end of 2022. Two-thirds of those infected live in Africa and the continent also bore most of the death burden. Some of the most affected countries in Africa have reportedly reached 20–30 per cent prevalence rates among the population at some point (see, e.g., WHO, 2025).

---

2 See Bill 124, Parliament 42, Session 1, Legislative Assembly of Ontario at Ontario (2019).
3 See the decision in *Ontario English Catholic Teachers Association v. Ontario (Attorney General)* (2024).

In 2022, an estimated 630 000 people (mid-range of estimates) died from HIV-related causes (WHO, 2023). As tragic as
it is, HIV-related mortality has decreased significantly from its
peak of approximately 2 million deaths in 2004 and 1.3 million in
2010. The turnaround has been made possible through greater
access to antiretroviral therapy: As of December 2022, an estimated 29.8 million people had access to such therapy (roughly
76 per cent of the infected population) compared to only 7.7 million
in 2010 (UNAIDS, 2023).

The process by which such improvement in access to antiretroviral therapy materialized is important to note and analyze.

First of all, public- and private-funded research and development (R&D) in pharmaceutical companies clearly played a crucial
role in this progress. However, R&D costs are in general high, and
pharmaceutical companies recoup those costs by charging high
prices on the resulting products for a certain number of years
while the product is granted patent protection. Once the patent expires, generic drug makers can legally produce the drugs
based on the same formulas, but in different, typically lower-cost,
production facilities. From an economic point of view, patents are
granted to incentivize profit-seeking private companies to invest
in R&D. Time is of the essence with deadly diseases, and without
the help of private resources (capital and human resources), it
would likely take much longer to find viable treatments and many
more lives would be lost in the meantime.

The success of new antiretroviral drugs around the year 2000
was much welcome news, as they would enable HIV-positive individuals to survive and live productive lives. However, the new
therapies came with a price tag of approximately USD $10,000–
$15,000 per year per patient ('t Hoen et al., 2011). With the
majority of infected persons and deaths located in Africa, in
some of the world's poorest countries, the outlook remained very
grim for those populations due to the lack of affordability.

Affordability was lacking because of the patent protections,
even though the marginal costs of producing the drugs on a
large scale (after the R&D has been successful and completed)

was low. Patent protections in the pharmaceutical business were strengthened by the 1994 round of international trade negotiations and the emergent Trade-Related Aspects of Intellectual Property Rights (TRIPS) agreement that became part of the establishment of the WTO in the same year.[1] High-income countries advocated for TRIPS, and with their strong bargaining position, developing countries that wanted to be part of the WTO and enjoy access to markets in high-income economies had to agree to TRIPS and the protections it afforded to drug companies.

Several developing countries, including South Africa, Brazil, and India, challenged TRIPS and the pharmaceutical companies in various ways on the grounds of public health licensing. Under compulsory licensing provisions for public health, authorities can compel pharmaceutical companies to license generic production for a set fee. The patent-holding companies in response sued the South African government of Nelson Mandela in 1998. In 2001, an Indian generic drug maker produced generic versions of antiretroviral therapies and made them available for about USD $350 per year per patient (i.e., less than USD $1 per day), which demonstrated to the world the marginal cost of production and the marked difference relative to the prices charged by the patent-holders.

Advocacy groups and associations of health care professionals organized public meetings and protests in response. The media attention and public pressure on the pharmaceutical companies was mounting until, in 2001, they dropped their lawsuit against the South African government for patent violations and agreed to provide the licensing to generic drug companies in developing countries at low cost (for more detail on related events and actions taken by different actors in this process, see 't Hoen et al., 2011; Gore et al., 2023).

In the face of preventable deaths and suffering, the global public deemed it unethical to deny treatment once it was successfully developed, and the pharmaceutical companies were forced to reconsider their stance on licensing due to bad publicity and mounting political pressure. In the meantime, many lives that

could have been saved under a more responsive system of intellectual property regulations were needlessly lost.

---

1   The full text of the TRIPS agreement is available at https://www.wto.org
    /english/docs_e/legal_e/27-trips_01_e.htm.

QUESTIONS FOR DISCUSSION AND FURTHER RESEARCH

1   Under what conditions can public and private sector service
    providers successfully coexist and benefit patients under single-
    payer public health insurance systems?
2   How are technological improvements and rising costs likely to
    affect health care policies in the future?
3   As illustrated by declining vaccination rates around the world and the
    word "anti-waxxer" now being an official word in dictionaries (defined
    by Merriam-Webster as "a person who opposes the use of some or
    all vaccines, regulations mandating vaccination, or usually both"[4]),
    demand for health care services can be a limiting factor in achieving
    the desired health outcomes, not just supply. What policies are likely
    to be effective or counterproductive in combating such trends?

BOX 8.4. EMPLOYING "NUDGING" IN THE IMPLEMENTATION OF POLICIES AND PROGRAMS

Government policies and programs often aim to induce behaviour
that is deemed to be socially desirable. The monitoring, administration, and enforcement of policies is often quite costly and unpopular among the electorate. Consequently, governments have been
looking for ways to reduce costs while also aiming to appear less
authoritarian or patronizing in the inducement of desired behaviour.

Some solutions have been offered through advancements in
behavioural economics. So-called "nudging" strategies, named

---

4   See anti-vaxxer, in *Merriam-Webster.com dictionary*, https://www.merriam-webster.
    com/dictionary/anti-vaxxer.

after the work of Thaler and Sunstein (2008), tend to focus on the manner in which options are structured and presented to individuals. The "choice architecture" is designed to make desired behaviour more appealing and inefficient choices less likely. Such strategies are commonly used in the area of public health, for example, to induce individuals to keep up with recommended vaccinations, choose healthy eating options, exercise, etc.

Another example of nudging strategies is to alter default options for certain programs. For instance, automatically enrolling people into retirement plans or into an organ donor program is likely to increase participation rates even if there is the possibility to opt out. The idea is that people are likely to remain under the default option because actively changing one's enrolment status involves transaction costs in terms of individual time and effort, and individuals find it more convenient to avoid those transaction costs.

Another option in nudging strategies is to artificially increase the transaction costs of engaging in undesirable behaviour by making it inconvenient to engage in certain activities. For example, governments may employ nudging strategies that involve restricting options, for example, where and when to buy or use cigarettes or alcoholic beverages.

Many governments and large agencies now have behavioural insight units that support the analysis and design of policies that aim to nudge individual behaviour to align with policy priorities (see, e.g., Halpern & Sanders, 2016). Due to this demand, behavioural public policy (BPP) has emerged as a subfield in the study and practice of public policy. The effectiveness of nudging strategies that are evolving across policy areas is highly context-dependent and can be limited in some cases due to the heterogeneity of preferences and individual agency.

In practice, binding mandates and behavioural modification strategies tend to complement each other. They can also backfire and create resistance by the public. Burgess (2012) and Banerjee et al. (2024) argue for the greater inclusion of individual agency, that is, the ability to form choices and to act on them, enhancing people's competence to make decisions. The design and evaluation of such strategies represents a growing area in the practice of public policy. Due to uncertainties about the distribution of individual preferences and response functions across populations, experimentation and learning through trial and error are integral to improving the efficacy of behavioural modification strategies used by the public sector to achieve policy objectives.

It should be noted that nudging strategies have also been employed by political strategists and campaigns and can affect election results. Growth in behavioural data harvested from online activities of individuals creates a wide range of opportunities for the design and implementation of nudging strategies by policy-makers, political parties, and resourceful interest groups trying to shape individual political and economic decisions.

QUESTIONS FOR DISCUSSION AND FURTHER RESEARCH

1 Can you provide examples of successful nudging strategies employed by policy-makers or political actors?
2 Can you identify instances in which the deployment of nudging strategies has created resistance by the target groups or yielded unintended consequences?

8.4 RETIREMENT

Demographic trends and structural change affect retirement policy. Life expectancy typically increases with per capita income and improvements in health care technology. As industrialization and urbanization accompany per capita income increases, these structural changes typically lead to lower birth rates and the disintegration of traditional families in which the children take care of their parents in old age. As a result, the demand for public pension systems increases with per capita income.

There are two main types of pension systems:

- *Pay-as-you-go systems*, in which the pension is a simple transfer/redistribution from the working population to the elderly
- *Fully funded or asset-backed systems*, which involve saving for retirement and investing the funds in well-diversified portfolios; the interest earned on the investment is added to the fund, and the retirees draw on their accumulated savings when reaching retirement

Size matters for retirement funds: The more resources from diverse populations are pooled together, the more viable a pension system/fund becomes. Pension systems can be public or private, with private pensions offered by large companies to their employees, or by financial institutions to individuals who are not employees of large companies.

Even if pensions are typically co-financed by employees and employers, it is important to keep in mind that, ultimately, employers look at total compensation – that is, if pension contributions are large, this is likely to have a negative impact on wages as a compensating mechanism.

As income per capita grows, life expectancy increases and the birth rate declines. There are several factors that contribute to increasing the opportunity costs of having children – for a refresher, see section 2.2 in chapter 2 – but the overall result is that the number of retirees relative to the working age population increases. Figure 8.2 captures this demographic trend from 1952 to 2022 and includes (medium-variant) projections for 2052 and 2082 for select countries. The demographic old-age to working-age ratio is defined as the number of individuals aged 65 and over per 100 people aged between 20 and 64 (OECD, 2023b). The figure shows dramatic changes in the ratio of the number of old-age persons to the working-age population in OECD countries and large developing countries with rapid economic growth in recent decades, such as China and India. Canada, the United States, the EU, and other average OECD countries are expected to reach 40–50+ per cent ratios of old-age to working-age persons by 2052 and over 60 per cent by 2082. South Korea's ratio is projected to reach nearly 120 per cent, which means the number of elderly will actually exceed

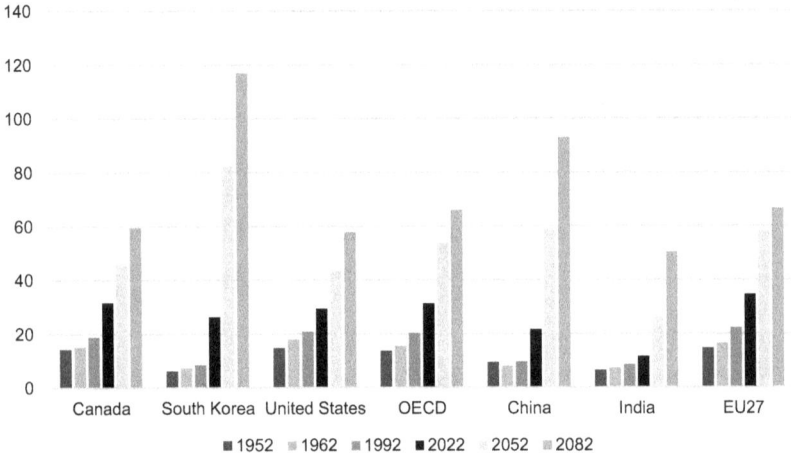

Figure 8.2. Demographic old-age to working-age ratio: historical and projected values, 1952–2082
Source: OECD (2023b).

the working-age population by nearly 20 per cent by 2082. China is a close second, with the elderly population nearly matching the working-age group at 93 per cent by that time.

Based on these projections, the *pay-as-you-go pension systems* that rely on the fact that the working-age population is large enough to finance the retirement benefits of the elderly are becoming insolvent. This has prompted many governments around the world to switch from pay-as-you-go pension systems to fully funded/asset-backed ones.

It is important to note that fully funded/asset-backed pension systems have not eliminated all the problems. Given that everyone is forced to save for retirement by policy (to avoid the moral hazard problem of individuals not saving and expecting the state to bail them out when they are old), large pools of savings are channelled into the same asset markets. This means that all the fully funded pension funds – no matter how well-diversified their portfolios are – are still exposed to *systemic risk* that cannot be eliminated. This was well illustrated by the 2007–9 financial crisis that started in the United States with its real estate market (see box 7.1 in chapter 7), which extended to financial institutions (banks, insurance companies, etc.) and quickly spread around the world, given how interconnected markets (especially financial markets) are in a globalized world.

In recognition of the risks involved in fully funded/asset-backed systems exposed to systemic risk, there has been another structural shift in pensions systems from those with *defined benefits* (guaranteed level of pension) to *defined contribution* systems (no guaranteed pension level and the retirees are exposed to the market risk).

In practical terms, this means that even if one does all the right things, saving for retirement throughout their productive years, they may end up with a significant shortfall in expected retirement benefits – depending on how the financial markets perform (grow, stagnate, or decline). Current and future retirees in high-income countries are likely to be worse off relative to previous generations. We also see the movement in policy from mandatory retirement at a specific age to either explicitly raising the normal retirement age or introducing more flexibility and encouraging workers to remain in the labour market longer. Some choose to work longer because they need to work (due to the negative wealth effects they have experienced as a result of market crashes), and others choose to work longer because their expected lifespan is longer and they want to remain active longer. It follows that the rate of labour force participation of the elderly is now on the rise in Canada and in other countries. The COVID-19 pandemic hampered this trend to some degree, given the disproportionate risks to the elderly from the disease, but there are indications that the rates of labour force participation by the elderly are returning to pre-pandemic levels.

While there have been government bailouts of financial institutions and car manufacturers in the face of financial crises in the late 2000s, there have not been government bailouts of pension systems (public or private) that experienced significant negative effects. Instead, retirees have been forced to bear the burden of the new risks – despite the fact that retirees tend to be more active voters than many other groups.

For an analysis of pension coverage trends in the Canadian market, including coverage by gender, age, level of education, and industry, see Drolet and Morissette (2014) and Statistics Canada (2023a). For broader international comparisons, see OECD (2023b).

BOX 8.5. DISABILITY AND PUBLIC POLICY

An informative example of the insurance analogy is enhancing accessibility and social support for people with disabilities. At any point in time, only a minority of people are, or have family members who are, disabled. Over time, however, most people are likely to become disabled in ways that limit their ability to engage in economic and social activities. Families and non-governmental social support networks provide some measure of insurance against the risks and costs of becoming disabled. People with relatively high income may be able to absorb the loss of income and substantive health care costs associated with a serious disability, but family and private networks and wealth would not be sufficient for most people. Limited information at the individual and family level about the likelihood and impacts of becoming disabled generates a suboptimal supply/demand state in provisioning for insurance for the possibility of physical or mental disability.

Complementary mechanisms have evolved that aim to mitigate against the risk a serious disability and/or health challenge poses to individuals and communities:

- *Safety regulations*: While some causes of disability are hard to predict and counteract, others are more predictable and may be preventable by reducing their incidence. Regulating safety of consumer products and workplaces aim to limit hazards to individual health and "accidents." Examples include banning dangerous chemicals associated with serious illnesses in consumer products or mandating hard hats in construction areas.
- *Benefits targeted at individuals*: Since having a disability has a large negative impact on earning capacity, disability benefits in terms of cash transfers are a form of insurance against the adverse impacts of the hard to predict state of the world. Determining who is sufficiently disabled (or not) to qualify for targeted disability benefits can be challenging, controversial, and costly. Means testing can also be used to target benefits at individuals and families that need it most versus the general population.

- *Accessibility policy*: Having a disability undermines opportunities for individuals to go to school, work, and participate in social activities. Policies that promote accessibility to public services and private workplaces aim to reduce the barriers to social and economic participation by individuals with disabilities. In addition to this private benefit, social policies that promote accessibility can have positive spillover effects by expanding the labour pool that is available to businesses, enriching workplaces, and minimizing the need to provide direct cash benefits to people who can support themselves. Making public and private spaces (physical spaces and virtual ones such as websites) accessible inherently increases construction and retrofitting costs to property owners, which means it would not be occurring without public mandates, but those may be unpopular and generate resistance to their implementation.

QUESTIONS FOR DISCUSSION AND FURTHER RESEARCH

1 In theory, open immigration could counter the effects of low birth rates in high-income countries and thus strengthen pension systems, but opposition to immigration is generally strong in most high-income countries. How can we explain this phenomenon?
2 What are the implications for labour mobility when pensions are largely private employer–based?
3 In 2023, the Alberta provincial government announced its plans to withdraw from the national Canada Pension Plan (CPP). What are the likely reasons for this proposal? What outcomes would you expect from such a move for Albertans, their government, the federal government, and other Canadians more broadly?

8.5 EDUCATION

Education is a long-term investment: It involves multi-year investment in the form of primary, secondary, and tertiary (post-secondary) education, and the payoffs accrue over one's lifetime. For the analysis of education as an investment, you can utilize the concepts of net present value (NPV) and discounting introduced in chapter 3, section 3.3.

Most of the payoffs from education are private benefits in the form of higher earnings, but education also has a positive impact on society – positive externalities for communities, producers, and other members of society in general ensure better health and economic and social outcomes, such as less crime and more inclusive societies.

Education is widely considered an equalizer in society as it empowers – economically, socially, and politically – those from disadvantaged backgrounds. Education can help equalize not just economic outcomes, in terms of incomes and wealth accumulation, but also social outcomes, through improving opportunities in life by preventing diseases that could otherwise lead to disability and/or shorter lifespans. For example, it is well documented that, especially in poor countries and poor communities with limited access to adequate infrastructure and health care, greater educational attainment by mothers leads to improved health outcomes and reduced mortality for children (see, e.g., Cleland & van Ginneken, 1988; Chen & Li, 2009; Shrestha, 2020).

Based on the above listed reasons, many societies choose to subsidize education through public funding. This means that education involves redistribution across generations and across economic groups.

Early education can have long-term impact, and therefore funding of primary education is often public, but different funding systems are more or less likely to be successful in promoting equity. For example, primary education in the United States is largely funded by local governments, which depend on real estate taxes as their main source of revenue. This implies that rich neighborhoods have more funding per student than poor neighborhoods, and this tends to reinforce inequality of opportunities and outcomes in American society.

In a world of global capital mobility, outsourcing of jobs to developing countries, and technology replacing tasks traditionally performed by workers, we see the demand for unskilled labour declining in high-income countries. This translates into lower wages, higher poverty, and growing inequality in high-income countries. Policies that aim to increase the share of the population with tertiary education are supposed to counter these trends.

According to OECD (2023a) data, Canada had one of the highest rates of tertiary educational attainment among adults aged 25–64 at 62.74 per cent in 2022. In comparison, the United States also ranks high, with 50 per cent of working-age adults having tertiary education as of 2022, while Germany had only 32.5 per cent (see figure 8.3).

Funding schemes likely have an impact on these outcomes: Universities and colleges in countries with predominantly public funding of tertiary education face stricter budget constraints and thus fewer available seats for students. This leads to more competition for those seats and a less inclusive tertiary education system, resulting in lower tertiary educational attainment.

Countries with public-private co-funding models have more capacity in colleges and universities, thus allowing more people to pursue tertiary education. Canada and the United States fall into this category. It is also interesting to note that this is true even in light of the much higher costs of tertiary education in the United States, resulting in higher debt burdens.

This leads us to the next question: Is it an economically viable decision in the United States to pursue costly tertiary education? The long answer to this question is that it likely depends on the type of university or college pursued, the costs involved, the reputational signal the degree and the institution send to employers, the discipline studied, the degree of transferable skills gained, labour market conditions, etc. Nevertheless, the short answer can also be gauged by looking at the economic outcomes for those with tertiary education compared to those with lower levels of education. This is demonstrated in figure 8.4 by the percentage of adults earning twice the median level,[5] broken down by the level of educational attainment, including having a bachelor's degree versus other, short-cycle tertiary education only. Those in countries on the left-hand side of figure 8.4 are most likely to enjoy the benefits of higher earnings associated with a bachelor's degree (or equivalent). The gap between the share of those with a bachelor's degree versus other/short-cycle tertiary education earning twice the median level is more pronounced in the United States than in Canada, suggesting that the earnings premium to a bachelor's degree is more significant in the United States.[6]

---

5   A reminder that median income level represents the mid-point of earnings in an economy with 50 per cent of income earners falling below it and 50 per cent above. The median shows a more accurate picture of income distribution than average earnings because averages can be skewed by high-income earners.

6   You can explore in-depth data on country-specific education systems and their outcomes at OECD's website, https://gpseducation.oecd.org/CountryProfile.

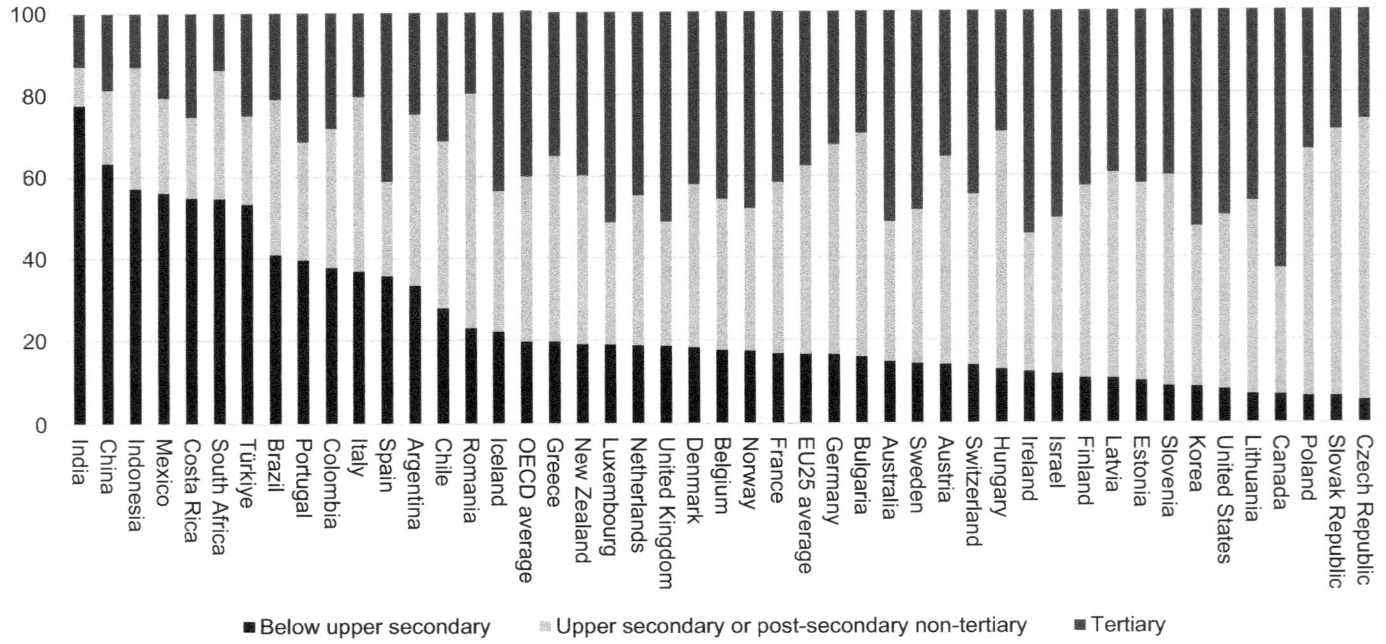
100
80
60
40
20
0
India
China
Indonesia
Mexico
Costa Rica
South Africa
Türkiye
Brazil
Portugal
Colombia
Italy
Spain
Argentina
Chile
Romania
Iceland
OECD average
Greece
New Zealand
Luxembourg
Netherlands
United Kingdom
Denmark
Belgium
Norway
France
EU25 average
Germany
Bulgaria
Australia
Sweden
Austria
Switzerland
Hungary
Ireland
Israel
Finland
Latvia
Estonia
Slovenia
Korea
United States
Lithuania
Canada
Poland
Slovak Republic
Czech Republic
Below upper secondary
Upper secondary or post-secondary non-tertiary
Tertiary

Figure 8.3. Educational attainment among 25–64 year olds as % of total population (2022)

Source: OECD (2023a).

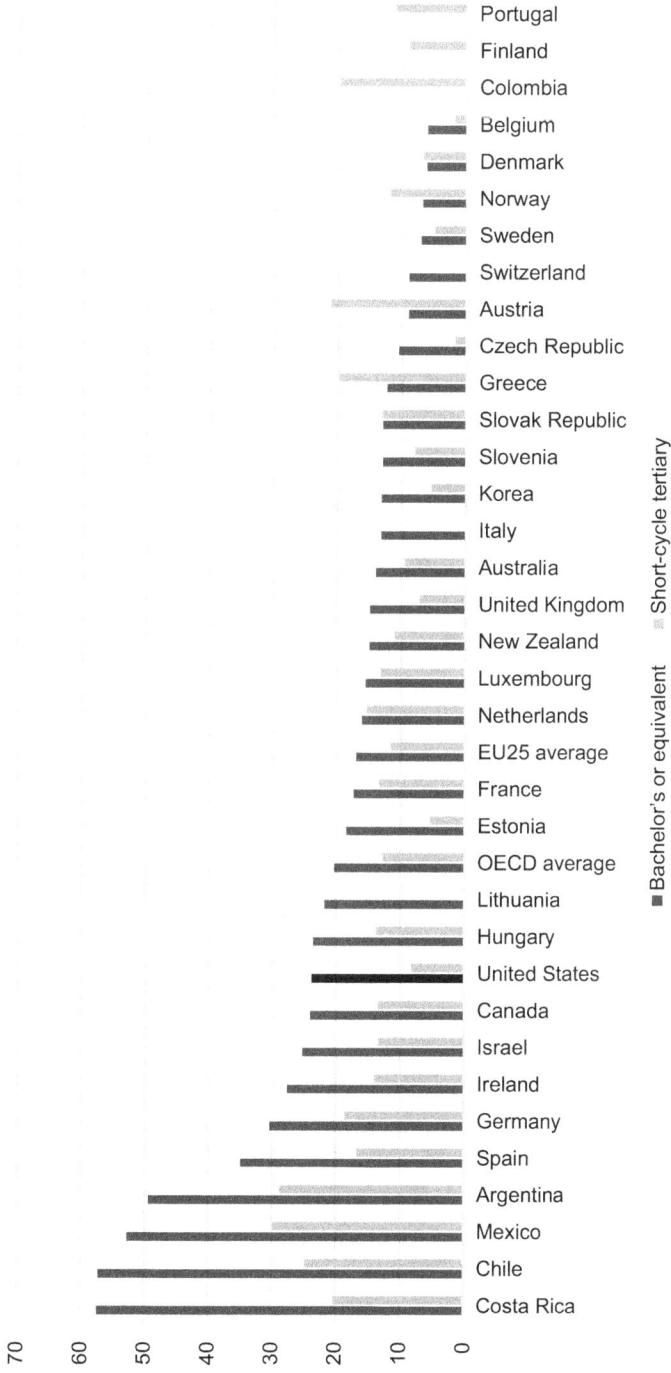

Figure 8.4. Percentage of adults earning more than twice the median by level of tertiary attainment (2021)

Source: OECD (2023a).

QUESTIONS FOR DISCUSSION AND FURTHER RESEARCH

1 What are the implications of elementary and high school teachers falling short of private sector wages commensurate with their education?

2 Legal challenges to affirmative action in university admissions in the United States have succeeded and gained ground in other jurisdictions. What is their likely impact?

BOX 8.6. ARTIFICIAL INTELLIGENCE TECHNOLOGY AND ITS IMPACT ON THE ECONOMY

Technological change, specifically developments in artificial intelligence (AI) and their rapid adoption, are generally considered an economic disruptor, as they can reduce the demand for certain types of labour and thus alter the return on education, which has been a driver of productivity and economic security as demonstrated in the section above.

In terms of its impact on employment, in general AI can substitute for existing jobs, complement existing jobs, and/or create new jobs and industries that did not exist before. The potential for AI to substitute for existing jobs has individual and social costs, while the other two effects of AI diffusion could actually enhance productivity and earnings. The magnitude and speed of the shifts will also matter since job creation and/or productivity enhancement need to keep pace with job losses. Reductions in the cost of AI – as demonstrated by the emergence of the Chinese-based DeepSeek on the global scene in early 2025 (Ng et al., 2025) – will help accelerate AI adoption.

The transaction costs of transitioning from declining to growing industries or jobs will also play a role and may increase demand for retraining and lifelong learning. Will older individuals be able to recoup the investment in this additional education (formal or informal)? Are governments going to provide subsidies and/or other incentives for retraining?

Is policy/regulation likely to limit the threat from AI job substitutions? Unlikely, as we have seen policy-makers engage in the international AI development and market dominance race by pledging to reduce so-called red tape and regulation.

Collective bargaining has been somewhat more successful (at least for now) in curbing AI as a substitute in creative industries in Hollywood, for example, but it came at the cost of several labour disruptions in 2024 (e.g., with the Writers Guild of America and Screen Actors Guild – American Federation of Television and Radio Artists) – and not all groups are able to organize effectively due to collective action problems, as discussed in chapter 5.

Can there be collective action in the form of boycotts and consumer demand deliberately shifting away from AI? That is also a possibility in times of social movements, but consumers in general do not have a good track record of effective collective action, especially that which is sustained over a long period of time.

If AI displaces labour on a mass scale, who will be affected? There are indications that in this case both unskilled and skilled labour might be replaced with AI (see, e.g., Mehdi & Frenette, 2024, for estimates in the Canadian context) and hence the impact would be felt by middle-income households in addition to lower-income households already affected by the outsourcing of manufacturing jobs to developing countries. Will this lead to greater public endorsement of (re)distributive policies and change in attitudes towards universal basic income (UBI) policies? And even if it does, can government revenue generation capabilities keep up with demand for (re)distributive policies? As outlined in chapter 6, taxable capacity is limited in a globalized world with free capital mobility, and public dislike for taxation has also limited the progressivity of tax systems in favour of reliance on regressive consumption taxes.

8.6 INTER-GENERATIONAL TENSIONS IN SOCIAL POLICY DEBATES

The focus of social policy in high-income countries has been traditionally the welfare of the elderly and children. High-income countries have reasonably well-developed pension systems, and most elderly also have a great deal of wealth embedded in the accumulated value of their homes.[7] The equity from home ownership can be converted to funds for elder care to supplement public social services.

However, younger generations of working adults have faced barriers to home ownership due to rising housing prices, costs of tertiary education and associated debt accumulation, and more volatile labour markets where employment is often more precarious rather than permanent. Younger generations are for the first time likely to be worse off compared to their parents, who enjoyed a comparatively long period of economic stability in their lifetime, especially during their productive years in the labour market.

At the same time, voter participation has been traditionally lower among young adults compared to older age groups. Political candidates across diverse political platforms have turned their attention to this untapped potential to boost their razor-thin electoral margins in highly polarized environments. The negative economic sentiments among the young electorate combined with the powers of social media to appeal to younger demographic groups have paved the way to new social policies directly benefiting younger generations.

In the United States, for example, the cost of university tuition is relatively high even for domestic students. This is illustrated in table 8.1 (based on excerpts from OECD, 2024, table C5.1) showing average (or most common) annual tuition fees for bachelor's degree programs in the 2022–3 academic year adjusted in purchasing power parity (PPP) terms for cross-country comparisons.

Most undergraduate students receive some form of aid in the United States, with the 2019–20 National Postsecondary Student Aid Study (NPSAS:20) showing that 64 per cent of students received grants and 36 per cent took out student loans, the majority of which are federal government supported. Among undergraduates who received any aid, the average total amount received was $14,100 (Cameron et al., 2023). Despite all these financial supports, federal student loan borrowers who completed their bachelor's degree in 2015–16 on average borrowed $45,300 and owed 78 per cent of the amount borrowed in 2020, according to the National Center for Education Statistics (2023).

---

7   In Canada, for example, the median net worth of households in the 65 years or older category is estimated to be $738,900 in 2023 (see Statistics Canada, 2024).

Table 8.1. Annual average (or most common) tuition fees for bachelor's or equivalent programs

Country/university type	Domestic students	Foreign students
US (public)	$9,596	$27,457
US (private)	$34,041	No differentiation
Canada (public)	$5,590	$30,697
Japan (public)	$5,645	No differentiation
Japan (private)	$10,104	No differentiation
Netherlands (public)	$3,041	$16,415
Spain (public)	$1,708	No differentiation
France (public)	$252	$4,109
Germany (public)	$157	-

Source: OECD (2024).

Note: In equivalent USD converted using PPPs, for full-time students, by type of institutions and level of education (2022–3).

President Biden made student debt forgiveness a campaign promise and once elected, embarked on implementing it. The debt relief policy included five different programs costing nearly $190 billion between 2021 and 2024 and covering approximately five million borrowers, according to Partridge and Weiss (2024).

Catherine and Yannelis (2023) analyzed the distributional effects of student loan forgiveness and found that full or partial forgiveness is actually regressive, because high earners took larger loans and because, for low earners, balances owed overestimate present values of outstanding debt. This is because under the Income-Based Repayment (IBR) plan, borrowers pay 15 per cent of their discretionary income (defined as income above 150 per cent of the poverty line) and outstanding balances are forgiven after 25 years.

Dinerstein et al. (2025) utilized administrative credit bureau data and estimated that forgiven borrowers' predicted monthly earnings were $115 higher than those of borrowers who did not receive forgiveness and $193 more than the general population. They also found that instead of reducing the overall debt burden, student loan forgiveness led to increases in mortgage, auto, and credit card debt by 9 cents for every dollar forgiven. Furthermore, borrowers' likelihood of employment and monthly earnings fell post-forgiveness.

The works of Catherine and Yannelis (2023) and Dinerstein et al. (2025) are consistent in their findings that the student debt forgiveness programs were regressive, benefiting relatively high-income earners, helping to explain their lack of popularity among the general public. According to the AP-NORC Center for Public Affairs Research (2024) survey, 39 per cent of the respondents indicated that it is extremely or very important for the federal government to forgive student loan debt, and only 30 per cent approved how the debt forgiveness was implemented by the Biden-Harris administration. Support for the debt forgiveness program was strongest among Democrats and those who were presently paying student loans.

In Canada, education, including university and college tuition and loans for tertiary education, fall under provincial jurisdiction and thus vary across the country. Nevertheless, the case of Ontario is interesting to explore because the Conservative government of Premier Doug Ford implemented a 10 per cent tuition cut in 2019, followed by a tuition freeze until the 2026–7 academic year at least. This period coincides with the COVID-19 pandemic and associated inflationary rises in costs, which has resulted in significant financial pressures on the entire tertiary education sector. While the tuition freeze appeals to students and parents with children attending university or college, the tuition freeze is not compensated by government funding. The shortfall in tuition revenue was initially covered by increases in tuition for international students and expanding international student recruitment, but new federal student visa restrictions introduced in 2024 have undermined this strategy. The combined effect of provincial and federal policies has led to budget cuts, layoffs, and program closures in the sector.

In Canada, housing affordability has become a major policy issue for young adults. Even though Canada has vast amounts of land, the population is largely concentrated in a few urban centres where demand for housing is very strong. In 2017, the federal Liberal government announced its National Housing Strategy, committing over $115 billion over ten years, mainly to expand housing supply.[8] Nevertheless, it takes time to increase the housing supply, and critics have expressed doubts as to whether the incentives to expand the housing supply would actually yield affordable housing units or simply expand the supply of homes for higher-income groups.

---

8   For more detail on the National Housing Strategy, see Government of Canada (2025).

According to Statistics Canada (2023b), the growth in renter house-holds between 2011 to 2021 was more than double that of owner house-holds (+8.4 per cent). Renters were also over twice as likely as owners to live in unaffordable housing. Unaffordable housing was defined as more than 30 per cent of pre-tax household income being spent on shelter costs. In 2021, recent renter households were most common in Canada's downtown cores, accounting for one-fifth (20.2 per cent) of all households living in downtowns. Young adults were more likely to live in recent renter households, with 25- to 29-year-olds representing the largest share of recent renters across age groups (15.2 per cent).

To curb demand for housing, especially demand for rental units, the federal Liberal government decided in early 2024 to impose significant cuts on international student visas (with provisions to limit the inflow of international students at the level of individual provinces) and to limit immigration more broadly (IRCC, 2024). As outlined above, the policy has had a dramatic impact on the financial situation of colleges and universities, especially in Ontario, and it remains to be seen if it will help alleviate the housing affordability crisis, especially for young adults, or deteriorate the university/college experience due to resource constraints.

The political participation of young adults and their electoral choices will continue to be carefully monitored by strategists to see whether policies aimed at directly benefiting this demographic will pay off.

QUESTIONS FOR DISCUSSION AND FURTHER RESEARCH

1 Can you think of other policy examples that involve intergenerational tensions or redistribution?
2 Can you identify other political and economic trends or divisions that shape the design of social policy in the twenty-first century?

RESEARCH ADVICE: A CHECKLIST FOR ANALYSTS OF SOCIAL POLICIES AND PROGRAMS

As analysts of social policy – whether in the public, non-profit, or private sectors – you should consider asking the following questions:

• What is the problem? Prepare a concise problem statement backed up with facts/data, if possible.

- What specific market/efficiency failures is social policy aiming to solve? Keep in mind that even when policies aim to tackle marginalization and/or discrimination, those are efficiency failures, because from a societal point of view, we achieve efficiency when all members can participate rather than being excluded. Exclusion leads to losses and unrealized potential.
- Are the (actual or proposed) policies tackling the root causes of problems or just their symptoms?
- Good intentions are not sufficient for sound policy, and hence: What is the potential for unintended consequences from a particular policy?
- What is the expected time horizon for the intended policy outcomes? Is it possible to measure them accurately, or are they measured too early?
- Are there both quantitative and qualitative measures included in evaluations for triangulation purposes? Keep in mind that context matters and some groups may be more or less accessible for participation in data collection. Aggregation also means that important information is inevitably lost.
- Are estimates of social benefits included in the data and analysis? Social costs are included based on budgetary spending data, but social benefits are often excluded due to their intangible nature and measurement challenges. For example, social rates of return to education should include measures of the positive externalities from education, but often only the private benefits of greater earnings are included in the calculation of the social rate of return on educational investment.
- If a policy has sound merits, is the implementation effective? Are there sufficient resources available for policy implementation, or does the policy/program suffer from "low dosage" problem?
- How can costs be mitigated without compromising the intended outcomes?
- Are the policies and programs financially and economically viable and sustainable? If the policies/programs rely on private markets in some way, are the policies incentive-compatible, that is, conducive to creating the right market conditions, or not? Are there any emergent risks that will affect market conditions?
- What is the public's attitude towards specific social policies and programs? Do they have accurate information about them? Is there a communication strategy in place to secure public support?

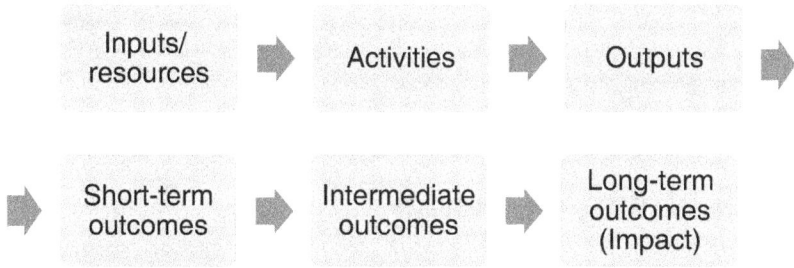

Figure 8.5. Basic components of a logic model

- Who opposes the policy and why? What are their organizational and communication strategies?

Borrowing from program evaluation literature, you may also consider constructing a logic model for visual representation of the policy/program design to ensure logical consistency and/or to identify inconsistencies in design and implementation.

Logic models also help keep the focus on outcomes as the ultimate objective, rather than brandishing the resources devoted to policies and programs (as politicians have an incentive to do) or confusing outputs with outcomes. Outcomes are the ultimate objective of policies and programs, which is the reason why the policies/programs are in place while outputs such as the number of program recipients served, for example, is only a metric in the monitoring and implementation process. Figure 8.5 illustrates the basic structure of a logic model in its simplest, linear form.

For more detail on logic models, data collection, and analysis methods in the evaluation of social policies and programs, please refer to the rich program evaluation literature.

CHAPTER NINE

Concluding Remarks

We live in a rapidly evolving policy environment. Political and economic structures, as well as social norms and belief systems that have long been stable and perceived as resistant to change, have been dramatically uprooted in recent years since the COVID-19 pandemic.

In your work as policy analysts, you will encounter issues and questions that have not been covered in this text. Nevertheless, I hope you will find that the text has prepared you to tackle these challenges by keeping in mind the following advice:

- Make sure to maintain an interdisciplinary approach by integrating research and concepts from a variety of disciplines.
- Identify the key theoretical concepts that play a role in the given policy issue or questions.
- Identify the key players, their preferences and endowments, and the main sources of tension.
- Assess critically the assumptions of the underlying theoretical frameworks and question your own explicit and implicit assumptions.
- Practical experience and front-line service work will make you a better policy analyst. Do not focus only on policy analyst positions while actively trying to avoid service-delivery roles.
- Do not assume irrationality on the part of any actors; look instead for missing information and factors that you are discounting as unimportant or unfounded.

- Take into consideration both explicit and implicit redistributive considerations.
- Remember to integrate economic, legal, and political factors into your analysis.
- Research thoroughly the institutional setting and its implications and consider if the formal and informal/de facto institutional settings are evolving.
- Expand your research to include the latest theoretical frameworks, methods, and data, but question their validity and applicability to the given setting.
- Never assume that markets are competitive; always actively investigate market structure.
- Always question the validity and reliability of your data and assess sampling bias.
- Take a holistic view of the analysis and adopt a general equilibrium frame of analysis that will account for intended and unintended consequences in all parts of the economy beyond the immediate economic and policy setting.
- Question whether you missed any important factors. Develop connections and keep in touch with practitioners to incorporate their insight and perspectives.
- Qualitative assessment is just as important as quantitative methods.
- Remember that history matters, but the past is not necessarily a good predictor of the future.
- Communicate the results of your analysis in a careful and considered manner, including its limitations and taking into consideration its potential uses and misinterpretations.
- If the average person cannot understand your communication pieces, make an effort to revise them to make them more accessible, because information is the most fundamental and consequential public good.
- If you are an outlier among policy analysts with your methods or findings, do not be intimidated by it. The pressure to conform can be strong, but groupthink makes us miss important factors.

References

Abbott, R. (2014, January 9). Fierce debate in congress on abortion funding. *Courthouse News Service*. https://www.courthousenews.com/fierce-debate-in-congress-on-abortion-funding/

Acemoglu, D. (2003). Why not a political Coase theorem? Social conflict, commitment, and politics. *Journal of Comparative Economics*, *31*(4), 620–52. https://doi.org/10.1016/j.jce.2003.09.003

Acemoglu, D., Johnson, S., & Robinson, J.A. (2001). The colonial origins of comparative development: An empirical investigation. *American Economic Review*, *91*(5), 1369–401. https://doi.org/10.1257/aer.91.5.1369

Acquisti, A., Taylor, C., & Wagman, L. (2016). The economics of privacy. *Journal of Economic Literature*, *54*(2), 442–92. https://doi.org/10.1257/jel.54.2.442

Adam, A., Delis, M.D., & Kammas, P. (2011). Are democratic governments more efficient? *European Journal of Political Economy*, *27*(1), 75–86. https://doi.org/10.1016/j.ejpoleco.2010.04.004

Adrian, T., Khan, A., & Menand, L. (2024). *A new measure of Central Bank Independence* (IMF Working Paper No. 24/35). https://www.imf.org/en/Publications/WP/Issues/2024/02/23/A-New-Measure-of-Central-Bank-Independence-545270

Ahmed, F. (2007). Shari'a, custom, and statutory law: Comparing state approaches to Islamic jurisprudence, tribal autonomy, and legal development in Afghanistan and Pakistan. *Global Jurist*, *7*(1), 1934–2640. https://doi.org/10.2202/1934-2640.1222

Akerlof, G.A. (1970). The market for "lemons": Quality uncertainty and the market mechanism. *Quarterly Journal of Economics*, *84*(3), 488–500. https://doi.org/10.2307/1879431

Akkoyunlu, S., & Ramella, D. (2020). Corruption and economic development. *Journal of Economic Development, 45*(2), 63–94.

Akman, S., Brandi, C., Dadush, U., Draper, P., Freytag, A., Kautz, M., Rashish, P., Schwarzer, J., & Vos, R. (2018). *Mitigating the adjustment costs of international trade*. Economics Discussion Papers, No. 2018-49. Kiel Institute for the World Economy. https://www.econstor.eu/bitstream/10419/179969/1/1025471024.pdf

Alesina, A., Devleeschauwer, A., Easterly, W., Kurlat, S., & Wacziarg, R. (2003). Fractionalization. *Journal of Economic Growth, 8*(2), 155–94. https://doi.org/10.1023/A:1024471506938

Alesina, A., & Perotti, R. (1995). The political economy of budget deficits. *International Monetary Fund Staff Papers, 42*(1), 1–31. https://www.elibrary.imf.org/view/journals/024/1995/001/article-A001-en.xml

Alesina, A., & Spolaore, E. (1997). On the number and size of nations. *The Quarterly Journal of Economics, 112*(4), 1027–56. https://doi.org/10.1162/003355300555411

———. (2003). *The size of nations*. MIT Press. https://doi.org/10.7551/mitpress/6261.001.0001

Allyn, B. (2024, April 12). Google blocks California news in response to bill that would force tech giant to pay. *NPR*. https://www.npr.org/2024/04/12/1244416887/google-blocks-california-news-payments-bill

Almond, D., Edlund, L., & Milligan, K. (2013). Son preference and the persistence of culture: Evidence from South and East Asian Immigrants to Canada. *Population and Development Review, 39*(1), 75–95. https://doi.org/10.1111/j.1728-4457.2013.00574.x

Alt, J.E., & Shepsle, K.A. (Eds.). (1990). *Perspectives on positive political economy*. Cambridge University Press. https://doi.org/10.1017/CBO9780511571657

Altman, D., & Castiglioni, R. (2009). Democratic quality and human development in Latin America: 1972–2001. *Canadian Journal of Political Science, 42*(2), 297–319. https://doi.org/10.1017/S0008423909090301

Alvarez, F., Argente, D., & van Patten, D. (2023). Are cryptocurrencies currencies? Bitcoin as legal tender in El Salvador. *Science, 382*(6677). https://doi.org/10.1126/science.add2844

Anand, P. (1993). The philosophy of intransitive preference. *The Economic Journal*, 337–46. https://doi.org/10.2307/2234772

Anderlini, J. (2013, March 7) Chinese National People's Congress has 83 billionaires, report says. *Washington Post*. https://www.washingtonpost.com/world/asia_pacific/chinese-national-peoples-congress-has-83-billionaires-report-says/2013/03/07/d8ff4a4e-8746-11e2-98a3-b3db6b9ac586_story.html

Annett, A. (2001). Social fractionalization, political instability and the size of government. *International Monetary Fund Staff Papers, 48*, 561–92. https://doi.org/10.2307/4621684

AP-NORC Center for Public Affairs Research. (2024, June). *Views toward student loan relief are tied to partisanship and experience with debt.* https://apnorc.org/projects/views-toward-student-loan-relief-are-tied-to-partisanship-and-experience-with-debt/

Arikan, G.G. (2008). How privatizations affect the level of perceived corruption. *Public Finance Review, 36*(6), 706–27. https://doi.org/10.1177/1091142107313302

Arsenych, A. (2024, March 5). "People are hurting": Premier Doug Ford calls on Bank of Canada to lower interest rates. *CTV News Toronto.* https://toronto.ctvnews.ca/people-are-hurting-premier-doug-ford-calls-on-bank-of-canada-to-lower-interest-rates-1.6796052

Austen-Smith, D., & Banks, J.S. (1998). Social choice theory, game theory, and positive political theory. *Annual Review of Political Science, 1*(1), 259–87. https://doi.org/10.1146/annurev.polisci.1.1.259

Austin v. Michigan Chamber of Commerce, 494 US 652 (1990). https://supreme.justia.com/cases/federal/us/494/652/

Bachas, P., Fisher-Post, M.H., Jensen, A., & Zucman, G. (2022). *Globalization and factor income taxation: Evidence from a macro-historical database.* National Bureau of Economic Research (No. w29819). https://www.nber.org/papers/w29819

Bakare, S.S., Adeniyi, A.O., Akpuokwe, C.U., & Eneh, N.E. (2024). Data privacy laws and compliance: A comparative review of the EU GDPR and USA regulations. *Computer Science & IT Research Journal, 5*(3), 528–43. https://doi.org/10.51594/csitrj.v5i3.859

Bakonyi, J. (2013). Authority and administration beyond the state: Local governance in southern Somalia, 1995–2006. *Journal of Eastern African Studies, 7*(2), 272–90. https://doi.org/10.1080/17531055.2013.776278

Banerjee, S., Grüne-Yanoff, T., John, P., & Moseley, A. (2024). It's time we put agency into behavioural public policy. *Behavioural Public Policy, 8*(4), 789–806. https://doi.org/10.1017/bpp.2024.6

Bank of Canada. (n.d.). *Key inflation indicators and the target range.* Retrieved August 5, 2025, at https://www.bankofcanada.ca/rates/indicators/key-variables/key-inflation-indicators-and-the-target-range/

Bank of Thailand. (n.d.). *Lessons learnt from the Asian Financial Crisis.* https://www.bot.or.th/en/our-roles/special-measures/Tom-Yum-Kung-lesson.html

Barnett, W.S., & Belfield, C.R. (2006). Early childhood development and social mobility. *The Future of Children, 16*(2), 73–98. https://doi.org/10.1353/foc.2006.0011

Barro, R.J., & Gordon, D.B. (1983). Rules, discretion and reputation in a model of monetary policy. *Journal of Monetary Economics, 12*(1), 101–21. https://doi.org/10.1016/0304-3932(83)90051-X

Barro, R.J. (1999). Determinants of democracy. *The Journal of Political Economy, 107*(6), S158–83. https://doi.org/10.1086/250107

Bauerly, C.L., & Hallstrom, E.C. (2012). Square pegs: The challenges for existing federal campaign finance disclosure laws in the age of the super pac. *NYU Journal of Legislation and Public Policy, 15,* 329.

Bearer-Friend, J. (2024). Race-based tax weapons. *UC Irvine Law Review, 14*(4). https://escholarship.org/content/qt3cn7g0cj/qt3cn7g0cj.pdf

Becker, G. (1968). Crime and punishment: An economic approach. *Journal of Political Economy, 76*(2), 169–217.

———. (1981). *A treatise on the family.* Harvard University Press.

Becker, G.S., & Stigler, G.J. (1974). Law enforcement, malfeasance, and compensation of enforcers. *The Journal of Legal Studies, 3*(1), 1–18. https://doi.org/10.1086/467507

Béland, D., Cantillon, B., Hick, R., & Moreira, A. (2021). Social policy in the face of a global pandemic: Policy responses to the COVID-19 crisis. *Social Policy & Administration, 55*(2), 249–60. https://doi.org/10.1111/spol.12718

Bello, W. (1999). The Asian financial crisis: Causes, dynamics, prospects. *Journal of the Asia Pacific Economy, 4*(1), 33–55. https://doi.org/10.1080/13547869908724669

Bidadanure, J.U. (2019). The political theory of universal basic income. *Annual Review of Political Science, 22*, 481–501. https://doi.org/10.1146/annurev-polisci-050317-070954

Blanchard, O., & Watson, M. (1982). *Bubbles, rational expectations, and financial markets* (NBER Working Paper No. 945). https://www.nber.org/system/files/working_papers/w0945/w0945.pdf

Blasco, J., Guillaud, E., & Zemmour, M. (2023). The inequality impact of consumption taxes: An international comparison. *Journal of Public Economics, 222*, 104897. https://doi.org/10.1016/j.jpubeco.2023.104897

Blaug, M. (1987). *Economic history and the history of economics.* New York University Press.

Blaydes, L., & Kayser, M.A. (2011). Counting calories: Democracy and distribution in the developing world. *International Studies Quarterly, 55*(4), 887–908. https://doi.org/10.1111/j.1468-2478.2011.00692.x

Bloomberg News (2012, February 27). China's billionaire congress makes its U.S. peer look poor. *Bloomberg News.* https://www.bloomberg.com/news/2012-02-26/china-s-billionaire-lawmakers-make-u-s-peers-look-like-paupers.html

Blundell, R., Dearden, L., Meghir, C., & Sianesi, B. (1999). Human capital investment: The returns from education and training to the individual, the firm and the economy. *Fiscal Studies, 20*(1), 1–23. https://doi.org/10.1111/j.1475-5890.1999.tb00001.x

Bordelon, B., & Ng, A. (2023, August 16). Tech lobbyists are running the table on state privacy laws. *Politico.* https://www.politico.com/news/2023/08/16/tech-lobbyists-state-privacy-laws-00111363

Brands, H. (2011). Crime, irregular warfare, and institutional failure in Latin America: Guatemala as a case study. *Studies in Conflict & Terrorism, 34*(3), 228–47. https://doi.org/10.1080/1057610X.2011.545937

Buchanan, J.M., & Yoon, Y.J. (2000). Symmetric tragedies: Commons and anticommons. *Journal of Law and Economics, 43*(1), 1–14. https://doi.org/10.1086/467445

Buchholz, T.G. (2021). *New ideas from dead economists: The introduction to modern economic thought* (4th ed.). Plume.

Burger, K. (2010). How does early childhood care and education affect cognitive development? An international review of the effects of early interventions for children from different social backgrounds. *Early Childhood Research Quarterly, 25*(2), 140–65. https://doi.org/10.1016/j.ecresq.2009.11.001

Burgess, A. (2012). "Nudging" healthy lifestyles: The UK experiments with the behavioural alternative to regulation and the market. *European Journal of Risk Regulation, 3*(1), 3–16. https://doi.org/10.1017/S1867299X00001756

Burke, E. (1774). *The Works of the Right Honourable Edmund Burke.* (Vols. 1–6). Henry G. Bohn, 1854–6. (Reprinted in P.B. Kurland & R. Lerner [Eds.], *The Founders' Constitution* [Vol. 1, Chap. 13, Document 7]. University of Chicago Press. https://press-pubs.uchicago.edu/founders/documents/v1ch13s7.html)

Bush v Gore, 531 US 98 (2000). https://supreme.justia.com/cases/federal/us/531/98/

Cagan, P. (1956). The monetary dynamics of hyperinflation. In M. Friedman (Ed.), *Studies in the quantity theory of money* (pp. 22–117). University of Chicago Press.

Calvo, G.A., & Reinhart, C.M. (2002). Fear of floating. *Quarterly Journal of Economics, 117,* 379–408. https://doi.org/10.1162/003355302753650274

Cameron, M., Johnson, R., Lacy, T.A., Wu, J., Siegel, P., Holley, J., & Wine, J. (2023). *2019–20 National Postsecondary Student Aid Study (NPSAS:20): First look at student financial aid estimates for 2019–20* (NCES 2023-466). U.S. Department of Education, National Center for Education Statistics. https://nces.ed.gov/pubsearch/pubsinfo.asp?pubid=2023466

The Canadian Press. (2024, January 17). Ontario preparing for next step in private clinic expansion. *CBC News.* https://www.cbc.ca/news/canada/toronto/ont-private-clinics-1.7086744

———. (2024, May 10). Trudeau points to fire fight, says Meta news ban degrades safety as it makes billions. *CTV News.* https://www.ctvnews.ca/politics/trudeau-points-to-fire-fight-says-meta-news-ban-degrades-safety-as-it-makes-billions-1.6882241

Carey, D., & Tchilinguirian, H. (2000). *Average effective tax rates on capital, labour and consumption* (OECD Economics Department Working Papers No. 258). OECD Publishing.

Castetter, M.D. (2003). Taking law into their own hands: Unofficial and illegal sanctions by the Pakistani tribal councils. *Indiana International & Comparative Law Review, 13*(2), 543–78. https://doi.org/10.18060/17769

Catherine, S., & Yannelis, C. (2023). The distributional effects of student loan forgiveness. *Journal of Financial Economics, 147*(2), 297–316. https://doi .org/10.1016/j.jfineco.2022.10.003

CBC News. (2015). *Canada's deficits and surpluses, 1963 to 2015.* https:// www.cbc.ca/news/multimedia/canada-s-deficits-and-surpluses -1963-to-2015-1.3042571

Chen, Y., & Li, H. (2009). Mother's education and child health: Is there a nurturing effect? *Journal of Health Economics, 28*(2), 413–26. https://doi .org/10.1016/j.jhealeco.2008.10.005

Chetty, R., & Finkelstein, A. (2013). Social insurance: Connecting theory to data. In *Handbook of public economics* (Vol. 5, pp. 111–93). Elsevier. https:// doi.org/10.1016/B978-0-444-53759-1.00003-0

Chrisp, J., Smyth, L., Stansfield, C., Pearce, N., France, R., & Taylor, C. (2022). *Basic income experiments in OECD countries: A rapid evidence review.* EPPI Centre, UCL Social Research Institute, University College London. https://eppi.ioe.ac.uk/cms/Default.aspx?tabid=3856

Citizens United v. Federal Election Commission, 558 US 310 (2010). https:// supreme.justia.com/cases/federal/us/558/310/

Cleland, J.G., & van Ginneken, J.K. (1988). Maternal education and child survival in developing countries: The search for pathways of influence. *Social Science & Medicine, 27*(12), 1357–68. https://doi.org/10.1016/0277 -9536(88)90201-8

Coase, R. (1960). The problem of social cost. *Journal of Law and Economics, 3*(1), 1–44.

Coates, D., Heckelman, J.C., & Wilson, B. (2007). Determinants of interest group formation. *Public Choice, 133*(3/4), 377–91. https://doi.org/10.1007 /s11127-007-9195-4

Coccia, M. (2010). Democratization is the driving force for technological and economic change. *Technological Forecasting & Social Change, 77*(2), 248–64. https://doi.org/10.1016/j.techfore.2009.06.007

Condorcet, M. (1785). *Essai sur l'application de l'analyse à la probabilité des décisions rendues à la pluralité des voix.*

Congleton, R.D. (2004). The median voter model. In *The encyclopedia of public choice* (pp. 707–12). Springer US. https://doi.org/10.1007/978-0-306-47828 -4_142

Cooter, R., & Ulen, T. (2011). *Law and economics* (6th ed.). Pearson.

Cunha, F., & Heckman, J. (2007). The technology of skill formation. *American Economic Review, 97*(2), 31–47. https://doi.org/10.1257/aer.97.2.31

d'Addio, A.C. (2007). *Intergenerational transmission of disadvantage: Mobility or immobility across generations? A review of the evidence for OECD countries.* Organization for Economic Cooperation and Development (OECD).

Dahl, R.A. (1971). *Polyarchy.* Yale University Press.

Dahlgren, P. (2005). The internet, public spheres, and political communication: Dispersion and deliberation. *Political Communication, 22*(2), 147–62. https://doi.org/10.1080/10584600590933160

Daily Mail Reporter. (2012, February 17). "Where are the women?" Outrage after birth control hearing is led by panel of five men. *Daily Mail*. https://www.dailymail.co.uk/news/article-2102411/Birth-control-hearing-Capitol-Hill-led-male-panel.html

DeStefano, F. (2007). Vaccines and autism: Evidence does not support a causal association. *Clinical Pharmacology and Therapeutics, 82*(6), 756–59. https://doi.org/10.1038/sj.clpt.6100407

Dickson, A. (2023, August 25). Brexit Wars part II: Tories plot British exit from Europe's human rights treaty. *Politico*. https://www.politico.eu/article/brexit-tories-rishi-sunak-european-convention-on-human-rights/

Dinerstein, M., Earnest, S., Koustas, D.K., & Yannelis, C. (2025). *Student loan forgiveness* (NBER Working Paper No. w33462). National Bureau of Economic Research. https://www.nber.org/system/files/working_papers/w33462/w33462.pdf

Djuric, M. (June 4, 2024). New Democrats want a price cap on grocery store staples – Liberals say it won't work. *CBC News*. https://www.cbc.ca/news/politics/ndp-price-cap-groceries-food-staples-1.7224870

Dobbs v Jackson Women's Health Organization, 597 US ___ (2022). https://supreme.justia.com/cases/federal/us/597/19-1392/

Downs, A. (1957). *An economic theory of democracy*. HarperCollins.

Drolet, M., & Morissette, R. (2014). New facts on pension coverage in Canada. Insights on Canadian Society, catalogue no. 75-006-X. *Statistics Canada*. https://www.statcan.gc.ca/pub/75-006-x/2014001/article/14120-eng.pdf

Dunmore, C. (2011, June 10). *Scrap biofuel support to curb food costs: Agencies*. Reuters. https://www.reuters.com/article/2011/06/10/us-biofuels-g-idUSTRE7593ZB20110610

Dür, A. (2008a). Interest groups in the European Union: How powerful are they? *West European Politics, 31*. https://doi.org/10.1080/01402380802372662

———. (2008b). Measuring interest group influence in the EU: A note on methodology. *European Union Politics, 9*(4), 559–76. https://doi.org/10.1177/1465116508095151

Dür, A., & De Bièvre, D. (2007). The question of interest group influence. *Journal of Public Policy, 27*(1), 1–12. https://doi.org/10.1017/S0143814X07000591

Egger, P.H., Nigai, S., & Strecker, N.M. (2019). The taxing deed of globalization. *American Economic Review, 109*(2), 353–90. https://doi.org/10.1257/aer.20160600

Eichengreen, B., & Hausmann, R. (1999). *Exchange rates and financial fragility* (NBER Working Paper No. 7418). National Bureau of Economic Research. https://ideas.repec.org/p/nbr/nberwo/7418.html

Elections Canada. (2011). *Estimation of voter turnout by age group and gender at the 2011 federal general election*. https://www.elections.ca/content.aspx?section=res&dir=rec/part/estim/41ge&document=report41&lang=e#p41

———. (2025). *Political financing*. Last modified at March 24, 2025. https://www.elections.ca/content.aspx?section=fin&&document=index&lang=e

Erbring, L., Goldenberg, E.N., & Miller, A.H. (1980). Front-page news and real-world cues: A new look at agenda-setting by the media. *American Journal of Political Science*, 16–49. https://doi.org/10.2307/2110923

Esty, D.C. (2001). Bridging the trade-environment divide. *Journal of Economic Perspectives*, *15*(3), 113–30. https://doi.org/10.1257/jep.15.3.113

European Court of Human Rights (ECHR). (n.d.). *European Convention on Human Rights*. Retrieved August 5, 2025, at https://www.echr.coe.int/european-convention-on-human-rights

———. (2024, April 9). *Verein KlimaSeniorinnen Schweiz and others v Switzerland*, ECHR Application no. 53600/20, Strasbourg. https://hudoc.echr.coe.int/eng?i=001-233206

European Parliament. (n.d.). *Treaty on European Union (TEU) / Maastricht Treaty*. Retrieved August 5, 2025, at https://www.europarl.europa.eu/about-parliament/en/in-the-past/the-parliament-and-the-treaties/maastricht-treaty

European Union. (n.d.-a). Court of Justice of the European Union (CJEU). Retrieved August 5, 2025, from https://european-union.europa.eu/institutions-law-budget/institutions-and-bodies/search-all-eu-institutions-and-bodies/court-justice-european-union-cjeu_en

———. (n.d.-b). *Types of institutions and bodies*. Retrieved August 5, 2025, from https://european-union.europa.eu/institutions-law-budget/institutions-and-bodies/types-institutions-and-bodies_en

Fan, S., Yu, B., & Saurkar, A. (2008). *Public spending in developing countries: Trends, determination and impact*. IFPRI; Johns Hopkins University Press.

Fearon, J.D., & Laitin, D.D. (2003). Ethnicity, insurgency, and civil war. *American Political Science Review*, *97*(1), 75–90. https://doi.org/10.1017/S0003055403000534

Feld, L.P., Fischer, J.A., & Kirchgassner, G. (2010). The effect of direct democracy on income redistribution: Evidence from Switzerland. *Economic Inquiry*, *48*(4), 817–40. https://doi.org/10.1111/j.1465-7295.2008.00174.x

Federal Deposit Insurance Corporation (FDIC). (n.d.). *Bank failures in brief – summary*. Retrieved August 5, 2025, at https://www.fdic.gov/resources/resolutions/bank-failures/in-brief/index.html

Federal Election Commission. (n.d.). *Campaign finance data*. Retrieved August 5, 2025, at https://www.fec.gov/data/

———. (2019–20). *Political action committee data summary tables, 2019–2020*. https://www.fec.gov/campaign-finance-data/political-action-committee-data-summary-tables/?year=2020&segment=12

———. (2020, April 3). *Statistical summary of 12-month campaign activity of the 2019–2020 election cycle* [Press release]. https://www.fec.gov/updates

/statistical-summary-12-month-campaign-activity-2019-2020-election
-cycle/.

Ferreira, F.H.G., & Walton, M. (2006). *Inequality of opportunity and economic development* (World Bank Policy Research Working Paper No. WPS 3816). World Bank.

Fleming, M. (1962). Domestic financial policies under fixed and floating exchange rates. *International Monetary Fund Staff Papers*, *9*, 369–80. https://www.elibrary.imf.org/view/journals/024/1962/003/article-A004-en.xml

Frankel, J.A., & Rose, A.K. (1998). The endogeneity of the optimum currency area criteria. *Economic Journal*, *108*, 1009–25. https://doi.org/10.1111/1468-0297.00327

Friedman, D. (1999). Why not hang them all: The virtues of inefficient punishment. *Journal of Political Economy*, *107*(S6), S259–69. https://doi.org/10.1086/250110

Fullerton, D., & Monti, H. (2013). Can pollution tax rebates protect low-wage earners? *Journal of Environmental Economics and Management*, *66*(3), 539–53. https://doi.org/10.1016/j.jeem.2013.09.001

García, J.L., Heckman, J., & Ronda, V. (2022). The lasting effects of early childhood education on promoting the skills and social mobility of disadvantaged African Americans and their children. *Journal of Political Economy*, *131*, 1477–506. https://doi.org/10.1086/722936

Garoupa, N., & Klerman, D. (2002). Optimal law enforcement with a rent seeking government. *American Law and Economics Review*, *4*(1), 116–40. https://doi.org/10.1093/aler/4.1.116

Geist, M. (2023, August 2). The lose-lose-lose-lose Bill C-18 outcome: Meta blocking news links on Facebook and Instagram in Canada. *Michael Geist* (website). https://www.michaelgeist.ca/2023/08/metablockslinks/

———. (2024, June 12). Sour grapes: Big media lobby wants to squash the new collective responsible for administering Google's $100 million online news act money. *Michael Geist* (website). https://www.michaelgeist.ca/2024/06/sour-grapes-big-media-lobby-wants-to-squash-the-new-collective-responsible-for-administering-googles-100-million-online-news-act-money/

Gilardi, F., Gessler, T., Kubli, M., & Müller, S. (2022). Social media and political agenda setting. *Political Communication*, *39*(1), 39–60. https://doi.org/10.1080/10584609.2021.1910390

Gilberstadt, H. (2020, August 19). More Americans oppose than favor the government providing a universal basic income for all adult citizens. *Pew Research Center*. https://www.pewresearch.org/short-reads/2020/08/19/more-americans-oppose-than-favor-the-government-providing-a-universal-basic-income-for-all-adult-citizens/

Glaeser, E.L., Ponzetto, G., & Shleifer, A. (2007). Why does democracy need education? *Journal of Economic Growth*, *12*(2), 77–99. https://doi.org/10.1007/s10887-007-9015-1

Gore, C., Morin, S., Røttingen, J.-A., & Kieny, M.P. (2023). Negotiating public-health intellectual property licensing agreements to increase access to health technologies: An insider's story. *BMJ Global Health, 8*(9), e012964. https://doi.org/10.1136/bmjgh-2023-012964.

Government of Canada. (2024, October 22). *Reporting your capital gains as a crypto-asset user.* https://www.canada.ca/en/revenue-agency/news/newsroom/tax -tips/tax-tips-2024/reporting-your-capital-gains-as-a-crypto-asset-user.html

———. (2025). About the national housing strategy. Last modified June 9, 2025, at https://housing-infrastructure.canada.ca/housing-logement /ptch-csd/about-strat-apropos-eng.html

Greijdanus, H., de Matos Fernandes, C.A., Turner-Zwinkels, F., Honari, A., Roos, C.A., Rosenbusch, H., & Postmes, T. (2020). The psychology of online activism and social movements: Relations between online and offline collective action. *Current Opinion in Psychology, 35*, 49–54. https:// doi.org/10.1016/j.copsyc.2020.03.003

Grossman, G.M., & Helpman, E. (1996). Rent dissipation, free riding and trade policy. *European Economic Review, 40*(3–5), 795–803. https://doi.org/10.1016 /0014-2921(95)00088-7

Haas, R., & Denmark, A. (2020, August 7). More pain than gain: How the US-China trade war hurt America. *The Brookings Institution.* https://www .brookings.edu/articles/more-pain-than-gain-how-the-us-china-trade -war-hurt-america/

Hainmueller, J., & Hangartner, D. (2013). Who gets a Swiss passport? A natural experiment in immigrant discrimination. *American Political Science Review, 107*(1), 159–87.

Halpern, D., & Sanders, M. (2016). Nudging by government: Progress, impact, & lessons learned. *Behavioral Science & Policy, 2*(2), 53–65. https:// behavioralpolicy.org/wp-content/uploads/2017/06/Sanders-web.pdf

Hambly, H., & Rajabiun, R. (2021). Rural broadband: Gaps, maps and challenges. *Telematics and Informatics, 60*, 101565. https://doi.org/10.1016 /j.tele.2021.101565

Hancké, B., Overbeke, T.V., & Voss, D. (2025). *Understanding political economy: Capitalism, democracy and inequality.* Edward Elgar. https://doi.org/10.4337 /9781035325085

Hatfield, M. (2020, October 28). What's wrong with the link tax? An FAQ. *OpenMedia.* https://openmedia.org/article/item/whats-wrong-with -the-link-tax-an-faq

Hausmann, R. (1999). Currencies: Should there be five or one hundred and five? *Foreign Policy, 116*, 65–79. https://doi.org/10.2307/1149644

Hayward, M.D., & Gorman, B.K. (2004). The long arm of childhood: The influence of early-life social conditions on men's mortality. *Demography, 41*(1), 87–107. https://doi.org/10.1353/dem.2004.0005

Hazard Owen, L. (2022, June 22). After 8 years, Google News returns to Spain. *NiemanLab.* https://www.niemanlab.org/2022/06/after-8-years-google-news-returns-to-spain/

He, M., Ditto, J.C., Gardner, L., Machesky, J., Hass-Mitchell, T.N., Chen, C., Khare, P., Bugra, S., Fortner, J.D., Plata, D., Drollette, B., Hayden, K., Wentzell, J., Mittermeier, R., Leithead, A., Lee, P., Darlington, A., Wren, S., Zhang, J., … Gentner, D.R. (2024). Total organic carbon measurements reveal major gaps in petrochemical emissions reporting. *Science, 383*(6681), 426–32. https://doi.org/10.1126/science.adj6233

Heilbroner, R.L. (1999). *The worldly philosophers: The lives, times, and ideas of the great economic thinkers* (7th ed.). Touchstone.

Heller, M.A. (1998). The tragedy of the anticommons: Property in the transition from Marx to markets. *Harvard Law Review, 111*(3), 621–88.

Henrich, J. (2000). Does culture matter in economic behavior? Ultimatum game bargaining among the Machiguenga of the Peruvian Amazon. *American Economic Review, 90*(4), 973–79.

Hillman, A.L. (2009). *Public finance and public policy.* Cambridge University Press. https://doi.org/10.1017/CBO9780511813788

Holcombe, R.G. (2018). The Coase theorem, applied to markets and government. *The Independent Review, 23*(2), 249–66.

Hourani, D., Millar-Powell, B., Perret, S., & Rammet, A. (2023). *The taxation of labour vs. capital income: A focus on high earners* (OECD Taxation Working Papers, No. 65). OECD Publishing. https://doi.org/10.1787/04f8d936-en

Immigration, Refugees and Citizenship Canada (IRCC). (2024, January 22). *Canada to stabilize growth and decrease number of new international student permits issued to approximately 360,000 for 2024* [News release]. https://www.canada.ca/en/immigration-refugees-citizenship/news/2024/01/canada-to-stabilize-growth-and-decrease-number-of-new-international-student-permits-issued-to-approximately-360000-for-2024.html

International Monetary Fund (IMF). (2009). *Balance of payments and international investment position manual* (6th ed., BPM6). International Monetary Fund Publication Services. https://www.imf.org/external/pubs/ft/bop/2007/bopman6.htm

Innis, H.A., Babe, R.E., & Comor, E. (2018). *Political economy in the modern state.* University of Toronto Press. https://doi.org/10.3138/9781487518905

Irvin, R.A. (2023). How dark is it? An investigation of dark money operations in U.S. nonprofit political advocacy organizations. *Nonprofit Policy Forum, 14*(2), 101–29. https://doi.org/10.1515/npf-2022-0032

Jickling, M., & Janov, P.H. (2003). *Criminal charges in corporate scandals.* Congressional Research Service (CRS) Report RL31866 for Congress, Library of Congress. https://www.everycrsreport.com/files/20031205_RL31866_8a3f9c7abb1de706078cf9591e78a92fca5e769b.pdf

Johnson, G.A., Shriver, S.K., & Goldberg, S.G. (2023). Privacy and market concentration: Intended and unintended consequences of the GDPR.

Management Science, 69(10), 5695–721. https://doi.org/10.1287
/mnsc.2023.4709

Jones, A. (2024, March 15). Ontario has to pay public sector workers $6B and counting in Bill 124 compensation. *CBC News*. https://www.cbc.ca/news
/canada/toronto/bill124-compensation-ford-government-1.7144793

Justesen, M.K. (2012). Democracy, dictatorship, and disease: Political regimes and HIV/AIDS. *European Journal of Political Economy, 28*(3), 373–89. https://
doi.org/10.1016/j.ejpoleco.2012.02.001

Kennedy, B., & Tyson, A. (2024, March 1). How Republicans view climate change and energy issues. *Pew Research Center*. https://www
.pewresearch.org/short-reads/2024/03/01/how-republicans-view
-climate-change-and-energy-issues/

Khadiagala, L. (2001). The failure of popular justice in Uganda: Local councils and women's property rights. *Development and Change, 32*(1),
55–76. https://doi.org/10.1111/1467-7660.00196

Kimakova, A. (2008a). Teaching law and economics from a positive perspective: The political economy of policy design in university curricula. *Global Jurist, 8*(2). https://doi.org/10.2202/1934-2640.1264

———. (2008b). The political economy of exchange rate regime choice: Theory and evidence. *Economic Systems, 32*(4), 354–71. https://doi
.org/10.1016/j.ejpoleco.2011.06.007

———. (2009). Government size and openness revisited: The case of financial globalization. *Kyklos, 62*(3), 394–406. https://doi.org/10.1111/j.1467
-6435.2009.00442.x

———. (2010). A political economy model of health insurance policy. *Atlantic Economic Journal, 38*(1), 23–36. https://doi.org/10.1007/s11293-009-9200-z

King, S.M., Chilton, B.S., & Roberts, G.E. (2010). Reflections on defining the public interest. *Administration & Society, 41*(8), 954–78. https://doi.org
/10.1177/0095399709349910

Kiser, E., & Karceski, S.M. (2017). Political economy of taxation. *Annual Review of Political Science, 20*(1), 75–92. https://doi.org/10.1146
/annurev-polisci-052615-025442

Klomp, J., & Haan, J.D. (2009). Is the political system really related to health? *Social Science & Medicine, 69*(1), 36–46. https://doi.org/10.1016/j.socscimed
.2009.03.033

Knight, J., Weir, S., & Woldehanna, T. (2003). The role of education in facilitating risk-taking and innovation in agriculture. *The Journal of Development Studies, 39*(6), 1–22. https://doi.org/10.1080
/00220380312331293567

Konyn, C. (2021, October 19). How Costa Rica reversed deforestation and became an environmental model. *Earth.org*. https://earth.org
/how-costa-rica-reversed-deforestation/

Kornai, J. (1992). *The socialist system: The political economy of communism.* Oxford University Press. https://doi.org/10.1515/9780691228020

Kraxberger, B. (2005). Strangers, indigenes and settlers: Contested geographies of citizenship in Nigeria. *Space and Polity, 9*(1), 19–27. https://doi.org/10.1080/13562570500078576

Kudrna, G., Tran, C., & Woodland, A. (2015). The dynamic fiscal effects of demographic shift: The case of Australia. *Economic Modelling, 50*, 105–22. https://doi.org/10.1016/j.econmod.2015.05.010

Kurmanaev, A., & Avelar, B. (2022, July 5). A poor country made bitcoin a national currency. The bet isn't paying off. *The New York Times.* https://www.nytimes.com/2022/07/05/world/americas/el-salvador-bitcoin-national-currency.html

Kurrild-Klitgaard, P. (2001). An empirical example of the Condorcet paradox of voting in a large electorate. *Public Choice, 107*(1–2), 135–45. https://doi.org/10.1023/A:1010304729545

Kuskova, P., Gingrich, S., & Krausmann, F. (2008). Long term changes in social metabolism and land use in Czechoslovakia, 1830–2000: An energy transition under changing political regimes. *Ecological Economics, 68*(1), 394–407. https://doi.org/10.1016/j.ecolecon.2008.04.006

Kydland, F.E., & Prescott, E.C. (1977). Rules rather than discretion: The inconsistency of optimal plans. *Journal of Political Economy, 85*, 473–91.

Laffont, J.J. (1999). Political economy, information and incentives. *European Economic Review, 43*(4–6), 649–69. https://doi.org/10.1016/S0014-2921(98)00130-5

Lake, D., & Baum, M. (2001). The invisible hand of democracy: Political control and the provision of public services. *Comparative Political Studies, 34*(6), 587–621. https://doi.org/10.1177/0010414001034006001

Leopold, J. (2002, May 16). Enron linked to California blackouts: Traders said manipulation began energy crisis. MarketWatch. https://www.marketwatch.com/story/enron-caused-california-blackouts-traders-say

Levine, M.E., & Forrence, J.L. (1990). Regulatory capture, public interest, and the public agenda: Toward a synthesis. *Journal of Law, Economics, & Organization, 6* [Special Issue: Papers from the Organization of Political Institutions Conference], 167–98. https://doi.org/10.1093/jleo/6.special_issue.167

Levy-Yeyati, E., & Sturzenegger, F. (2003). To float or fix: Evidence on the impact of exchange rate regimes on growth. *American Economic Review, 93*, 1173–93.

———. (2005). Classifying exchange rate regimes: Deeds versus words. *European Economic Review, 49*, 1603–35. https://doi.org/10.1016/j.euroecorev.2004.01.001

Lipscy, P.Y., & Lee, H.N.K. (2019). The IMF as a biased global insurance mechanism: Asymmetrical moral hazard, reserve accumulation, and

financial crises. *International Organization, 73*(1), 35–64. https://www
.lipscy.org/lipscyleeIMFbiasIO.pdf

Lowi, T.J. (1964). American business, public policy, case-studies, and political
theory. *World Politics, 16*(4), 677–715. https://doi.org/10.2307/2009452

Majó-Vázquez, S., Cardenal, A.S., & González-Bailón, S. (2017). Digital news
consumption and copyright intervention: Evidence from Spain before
and after the 2015 "link tax." *Journal of Computer-Mediated Communication,
22*(5), 284–301. https://doi.org/10.1111/jcc4.12196

Mamudi, S. (2008, September 15). Lehman folds with record $613 billion
debt. *MarketWatch*. https://www.marketwatch.com/story/lehman-folds
-with-record-613-billion-debt

Mandler, M. (2005). Incomplete preferences and rational intransitivity of
choice. *Games and Economic Behavior, 50*(2), 255–77. https://doi.org/10.1016
/j.geb.2004.02.007

Martinelli, C. (2007). Rational ignorance and voting behavior. *International
Journal of Game Theory, 35*(3), 315–35.

Masnick, M. (2021, June 17). Australian official admits that of course
Murdoch came up with link tax, but insists the bill is not a favor to News
Corp. *TechDirt*. https://www.techdirt.com/2021/06/17/australian-official
-admits-that-course-murdoch-came-up-with-link-tax-insists-bill-is-not
-favor-to-news-corp/

Maslin, M. (2008). *Global warming: A very short introduction* (2nd ed.). Oxford
University Press. https://doi.org/10.1093/actrade/9780199548248.001.0001

McCain, R.A. (2015). *Game theory and public policy* (2nd ed.). Edward Elgar.
https://doi.org/10.4337/9781784710903

McGuire, J.W. (2010). *Wealth, health, and democracy in East Asia and Latin
America*. Cambridge University Press. https://doi.org/10.1017
/CBO9780511750656

——– (2013). Political regime and social performance. *Contemporary Politics,
19*(1), 55–75. https://doi.org/10.1080/13569775.2013.773203

McKinnon, R. (1963). Optimal currency areas. *American Economic Review, 53*,
717–24.

McRae, M. (2017, May 31). *The Chinese head tax and the Chinese Exclusion Act*.
Canadian Museum for Human Rights. https://humanrights.ca/story
/chinese-head-tax-and-chinese-exclusion-act

Mehdi, T., & Frenette, M. (2024). *Exposure to artificial intelligence in Canadian
jobs: Experimental estimates*. Economics and Social Reports, Statistics
Canada. https://doi.org/10.25318/36280001202400900004-eng

Meloche, J.P., & Vaillancourt, F. (2021). *Municipal financing opportunities in
Canada: How do cities use their fiscal space?* Institute on Municipal Finance
and Governance. University of Toronto. https://utoronto.scholaris.ca
/server/api/core/bitstreams/a54ea1b6-8de8-4d82-a563-5d81881e44c5
/content

Milanovic, B. (1998). *Income, inequality, and poverty during the transition from planned to market economy* (World Bank Technical Paper No. 394). World Bank.

Moene, K.O., & Wallerstein, M. (2001). Inequality, social insurance, and redistribution. *American Political Science Review, 95*(4), 859–74. https://doi .org/10.1017/S0003055400400067

Moncada, E. (2013). Business and the politics of urban violence in Colombia. *Studies in Comparative International Development, 48*(3), 308–30. https://doi .org/10.1007/s12116-013-9135-x

Morris-Grant, B. (2024, March 12). Meta blocked news from Facebook and Instagram in Canada – could they do the same in Australia? *ABC News.* https://www.abc.net.au/news/2024-03-13/could-meta-block-news-in -australia-after-canada-ban/103576038

Mortimer, C. (2017, April 24). Brexit campaign was largely funded by five of UK's richest businessmen. *Independent.* https://www.independent.co.uk /news/uk/politics/brexit-leave-eu-campaign-arron-banks-jeremy -hosking-five-uk-richest-businessmen-peter-hargreaves-robert-edmiston -crispin-odey-a7699046.html

Motel, S. (2014, September 23). Polls show most Americans believe in climate change, but give it low priority. *Pew Research Center.* https://www .pewresearch.org/short-reads/2014/09/23/most-americans-believe -in-climate-change-but-give-it-low-priority/

Mumtaz, K. (2010). Post-Saddam democratization in Iraq: An assessment of March 2010 elections. *Strategic Studies, 30*(1–2), 208–38. https://www.jstor .org/stable/48527672

Munck, G.L., & Verkuilen, J. (2002a). Conceptualizing and measuring democracy: Evaluating alternative indices. *Comparative Political Studies, 35*(1), 5–34. https://doi.org/10.1177/001041400203500101

Munck, G., & Verkuilen, J. (2002b). Generating better data: A response to discussants. *Comparative Political Studies, 35*(1), 52–7. https://doi .org/10.1177/001041400203500105

Mundell, R. (1961). The theory of optimum currency areas. *American Economic Review, 51*, 657–61.

———. (1963). Capital mobility and stabilization policy under fixed and flexible exchange rates. *Canadian Journal of Economics and Political Science, 29*, 475–85. https://doi.org/10.2307/139336

Nash, J. (1950a). Equilibrium points in n-person games. *Proceedings of the National Academy of Sciences of the United States of America, 36*(1):48–9. https://doi.org/10.1073/pnas.36.1.48

———. (1950b). The bargaining problem. *Econometrica, 18*(2), 155–62. https:// doi.org/10.2307/1907266

———. (1951). Non-cooperative games. *The Annals of Mathematics, 54*(2), 286–95. https://doi.org/10.2307/1969529

National Center for Education Statistics. (2023). Loans for undergraduate students and debt for bachelor's degree recipients. In *Condition of education*. U.S. Department of Education, Institute of Education Sciences. https://nces.ed.gov/programs/coe/indicator/cub

Nederman, C.J., & Bogiaris, G. (Eds.). (2024). *Research handbook on the history of political thought*. Edward Elgar. https://doi.org/10.4337/9781800373808

Neef, T. (2020). What's new about income inequality in Russia (1980–2019)? Trends in comparison to Eastern Europe. *World Inequality Lab*. Issue Brief 2020/05. https://wid.world/document/update-on-income-inequality-in -russia-compared-to-eastern-europe-1980-2019/

The New York Times. (2014, January 3). Abortion restrictions passed by states. *The New York Times*. https://www.nytimes.com /interactive/2014/01/03/us/abortion-restrictions-passed-by-states.html

Ng, K., Drenon, B., Gerken, T., & Cieslak, M. (4 February 2025). DeepSeek: The Chinese AI app that has the world talking. *BBC News*. https://www .bbc.com/news/articles/c5yv5976z9po

Oates, W.E. (1972). *Fiscal federalism*. Harcourt Brace Jovanovich.

OECD. (2003). *Using micro-data to assess average tax rates* (OECD Tax Policy Studies No. 8). OECD Publishing. https://doi.org/10.1787 /9789264199811-en

———. (2013). General government expenditure by function. In *National accounts at a glance 2013*. OECD Publishing. https://doi.org/10.1787 /na_glance-2013-19-en

———. (2014). *Social expenditure update: Social spending is falling in some countries, but in many others it remains at historically high levels*. Insights from the OECD Social Expenditure Database (SOCX). Directorate for Employment, Labour and Social Affairs. OECD.

———. (2023a). *Education at a glance 2023: OECD indicators*. OECD Publishing. https://doi.org/10.1787/e13bef63-en

———. (2023b). *Pensions at a glance 2023: OECD and G20 indicators*. OECD Publishing. https://doi.org/10.1787/678055dd-en

———. (2024). *Education at a glance 2024: OECD indicators*, OECD Publishing. https://doi.org/10.1787/c00cad36-en

Office of the Federal Register. (2000). 2000 electoral college results. *U.S. National Archives and Records Administration*. https://www.archives.gov /electoral-college/2000

Olson, M. (1965). *The logic of collective action: Public goods and the theory of groups*. Harvard University Press. https://doi.org/10.4159/9780674041660

———. (1982). *The rise and decline of nations: The political economy of growth, stagflation, and social rigidities*. Yale University Press.

Ontario. (2019). Bill 124, *Protecting a Sustainable Public Sector for Future Generations Act, 2019*, 1st sess, 42nd leg. https://www.ola.org/en /legislative-business/bills/parliament-42/session-1/bill-124/status

Ontario English Catholic Teachers Association v Ontario (Attorney General). (2024). ONCA 101. https://coadecisions.ontariocourts.ca/coa/coa/en /item/22091/index.do.

Ostrogorski, M. (1902). *Democracy and the organization of political parties* (2 Vols.).

Papaioannou, E., & Siourounis, G. (2008). Economic and social factors driving the third wave of democratization. *Journal of Comparative Economics, 36*(3), 365–87. https://doi.org/10.1016/j.jce.2008.04.005

Parisi, F. (2004). Positive, normative and functional schools in law and economics. *European Journal of Law and Economics, 18*(3), 259–72. https:// doi.org/10.1007/s10657-004-4273-2

Park, J., McCabe, B.C., & Feiock, R.C. (2010). Direct democracy provisions and local government fiscal choices. *The American Review of Public Administration, 40*(4), 400–10. https://doi.org/10.1177/0275074009350676

Parker, S., Park, S., Pehlivan, Z., Abrahams, A., Desblancs, M., Owen, T., Phillips, J., & Bridgman, A. (2024). *When journalism is turned off: Preliminary findings on the effects of Meta's news ban in Canada.* The Media Ecosystem Observatory, McGill University and the University of Toronto. https://doi .org/10.31235/osf.io/eqn45

Partridge, S., & Weiss, M. (2024, September 4). *Tracker: Student loan debt relief under the Biden-Harris administration.* Center for American Progress. https://www.americanprogress.org/article/tracker-student-loan-debt -relief-under-the-biden-harris-administration/

Pay Equity Commission. (2012, September 18). *Gender wage gap.* https://web .archive.org/web/20150309030105/www.payequity.gov.on.ca/en/about /pubs/genderwage/wagegap.php

Persson, M., & Siven, C.H. (2007). The Becker paradox and Type I versus Type II errors in the economics of crime. *International Economic Review, 48*(1), 211–33. https://doi.org/10.1111/j.1468-2354.2007.00423.x

Persson, T., Roland, G., & Tabellini, G. (1998). Towards micropolitical foundations of public finance. *European Economic Review, 42,* 685–94. https://doi.org/10.1016/S0014-2921(97)00145-1

Persson, T., & Tabellini, G. (1999). The size and scope of government: Comparative politics with rational politicians. *European Economic Review, 43,* 699–735. https://doi.org/10.1016/S0014-2921(98)00131-7

Peters, J.W. (2014, January 19). House votes to restrict payments for abortions. *The New York Times.* https://www.nytimes.com/2014/01/29/us/politics /house-votes-tighter-restrictions-on-federal-payments-for-abortions.html

Petri, M., Taube, G., & Tsyvinski, A. (2002). *Energy sector quasi-fiscal activities in the countries of the former Soviet Union* (No. 2002–2060). International Monetary Fund.

Pew Research Center. (2006). *Many Americans uneasy with mix of religion and politics.* https://www.people-press.org/2006/08/24/section-i-religion -and-public-life/#religion-and-american-law

———. (2011). American exceptionalism subsides: The American-Western European values gap. *Global Attitudes Survey*. https://www.pewglobal.org/2011/11/17/the-american-western-european-values-gap/

———. (2012, February 23). Auto bailout now backed, stimulus divisive: Mixed views of regulation, support for Keystone pipeline. https://www.people-press.org/2012/02/23/auto-bailout-now-backed-stimulus-divisive/

———. (2013, June 24). Climate change and financial instability seen as top global threats: Survey report. https://www.pewglobal.org/2013/06/24/climate-change-and-financial-instability-seen-as-top-global-threats/

———. (2014a). *Political polarization in the American public*. https://www.people-press.org/2014/06/12/political-polarization-in-the-american-public/

———. (2014b, June 12). Section 1: Growing ideological consistency. https://www.pewresearch.org/politics/2014/06/12/section-1-growing-ideological-consistency/

Phillips, A.W. (1958). The relation between unemployment and the rate of change of money wage rates in the United Kingdom, 1861–1957. *Economica*, *25*(100), 283–99. https://doi.org/10.2307/2550759

Pieters, R., & Baumgartner, H. (2002). Who talks to whom? Intra- and interdisciplinary communication of economics journals. *Journal of Economic Literature*, *40*(2), 483–509. https://doi.org/10.1257/002205102320161348

Pinkerton, J. (2024, March 21). The history of bitcoin, the first cryptocurrency. *U.S. News*. https://money.usnews.com/investing/articles/the-history-of-bitcoin

Posner, R. (2011). *Economic analysis of law* (8th ed.). Aspen.

Powlen, K.A., & Jones, K.W. (2019). Identifying the determinants of and barriers to landowner participation in reforestation in Costa Rica. *Land Use Policy*, *84*, 216–25. https://doi.org/10.1016/j.landusepol.2019.02.021

Price, C.S., Thompson, W.W., Goodson, B., Weintraub, E.S., Croen, L.A., Hinrichsen, V.L., Marcy, M., Robertson, A., Eriksen, E., Lewis, E., Bernal, P., Shay, D., Davis, R., & DeStefano, F. (2010). Prenatal and infant exposure to thimerosal from vaccines and immunoglobulins and risk of autism. *Pediatrics*, *126*(4), 656–64. https://doi.org/10.1542/peds.2010-0309

Rai, S. (2001, August 25). India-U.S. fight on basmati rice is mostly settled. *The New York Times*. https://www.nytimes.com/2001/08/25/business/india-us-fight-on-basmati-rice-is-mostly-settled.html

Raiser, K., Kornek, U., Flachsland, C., & Lamb, W.F. (2020). Is the Paris Agreement effective? A systematic map of the evidence. *Environmental Research Letters*, *15*(8), 083006. https://www.doi.org/10.1088/1748-9326/ab865c

Rajabiun, R. (2009). Private enforcement of law. In N. Garoupa (Ed.), *Encyclopedia of law and economics. Criminal law and economics*. Edward Elgar.

Rajabiun, R., & Middleton, C. (2015). Regulation, investment and efficiency in the transition to next generation broadband networks: Evidence from the European Union. *Telematics and Informatics, 32*(2), 230–44.

Rajvanshi, A. (2024, May 1). How a group of elderly Swiss women charted a new path for climate legislation. *Time*. https://time.com/6972924/climate -change-legislation-switzerland/?utm_source=pocket-newtab-en-us

Rausch, S., & Schwarz, G.A. (2016). Household heterogeneity, aggregation, and the distributional impacts of environmental taxes. *Journal of Public Economics, 138*, 43–56. https://doi.org/10.1016/j.jpubeco.2016.04.004

Rehm, P. (2011). Social policy by popular demand. *World Politics, 63*(2), 271–99.

Reinhart, C.M., & Rogoff, K.S. (2004). The modern history of exchange rate arrangements: A reinterpretation. *Quarterly Journal of Economics, 119*, 1–48. https://doi.org/10.1162/003355304772839515

Reno, W. (2009). Illicit markets, violence, warlords, and governance: West African cases. *Crime, Law, and Social Change, 52*(3), 313–22. https://doi .org/10.1007/s10611-009-9199-8

Robbins, L.R., & London School of Economics and Political Science. (1998). *A history of economic thought: The LSE lectures* (S.G. Medema & W.J. Samuels, Eds.). Princeton University Press.

Roberts, G., & Doran, M. (2024, February 29). Meta won't renew commercial deals with Australian news media. *ABC News*. https://www.abc.net.au /news/2024-03-01/meta-won-t-renew-deal-with-australian-news-media /103533874

Rode, M., & Gwartney, J.D. (2012). Does democratization facilitate economic liberalization? *European Journal of Political Economy, 28*(4), 607–19. https:// doi.org/10.1016/j.ejpoleco.2012.07.001

Rodgers, D. (2006). The state as a gang: Conceptualizing the governmentality of violence in contemporary Nicaragua. *Critique of Anthropology, 26*(3), 315–30. https://doi.org/10.1177/0308275X06066577

Rodrik, D. (1998). Why do more open economies have bigger governments? *The Journal of Political Economy, 106*, 997–1032. https://doi .org/10.1086/250038

Roe v Wade, 410 US 113. (1973). https://supreme.justia.com/cases/federal/us /410/113/

Rosegrant, M.W. (2008). *Biofuels and grain prices: Impacts and policy responses*. International Food Policy Research Institute.

Ross, M. (2006). Is democracy good for the poor? *American Journal of Political Science, 50*(4), 860–74. https://doi.org/10.1111/j.1540-5907.2006.00220.x

Rothschild, M., & Stiglitz, J.E. (1976). Equilibrium in competitive insurance markets: An essay on the economics of imperfect information. *Quarterly Journal of Economics, 90*(4), 630–49. https://doi.org/10.2307/1885326

Russell, A., Jarvis, C., Wrobel, M., Sargent, E., & Jackson, K. (2022, May 28). Inside Ontario's "scary" child-welfare system where kids are

commodities. *Global News*. https://globalnews.ca/news/8874449
/ontario-child-welfare-system-serious-occurence-reports/

Sachs, J.D. (1993). Comments on privatizing Russia by Boycko, M., A. Shleifer
and R.W. Vishny. *Brookings Papers on Economic Activity, 1993*(2), 184–88.

Sanchez-Jankowski, M. (2003). Gangs and social change. *Theoretical
Criminology, 7*(2), 191–216. https://doi.org/10.1177/1362480603007002413

Sandmo, A. (2011). *Economics evolving: A history of economic thought*. Princeton
University Press.

Sargeson, S. (2008). Women's property, women's agency in China's "New
enclosure movement": Evidence from Zhejiang. *Development and Change,
39*(4), 641–65. https://doi.org/10.1111/j.1467-7660.2008.00499.x

Schumpeter, J.A. (1950). *Capitalism, socialism, and democracy* (3rd ed.).
HarperCollins.

Schwab, L. (2024, January 14). Conditions of for-profit immigrant detention
centers: Are human rights abandoned at the border? *Immigration and
Human Rights Law Review*. https://lawblogs.uc.edu/ihrlr/2024/01/14
/conditions-of-for-profit-immigrant-detention-centers-are-human-rights
-abandoned-at-the-border/

Shafiq, M.N. (2010). Do education and income affect support for democracy
in Muslim countries? Evidence from the Pew Global Attitudes Project.
Economics of Education Review, 29(3), 461–69. https://doi.org/10.1016/j
.econedurev.2009.05.001

Sherman, N., Epstein, K., & Fleury, M. (2024, March 28). Fallen "Crypto
King" Sam Bankman-Fried gets 25 years for fraud. *BBC News*. https://
www.bbc.com/news/business-68677487

Shrestha, V. (2020). Maternal education and infant health gradient: New
answers to old questions. *Economics & Human Biology, 39*, 100894. https://
doi.org/10.1016/j.ehb.2020.100894

Skarbek, D. (2011). Governance and prison gangs. *American Political Science
Review, 105*(4), 702–16. https://doi.org/10.1017/S0003055411000335

Skutnabb-Kangas, T. (2012). Indigenousness, human rights, ethnicity,
language and power. *International Journal of the Sociology of Language,
2012*(213), 87–104. https://doi.org/10.1515/ijsl-2012-0008

Slonim, R., & Roth, A.E. (1998). Learning in high stakes ultimatum games:
An experiment in the Slovak Republic. *Econometrica*, 569–96. https://doi
.org/10.2307/2998575

Smith, M.G. (2014). *Three essays on the political economy of corporate bailouts*
(Publication No. 3621006) [Doctoral dissertation, Columbia University].
ProQuest Dissertations & Theses. https://www.proquest.com/openview
/3f88916255f0ed36b069badb68595a18/1?pq-origsite=gscholar&cbl=18750

Smith, P. (1991). Lessons from the British poll tax disaster. *National Tax
Journal, 44*(4), 421–36.

Smith, V.L. (1962). An experimental study of competitive market behavior.
Journal of Political Economy, 70, 111–37. https://doi.org/10.1086/258609

———. (1982). Microeconomic systems as an experimental science. *American Economic Review, 72,* 923–55.

———. (1991a). Rational choice – the contrast between economics and psychology. *Journal of Political Economy, 99,* 877–97. https://doi .org/10.1086/261782

———. (1991b). *Papers in experimental economics.* Cambridge University Press.

Statistics Canada (2023a). Pension plans in Canada, as of January 1, 2022. *The Daily.* https://www150.statcan.gc.ca/n1/daily-quotidien/230623 /dq230623b-eng.htm

———. (2023b). *A tale of two renters: Housing affordability among recent and existing renters in Canada.* https://www12.statcan.gc.ca/census -recensement/2021/as-sa/98-200-X/2021016/98-200-x2021016-eng.cfm

———. (2024). Table 1: Total and median net worth by age of main income earner and family type. *The Daily,* last modified October 29, 2024, at https://www150.statcan.gc.ca/n1/daily-quotidien/241029/t001a-eng.htm

Stehr-Green, P., Tull, P., Stellfeld, M., Mortenson, P.B., & Simpson, D. (2003). Autism and thimerosal-containing vaccines: Lack of consistent evidence for an association. *American Journal of Preventive Medicine, 25*(2), 101–6. https://doi.org/10.1016/s0749-3797(03)00113-2

Stilwell, F. (2011). *Political economy: The contest of economic ideas* (3rd ed.). Oxford University Press.

Strotz, R.H. (1956). Myopia and inconsistency in dynamic utility maximization. *Review of Economic Studies, 23,* 165–80. https://doi .org/10.2307/2295722

Stubbs, T., Kentikelenis, A., Ray, R., & Gallagher, K.P. (2022). Poverty, inequality, and the international monetary fund: How austerity hurts the poor and widens inequality. *Journal of Globalization and Development, 13*(1), 61–89. https://doi.org/10.1515/jgd-2021-0018

Svoboda, E. (2018, August 16). The "neuropolitics" consultants who hack voters' brains. *MIT Technology Review.* https://www.technologyreview .com/s/611808/the-neuropolitics-consultants-who-hack-voters-brains/

Swinton, J.R., & Thomas, C.R. (2001). Using empirical point elasticities to teach tax incidence. *The Journal of Economic Education, 32*(4), 356–68. https://doi.org/10.1080/00220480109596114

Terren, L., & Borge-Bravo, R. (2021). Echo chambers on social media: A systematic review of the literature. *Review of Communication Research, 9,* 99–118. https://doi.org/10.12840/ISSN.2255-4165.028

Thaler, R.H., & Sunstein, C.R. (2008). *Nudge: Improving decisions about health, wealth, and happiness.* Yale University Press.

't Hoen, E., Berger, J., Calmy, A., & Moon, S. (2011). Driving a decade of change: HIV/AIDS, patents and access to medicines for all. *Journal of the International AIDS Society, 14,* 15. https://doi.org/10.1186/1758-2652-14-15

Tørstad, V.H. (2020). Participation, ambition and compliance: Can the Paris Agreement solve the effectiveness trilemma? *Environmental Politics, 29*(5), 761–80. https://doi.org/10.1080/09644016.2019.1710322

Tridimas, G., & Winer, S.L. (2005). The political economy of government size. *European Journal of Political Economy, 21*(3), 643–66. https://doi.org/10.1016/j.ejpoleco.2004.11.003

Tversky, A., & Kahneman, D. (1974). Judgment under uncertainty: Heuristics and biases. *Science, 185,* 1124–31. https://doi.org/10.1126/science.185.4157.1124

———. (1986). Rational choice and framing of decisions. *Journal of Business, 59,* S252–78. https://doi.org/10.1086/296365

UNAIDS. (2023). *Fact sheet: Global HIV statistics.* https://www.humanitarianlibrary.org/sites/default/files/2023/10/UNAIDS_FactSheet_en.pdf

United Nations. (n.d.). *The Paris Agreement: What is the Paris Agreement?* Retrieved August 5, 2025, at https://unfccc.int/process-and-meetings/the-paris-agreement

———. (2015, December 12). *Chapter XXVII: Environment, 7. d Paris Agreement.* https://treaties.un.org/Pages/ViewDetails.aspx?src=TREATY&mtdsg_no=XXVII-7-d&chapter=27&clang=_en#EndDec

———. (2019, November 4). *United States of America: Withdrawal.* https://treaties.un.org/doc/Publication/CN/2019/CN.575.2019-Eng.pdf

———. (2021, January 20). *United States of America: Acceptance.* https://treaties.un.org/doc/Publication/CN/2021/CN.10.2021-Eng.pdf

US Government Accountability Office. (2013). *Financial regulatory reform: Financial crisis losses and potential impacts of the Dodd-Frank Act.* https://www.gao.gov/products/gao-13-180

Vaubel, R. (1983). The moral hazard of IMF lending. *The World Economy, 6*(3), 291–304. https://doi.org/10.1111/j.1467-9701.1983.tb00015.x

Venkatesh, S. (2008). *Gang leader for a day: A rogue sociologist takes to the streets.* Penguin Press.

Warden-Fernandez, J. (2001). Indigenous communities and mineral development. *Mining, Minerals, and Sustainable Development, 59,* 1–30.

Whitehead, A., & Tsikata, D. (2003). Policy discourses on women's land rights in Sub–Saharan Africa: The implications of the re–turn to the customary. *Journal of Agrarian Change, 3*(1–2), 67–112. https://doi.org/10.1111/1471-0366.00051

The White House. (2025, January 20). *Putting America first in international environmental agreements.* Presidential Actions. https://www.whitehouse.gov/presidential-actions/2025/01/putting-america-first-in-international-environmental-agreements/

Whiteside, H. (Ed.). (2020). *Canadian political economy.* University of Toronto Press.

World Bank. (2018). *The state of social safety nets 2018*. World Bank. https://hdl.handle.net/10986/29115

———. (2020, February 19). *Anticorruption fact sheet*. https://www.worldbank.org/en/news/factsheet/2020/02/19/anticorruption-fact-sheet

———. (2024, May 9). *Heavily indebted poor countries (HIPC) initiative*. https://www.worldbank.org/en/topic/debt/brief/hipc

———. (2025a). *Gender statistics*. World Bank, DataBank. https://databank.worldbank.org/source/gender-statistics

———. (2025b). *World development indicators*. World Bank, DataBank. https://databank.worldbank.org/source/world-development-indicators

World Health Organization (WHO). (2014, May 5). *WHO statement on the meeting of the International Health Regulations Emergency Committee concerning the international spread of wild poliovirus. Media release*. World Health Organization. https://www.who.int/news/item/05-05-2014-who-statement-on-the-meeting-of-the-international-health-regulations-emergency-committee-concerning-the-international-spread-of-wild-poliovirus

———. (2023, July 13). *HIV and AIDS: Key facts*. https://www.who.int/news-room/fact-sheets/detail/hiv-aids

———. (2025). *HIV – Prevalence of HIV among adults aged 15 to 49 (%)*. The Global Health Observatory. https://www.who.int/data/gho/data/indicators/indicator-details/GHO/prevalence-of-hiv-among-adults-aged-15-to-49-(-)

World Trade Organization (WTO). (2015). *Special topic: Tariff accumulation, effective protection and export competitiveness in global production*. https://www.wto.org/english/res_e/statis_e/wtp2015_special_topic_e.pdf

Zaidi, J. (2024, June 7). How we're moving forward with the Canadian news ecosystem. *Google Canada Blog*. https://blog.google/intl/en-ca/company-news/outreach-initiatives/how-were-moving-forward-with-the-canadian-news-ecosystem/

Zilberman, D., Hochman, G., Rajagopal, D., Sexton, S., & Timilsina, G. (2012). The impact of biofuels on commodity food prices: Assessment of findings. *American Journal of Agricultural Economics, 95*(2), 257–81. https://doi.org/10.1093/ajae/aas037

Index

Note: The letter *f* following a page number denotes a figure; the letter *t*, a table and the letter *b* a box.